1987

Springer Series on ADULTHOOD and AGING

Series Editor: Bernard D. Starr, Ph.D.

Advisory Board:
Paul D. Baltes, Ph.D., Jack Botwinick, Ph.D., Carl Eisdorfer, M.D., Ph.D., Donald E. Gelfand, Ph.D., Lissy Jarvik, M.D., Ph.D., Robert Kastenbaum, Ph.D., Neil G. McCluskey, Ph.D., K. Warner Schaie, Ph.D., Nathan W. Shock, Ph.D., and Asher Woldow, M.D.

Raymond T. Coward, Ph.D., is currently Research Professor in the Center for Rural Studies, and Professor of Social Work in the College of Education and Social Services at The University of Vermont. He received his degree from Purdue University in 1974. His professional experiences included public school teaching, and faculty and administrative appointments at Purdue University and The University of Vermont. Dr. Coward is Editor-in-Chief of the *American Journal of Rural Health* and is the author of *The Rural Elderly: Program Planning Guidelines;* in addition, he has edited six other volumes, including *The Family in Rural Society and Family Services: Issues and Opportunities in Contemporary Rural America.* His primary research interests are in the development, delivery, and evaluation of health and human services in small towns and rural America.

Gary R. Lee, Ph.D., completed his degree at the University of Minnesota in 1973. Currently, he is Professor of Sociology and Rural Sociology, and Director of Research on Aging for the Social Research Center at Washington State University. A former chair of the section on the rural elderly of the Rural Sociological Society, Dr. Lee is now a member of the board of directors and chairperson of the International Section of the National Council of Family Relations. He is an associate editor of the *Journal of Marriage and the Family* and has written on comparative family sociology, kinship, intergenerational relations, and aging. Dr. Lee is the author of *Family Structure and Interaction: A Comparative Analysis.* His current research focuses on cross-cultural antecedents of family structure and on primary relations and life course transitions among the elderly.

THE ELDERLY
IN RURAL SOCIETY
Every Fourth Elder

Raymond T. Coward, Ph.D.
Gary R. Lee, Ph.D.

Editors

SPRINGER PUBLISHING COMPANY
New York

Springer Publishing Company, Inc.
200 Park Avenue South
New York, New York 10003

85 86 87 88 89 / 10 9 8 7 6 5 4 3 2 1   ·

Library of Congress Cataloging in Publication Data
Main entry under title:

The Elderly in rural society.
  (Springer series on adulthood and aging ; v. 13)
  Includes bibliographies and index.
  1. Rural aged—United States.   2. Rural aged—United States—Social conditions.
3. Rural aged—United States—Care and hygiene.   4. Rural aged—Services for—
United States.   I. Coward, Raymond T.   II. Lee, Gary R.   III. Series: Springer
series on adulthood and aging ; 13.
HQ1064.U5E42   1985   305.2'6'0973   84-13936
ISBN 0-8261-4120-X

Printed in the United States of America

mentor \'men-,tö(ə)r, 'ment-ər\ n [L, fr. Gk Mentōr] 1 cap: a friend of Odysseus entrusted with the education of Odysseus' son Telemachus 2a: a trusted counselor or guide b: TUTOR, COACH

Early in our careers, both of us were fortunate to study with senior scholars who brilliantly fulfilled the role of *mentor*. As action models they embodied the foremost traits of scholarship—inquisitiveness, rigor, ethics, high standards, hard work, dedication, and personal sacrifice. Their teachings by example have served as the touchstone for all of our own subsequent scholarly pursuits. This book is dedicated to these (gentle) men:

Victor G. Cicirelli
Purdue University

Reuben Hill
The University of Minnesota

Ira L. Reiss
The University of Minnesota

Contents

Contributors

Robert A. Bylund, Assistant Professor, Department of Sociology, Morehead State University, Kentucky.

Margaret L. Cassidy, Assistant Professor, Department of Sociology, University of Wisconsin at Eau Claire.

William B. Clifford, Professor, Department of Sociology, North Carolina State University, Raleigh.

Cynthia Dobson, Assistant Professor and Social Sciences Bibliographer, Library, Iowa State University, Ames.

Glenn V. Fuguitt, Professor, Department of Rural Sociology, University of Wisconsin at Madison.

Willis J. Goudy, Professor, Department of Sociology and Anthropology, Iowa State University, Ames.

Tim B. Heaton, Assistant Professor, Department of Sociology, Brigham Young University, Provo, Utah.

Vira R. Kivett, Associate Professor, Department of Child Development and Family Relations, The University of North Carolina at Greensboro.

Marie L. Lassey, Associate Professor, Department of Sociology and Anthropology, University of Idaho, Moscow.

William R. Lassey, Professor and Rural Sociologist, Departments of Sociology and Rural Sociology, Washington State University, Pullman.

Eloise Rathbone-McCuan, Associate Professor of Social Work and

Coordinator of the Social Work Program, College of Education and Social Services, The University of Vermont, Burlington.

Rick J. Scheidt, Associate Professor, Department of Family and Child Development, Kansas State University, Manhattan.

Philip Taietz, Professor Emeritus, Department of Rural Sociology, Cornell University, Ithaca, New York.

Paul R. Voss, Assistant Scientist, Department of Rural Sociology, University of Wisconsin at Madison.

Dennis A. Watkins, Associate Professor, Department of Agricultural and Resource Economics, University of Maine at Orono.

Julia M. Watkins, Associate Professor of Social Welfare and Coordinator of the Social Work Program, University of Maine at Orono.

Preface

The rural elderly, despite their absolute magnitude (59 million) and relative frequency (one in every four elders), remain a rather poorly understood and mythologized population. Traditional images of the life of elders in "the country" stand in stark contrast to the realities of contemporary rural America. As a consequence, there is a desperate need to collate and assess the information and assumptions that exist about the elderly in rural society, so that research, services, and policy development can proceed from a firm and accurate foundation of knowledge.

In August 1980, at the Annual Meeting of the rural Sociological Society in Ithaca, New York, a group of colleagues decided to have dinner together—a common event at such gatherings. What was unusual about this group was that all six of the individuals assembled that evening had an interest in rural gerontology. In attendance were Bill Lassey (Washington State University), Marie Lassey (University of Idaho), Bob Bylund (Morehead State University), John Krout (State University of New York at Fredonia), and the two editors of this volume.

Throughout the evening each of us commented on the phenomenal growth in the number of published pieces that were appearing pertinent to the special needs of life circumstances of those elders who lived in small towns and rural communities. We each lamented the difficulty of "keeping on top" of these diverse materials—many of which had appeared in obscure, renegade sources. There was complete consensus that there was a need to bring these materials together in one, readily available place—much as Grant Youmans had done more than a decade earlier in his now classic collection entitled *Older Rural Americans: A Sociological Perspec-*

tive (University of Kentucky Press, 1967). The group envisioned a collection much like the Youmans volume, covering many of the same issues but introducing certain selected topics that had emerged since the earlier work. Furthermore, the group agreed that the release of data from the 1980 Census represented an important vantage point from which to base new understandings of the life circumstances of the rural elderly. We all concurred that the census data, in combination with the increasing amount of research focused on the rural elderly that had recently been published, provided a firm empirical base from which to draw generalizations.

During the fall of 1980, we developed a set of materials that summarized our discussions in Ithaca and a tentative outline for the proposed book. We circulated these to more than 50 colleagues in sociology and/or social gerontology. We asked them for their review and comments on the preliminary materials. From these responses, we again revised the materials, prepared a prospectus, and in the early summer of 1981 began to approach prospective publishers. We were pleasantly surprised by the favorable reception we received from several publishing houses. In August 1981 we returned to the Annual Meeting of the Rural Sociological Society (just one year from our original discussions) with a signed contract with Springer Publishing Company, Inc.

We have developed this volume for those students and professionals who share our interest in the distinctive features of the process of aging as it occurs in small towns and rural communities throughout the United States. For current researchers, students, and service providers, the collection is intended as a comprehensive reference that will permit them to perceive their own work within a broader context. For academicians, the book may be a resource for the preservice training of students in a wide range of disciplines including rural sociology, gerontology, sociology, social work, and human services.

Each of the chapters in this book is an original manuscript which was commissioned exclusively for this volume. The authors are leaders in their respective fields of inquiry and represent the highest caliber of scholarship in the field. In attempting to shape these individual contributions into a coherent, integrated whole, we adhered to the following guidelines:

- Although we did not specifically articulate a theoretical framework for the book (nor did we choose authors from a predefined theoretical orientation), there was a basic premise that was significant in the overall development of the book. Simply stated, we held that the unique implications of rural residence could not be apprehended without an examination of the differences between rural and urban persons. Consequently, we encouraged each author to concentrate on those studies, when available, which dealt with rural–urban differences on selected variables and on the implications of those differences for the elderly as individuals and as a population.

- We recommended that individual authors draw heavily on the research literature. We believed that a research-based approach to the discussion of the rural elderly would be a major strength of this collection. On the other hand, we were not interested (and did not believe that the potential audience would be interested) in the simple regurgitation of the results of a long litany of research projects. Rather, we were interested in the *integration* of studies. We wanted the chapters to present clear, concise reviews of past work and to provide readers with a structure for organizing this knowledge base.

- We did not want chapters to be reports of individual studies. At the same time, we did not want authors to get carried away with references. There are cheaper ways to print comprehensive bibliographies than in a hardback book. We expected authors to include only the most significant contributions and to refer readers to those places where they could find more comprehensive bibliographies.

- Finally, we requested authors to refrain from the overuse of jargon. We did not ask them to compromise the scholarly integrity of their contributions. Indeed, we wanted thoughtful, scholarly, research-based manuscripts on these important topics. But from the outset our intended audience for the book was diverse (i.e., from different disciplines as well as different levels of experience) and, therefore, we wanted to be sensitive to the language used in the volume. Where possible we have used straightforward descriptions. When more sophisticated language was necessary, we have tried to provide definitions or references that will direct the reader to more basic materials.

These, in brief, were our objectives. We have not, of course, perfectly or consistently succeeded in attaining all of them. We feel, however, that the chapters which follow all represent reasonably close approximations of these ideals and that the emerging discipline of rural gerontology will benefit from the integration and synthesis of knowledge contained in this volume.

The subtitle of this book, "Every Fourth Elder," owes its origins to a publication distributed by the Select Committee on Aging of the U.S. House of Representatives (Committee Publication No. 97-332, July 1982). Their bulletin was entitled "Every Ninth American" to reflect the fact that at the beginning of 1982 older Americans made up over 11 percent of the population of the United States. When we discovered this publication, we were impressed by this straightforward and eye-catching technique for expressing a statistic with enormous implications. We adopted, therefore, a variation of their theme for our own purposes. The 1980 Census confirmed that "every fourth elder" lived in a rural environment (see Table 2.1 in Chapter 2) and thus emphasized the significant size of this segment of elders and our need to understand the special life circumstances of those individuals.

The development of a collection of readings of this scope and magnitude is a major undertaking and requires the support and commitment of many individuals. It would be impossible to list all those who have contributed directly or indirectly to the creation of this volume. However, certain key individuals merit recognition.

First and foremost are the contributors. Each of them has performed to the highest standards of professionalism. They have all worked diligently to prepare their chapters in a style and format that maximized the overall integration of the separate pieces. We are sincerely grateful for their hard work, tenacity, and patience.

In addition, the support and encouragement of close friends and professional colleagues are crucial during a project of this duration. Although many people have served this role, some deserve special mention and thanks: Robert W. Jackson, Eloise "Lee" Rathbone-McCuan, Kevin L. DeWeaver, Steven R. Rose, Martha F. Knight, Charles A. Tesconi, Don A. Dillman, Robert E. Howell, Irving Tallman, Marilyn Ihinger-Tallman, Steven R. Burkett, and Louis N. Gray. Similarly, the encouragement and tolerance of an institutional structure are necessary and in this regard we are obliged to the Center for Rural Studies and the College of Education and Social Services at the University of Vermont, and the Department of Rural Sociology at Washington State University.

We have received many years of capable secretarial support. From the beginning of this project, Cecile Fennell (The University of Vermont) has assumed responsibility for all aspects of the production of the manuscript. She has accepted each demand and impossible deadline with propriety, poise, and proficiency. Our deepest appreciation is extended to her for tolerating many, and often delinquent, revisions to the manuscript.

As is so often the case, our most ardent gratitude is reserved for our wives (Andrea Sushok Coward and Naomi Lee) and our children (Ryan Wells Coward, Carrie Elizabeth Coward, and Laura Lee). It is their patience, support, and sacrifice that constantly provide the *means* for our work—and it is their love that provides the *meaning* for our lives.

These people, with whom we work and live, are responsible for whatever strengths this book may contain. For the errors, inadequacies, and sins of omission and commission which inevitably remain in this volume, we have no one to blame but each other.

R.T.C.
G.R.L.

THE ELDERLY
IN RURAL SOCIETY

Part I

The Elderly in Rural Society

The three chapters in this section set the context and the tone for the text that follows. They describe and analyze some basic parameters of the rural elderly population which have critical implications for other issues and also identify reasons for, and approaches to, the study of the rural elderly.

Coward and Lee, in Chapter 1, examine recent increases in attention to the rural elderly from the perspectives of both research and policy. The problems of the rural elderly are receiving more widespread examination as the knowledge of these problems becomes more available. Awareness of the special needs of the rural elderly has increased along with the size and visibility of the elderly population generally and the overall importance of the problems of the elderly in the context of American life. Research on the rural elderly has also become more common and, in some ways, more adequate in recent years, although our abilities to understand, explain, or even describe the lives of the rural elderly are still in embryonic forms. Coward and Lee also argue that future research on the rural elderly, to be useful and productive, must be comparative and consider the entire spectrum of residential locations and populations. Research which focuses exclusively on the rural elderly thereby fails to treat residence as a variable and cannot go beyond the descriptive level in terms of promoting an understanding of the implications of residence for the lives of the elderly.

In Chapter 2, Clifford, Heaton, Voss, and Fuguitt investigate demographic processes which have influenced the size and residential distribution of the elderly population in the United States. They indicate that the smallest areas in terms of community size have the highest concentrations of elderly persons in their populations. Even though the substantial majority of the elderly live in urban areas, the elderly constitute a higher proportion of the populations of small towns and open country areas. Furthermore, although residential mobility is rather uncommon among the elderly as compared to the younger population, older people who do move are now relatively more likely to move from urban to rural areas than the reverse. This was true of the residentially mobile population in general during the 1970s, but the trend was apparent among the elderly even prior to the last decade. If it continues, this "migration turnaround" will have major implications for those rural communities most affected by the inmigration of elderly residents.

Chapter 3, by Goudy and Dobson, explores the economic exigencies of old age in rural areas. Contrary to popular belief, the rural elderly are markedly disadvantaged in economic terms relative to the urban elderly. Goudy and Dobson document this fact and examine some of the factors that contribute to these circumstances. The relatively low economic and financial status of the rural elderly is inextricably linked to many of the other problems they face—e.g., poor housing, poor health, and a generally lower standard of living than the urban elderly enjoy. Goudy and Dobson also look at the nature of retirement in rural areas and compare the rural retirement experience with the urban.

These chapters set the stage for the discussions that follow in the next two parts of the book. They establish the basic characteristics of the population with which we are concerned, the rural elderly, in demographic, occupational, and economic terms. They also establish the orientation of this book toward the study of the rural elderly and impart an idea of why the importance of the topic is likely to increase in the near future.

1

An Introduction to Aging in Rural Environments

Raymond T. Coward and Gary R. Lee

Over the past decade the special life circumstances of elders in the United States have received considerable attention from scholars, policy-makers, and service providers. This broad spotlight, however, has failed to illuminate the distinctive needs of subgroups of the elderly such as the frail elderly, isolated elders, the elderly in certain ethnic minorities, and *the elderly in rural society*. This latter category, those more than 59 million elders who reside in and around the small towns and rural communities of the contemporary United States, form the focus of this collection of original manuscripts.

Since the mid-1970s there has been a flurry of research, debate, and publication regarding the rural elderly. This activity has not reversed the still overwhelming urban bias of the gerontological literature (Coward, 1979), nor has it erased the major gaps that exist in our knowledge base concerning the rural elderly (Lee & Lassey, 1982), but it has signaled the apparent end to a period where the special needs and distinctive features of aging in rural society were virtually ignored by social gerontologists.

As more and more research on the rural elderly has been completed and the results of these efforts have become more visible, Americans have been confronted with a disheartening set of realities. The lives of many millions of the rural elderly are contrary to popular images of the "good life"—impressions that cast Grandmom and Grandpop whiling away their remaining years in the rocker on the expansive two-sided porch of the immaculately painted white farmhouse, surrounded by their land and their grandchildren, and their futures protected by the prosperity that they accumulated from their years of hard labor. Despite these romantic images of peaceful, quiet country living for the retired, the results of research have illuminated a harsher set of realities:

- On the average the income of the rural elderly is consistently lower than that of their urban counterparts (Kim, 1981) and a much higher proportion of the rural than the urban elderly have incomes below the poverty level (Lee & Lassey, 1980).
- The rural elderly occupy a disproportionate share of the nation's substandard and dilapidated housing (Atchley & Miller, 1979; Montgomery, Stubbs, & Savannah, 1980; Weicher, 1980).
- The rural elderly exhibit a larger number of health problems that tend to be more severe in comparison with the urban elderly and that result in a larger percentage of them retiring for health reasons (Davenport & Davenport, 1977; Lassey, Lassey, & Lee, 1980; McCoy & Brown, 1978)—although this does not necessarily translate into lower life expectancies (Kwan & Bertrand, 1978).
- Studies of the consumption of alcohol indicate a significantly higher percentage of "heavy drinkers" among the rural elderly when compared to their urban counterparts (Bainton, 1981; Christopherson, 1980).
- The health and mental health impairments of the elderly are not as readily treated in rural areas; indeed, rural health and human services are less abundant, less accessible, and more costly to deliver than in urban areas (Nelson, 1980; Rathbone-McCuan, 1981).
- Public transportation is more necessary for, but less available to, the rural elderly (McKelvey, 1979; Patton, 1975; Stuetze, 1977).
- Studies of the kin relationships of the elderly do not indicate that they are significantly stronger in rural society (Lee & Cassidy, 1981).

For many, these new insights into rural aging shatter nostalgic, romantic images of life in the country. The research findings that have emerged over the past decade have, nevertheless, cleared our vision and permitted us to move forward with a more accurate and realistic appreciation of the diversity of rural life.

Recent Rural Initiatives

Prior to the mid-1970s there was a small cadre of scientists interested in the rural elderly. For the most part, however, their work remained on the academic fringe of two professional disciples: gerontology and rural sociology. A clear exception to this anonymity was a book published in 1967 by the University of Kentucky Press entitled *Older Rural Americans: A Sociological Perspective.* This now classic collection of original manuscripts, edited by E. Grant Youmans, served for years as the benchmark from which all subsequent work was measured and made a significant and lasting contribution to the discipline. However, the changing circumstances of the rural elderly since this work appeared in 1967 and, perhaps more importantly, the significant advances in our scientific knowledge of these circumstances, warrant a new examination and synthesis of our understanding of the implications of rural residence for the elderly.

The increased interest in the rural elderly has manifested itself in three distinct areas: legislative intiatives, community services, and scholarly research and publication. The magnitude and significance of the efforts in each of these areas has precipitated the need for this book. In the sections that follow, some of the major contributions that have occurred are examined. This brief review of events will demonstrate the recent escalation of interest in the distinctive features of aging in rural environments while simultaneously illustrating the range of activities that have transpired and which form the underpinnings for this collection.

Legislative Initiatives

As the needs and life circumstances of the general population of elders have become more widely and better understood, local, state, and federal representatives of rural areas have been made to understand that their communities contained elders in need of assistance. Furthermore, elected rural officials soon became aware that their constituencies were not receiving their "fair share" of the burgeoning federal resources being spent on the elderly. In the mid-1970s, a bipartisan group of 100 members of Congress formed the Congressional Rural Caucus to coalesce their political powers on behalf of rural issues. The special needs of the rural elderly represented one of the major concerns of this group (Tsutras, 1978). Kivett and Learner (1981) have noted, however, that although

nearly one-third of all American elders live in nonmetropolitan
communities:

> As recently as 1979, rural areas were receiving only 11% of the total
> funds legislated to the Administration on Aging, the major economic
> source for programs and services for older Americans (National Coun-
> cil on Aging, 1979). . . . Similarly, it has been observed that the per
> capita federal outlays for health services in the 1970's were four times
> greater in metropolitan counties than in nonmetropolitan ones; wel-
> fare payments were four times greater; and worker training and de-
> velopment expenditures were three times greater (U.S. Department of
> Agriculture, 1971). (p. 103)

As a consequence of greater awareness of the needs of rural
elders, and a desire to reduce the discrepancy between federal and
state metropolitan and nonmetropolitan outlays, several pieces of
legislation were introduced to correct the inequities. For example,
Title III, Sections 307 and 421, of the Comprehensive Older Americans Act Amendments of 1978 increased allocations to rural areas
(mandated an additional 5%) and required special considerations to
be given to the implementation of rural model projects. Unfortunately, the effect of the mandated increase in funding levels on
services was probably negligble because the base upon which the
increase was calculated was preposterously small. Nevertheless,
the action indicated that there was an increased consciousness
(even if small) among legislators about the special needs of rural
elders.

Similarly, in January 1979, as part of the White House Rural
Development Initiatives announced by the Carter Administration
(Carter Administration, 1979), $12.5 million in funds was allocated
to construct 10 demonstration rural elderly congregate housing projects that included provisions for the delivery of social services on site
(referred to as the White House Rural Elderly Housing Initiative). In
that same year, the Farmers Home Administration (FmHA) increased the level of 504 low-income housing repair loans and grants
from $24 million in 1978 to $43 million in 1979 to better meet the
special needs of older rural Americans.

The availability and accessibility of health care facilities is a
critical factor in determining the quality of life for many older
Americans, and the continuing inadequacies of facilities and services for many rural communities is well documented (Miller,
1982). In the late 1970s several federal initiatives were enacted
that were intended to alleviate some of these problems. In Decem-

ber 1977, for example, the Rural Health Clinic Services Act was adopted. One of the many highlights of that legislation was the authority to provide Medicare/Medicaid reimbursement to nurse practitioners and physician assistants—a critical need in small, rural clinics which are often unable to attract and maintain a physician. The following year, the then Department of Health, Education and Welfare, in cooperation with the FmHA, announced plans to finance the construction and/or rehabilitation of 300 primary care health clinics in rural areas. This comprehensive, four-year program included funds to train health care professionals to staff the clinics.

These are but a smattering of examples of the federal initiatives that were adopted during this era. Similar actions were occurring at the state and local levels across the nation. It was during this era that, for the first time in the history of this country, our national leadership announced a comprehensive "Small Community and Rural Development Policy" (Carter Administration, 1979). In the document announcing the policy, President Carter detailed the reasons why he believed our nation needed a rural policy. Some of these points, we believe, are worth repeating here:

- Many rural areas are in the midst of significant economic and demographic change—change that is creating new demands, new problems, as well as new opportunities. A forward-looking policy is needed to manage the effects of such change—to enable individuals and communities to solve their problems and to capitalize on their opportunities.
- Rural people and communities have proportionately greater unmet basic human needs than do other parts of the nation. We must seek to assure that, to the maximum extent our resources allow, we address these needs and redress inequities. . . .
- Confused and often contradictory policy goals and implementation responsibilities have frustrated past efforts to address rural needs both within the federal government and between the federal government and local governments and community-based organizations. We need clear policy direction and a framework for integrating current federal efforts and reviewing future policy initiatives in order to evaluate the impact of actions we take and resources we commit.
- Frequently, past rural programs have been developed in Washington, D.C., on the basis of inadequate and out-of-date information. We need to improve our rural data base. We also need

to assure that diverse rural perspectives are available to federal policy makers and program managers. This continuous source of input is particularly important now when rural America is in transition. (Carter Administration, 1979, p. 5)

Community Services

Observations have repeatedly demonstrated deficiencies in the health and human services that are available in nonmetropolitan communities when compared to their metropolitan neighbors (Coward & Smith, 1983; Flax, Wagenfeld, Ivens, & Weiss, 1979; Ginsberg, 1976; Hassinger & Whiting, 1976; Johnson, 1980; Keller & Murray, 1982; Nelson, 1980; Sauer, 1983; Wagenfeld, 1981). Services for many rural residents are less accessible, more costly to deliver, narrower in range and scope, and fewer in number. This pattern of deficiencies is persistent across a spectrum of services and professions including physicians, dentists, and nurses (Ahern, 1979); social workers (Ginsberg, 1976); child care-givers (Schoffner, 1979); mental health workers (Wagenfeld & Wagenfeld, 1981); psychiatrists (National Institute of Mental Health, 1973); psychologists (Keller, Zimbelman, Murray, & Feil, 1980); professionals trained in developmental disabilities (DeWeaver, 1983); youth workers (Libertoff, 1983); and services for the aged (Nelson, 1980). This does not mean that health and human services are completely absent from rural environments; rather, relative to their more urban counterparts, many rural residents suffer a disadvantage in their ability to utilize the formal helping structure during periods of crisis.

The quantity and diversity of rural social services has, however, increased in recent years. The numerous legislative initiatives that have occurred (illustrated in the previous section) have resulted in *real* progress. Many rural communities have witnessed a significant rise in the number of services for the elderly. In one of the few studies of gerontological services over time and across rural–urban residences, Taietz and Milton (1979) reported data from 53 upstate New York counties (16 urban and 36 rural) collected at two different times (1967 and 1976). For each county, the availability of 25 services for the elderly was determined in both years. Analyses demonstrated that the greatest growth during this nine-year period in the number of services offered occurred in the *rural* counties. For 21 of the 25 services surveyed, the increases in the rural counties exceeded those in their urban counterparts. The authors noted that "while urban counties still provide more services for the elderly than do rural counties, the differences are less than they were in 1967" (p. 432).

The progress that has been made is very real and very important, but the differences that remain are equally real and important. Using completed questionnaires from a stratified national sample of 137 Area Agencies on Aging (AAAs), Nelson (1980) made rural/urban comparisons on the availability of specific services, the range of services offered, and specialized services for the "at-risk" aged. His analyses demonstrated significant rural–urban differences in the availability of 14 specific services. The average number of services offered by urban AAAs was 6.1 while the comparable figure for rural agencies was 4.7 (see Table 9.3 for a list of the services and rural–urban comparisons). In each of the categories of services examined, the urban agencies demonstrated a higher degree of service provision than did the rural areas. These discrepancies appear most acute in those service categories aimed at maintaining the independent living status of elders: day care, homemaker/chore services, and meal preparation.

The increased interest in the development and delivery of community services for the rural elderly is also illustrated by a January 1979 meeting entitled the "National Rural Strategy Conference to Improve Service Delivery to Rural Elderly" (Ambrosius, 1979). This gathering in Des Moines, Iowa, brought together representatives from the states to examine alternative strategies for mobilizing resources on behalf of rural elders. Similarly, the creation by the National Council on Aging of the National Center on Rural Aging depicts the commitment of that organization to the special needs and circumstances of the millions of elders residing in rural America.

Scholarly Research and Publication

Building on the contributions in Youmans (1967), a number of scholars have created products that have served to sharpen our understanding of the aging process as it occurs in rural environments. Their work has helped to cast off the shrouds of folklore and to systematically remove the layers of myth as one might peel an onion.

The many and varied contributions of researchers have been assembled and collected in several recent, excellent annotated bibliographies. The National Gerontology Resource Center (1980) in a review of literature on rural aging identified three documents that they found particularly valuable: Yenerall and Hayes (1975); Wilkinson (1978); and Kim and Lamprey (1979). Since that review, Wilkinson (1982) has published an update on her work. Collectively, these four bibliographies provide a comprehensive inventory of previous research and writing and are excellent resources for the newcomer to rural gerontology.

In addition to the annotated bibliographies, several very fine reviews of literature have appeared. These reviews have attempted to integrate a wide range of divergent literature and bring that knowledge to bear on particular issues. For example, Coward and Kerckhoff (1978), and in a shorter version Coward (1979), reviewed research on the elderly in an attempt to identify the major implications of those efforts for the delivery of gerontological services in rural communities. Similarly, the New York State Senate Research Service (1980) completed a review of literature to establish a foundation on which the state legislature could base programs for their older, rural constituents. The report offered 20 recommendations for addressing the most critical needs identified through their research. The federal government has also contracted for an extensive review of the literature on the life circumstances of rural elders, the uniquenesses of service delivery in rural areas, and the need for public policy development (Ecosometrics, Inc., 1981). In addition, both the U.S. Senate and the House of Representatives have sponsored numerous hearings on the special needs of the rural elderly (see Wilkinson, 1982, pp. 57–64 for summaries of many of the documents that have resulted from those efforts).

On other issues, Kim and Wilson (1981) have assembled a collection of original manuscripts summarizing the state of our knowledge regarding the mental health of the rural elderly. Lee and Lassey (1980) have reviewed previous research on differences in economic, social, and subjective factors between elderly persons residing in urban and rural locations. In a special issue of the *Annals of the American Academy of Political and Social Science* focused on "The New Rural America," Youmans (1977) summarized the current scholarly perspectives on the rural aging experience.

In addition to the attempts at integration that have appeared in journals, several special conferences have been held to permit researchers to exchange information and coalesce their knowledge on the rural aged. In 1975 the Gerontological Society joined with the Kentucky Aging Program and the Sanders-Brown Gerontology Center at the University of Kentucky to sponsor an invited conference. The proceedings from that conference, edited by Robert C. Atchley and Thomas O. Byerts (1975), contain an excellent set of reviews on the rural elderly and their relationships to family and friends, community facilities and services, nutrition, and transportation.

In the Northeastern United States, scientists from the land-grant university system gathered in May 1977 at The Pennsylvania State University to "detail priority research topics in rural gerontology" (Watkins & Crawford, 1978, p. 1). Under the sponsorship of the Northeast Regional Center for Rural Development (Cornell University) and the Farm Foundation, position papers were prepared on the needs and special life circumstances of the rural elderly; innovative organizational structures for meeting those needs; and demonstration or implementation strategies for delivering services.

In April 1979 an invited conference was sponsored by the Western Rural Development Center (Oregon State University) in cooperation with the University of Idaho, Washington State University, and the Western Gerontological Society. The focus of the position papers prepared for that gathering, and the discussions which followed, was the linkage between research and the development and delivery of public services for the rural elderly. The published proceedings from that meeting, edited by Lassey, Lassey, Lee, and Lee (1980), constitute an informative and provocative set of readings.

Finally, collections of work on the rural elderly have appeared as entire special issues of journals. For example, the October–December 1980 issue of *Educational Gerontology: An International Quarterly* (Volume 5, Number 4) was devoted to "Rural Aging and Education"; the January/February 1978 issue of *Perspective on Aging* (Volume 7, Number 1) was organized around the theme "A Look at Rural Realities"; and the Fall 1977 issue of *Generations* (Volume 2, Number 3) was a special issue on "Aging in Rural America."

Each of the bibliographies, literature reviews, conferences, and special issues of professional journals is tangible evidence of the increased attention being directed by scholars toward the distinctive lifestyles of the rural elderly. Many other examples exist and have not been listed. The sample above simply illustrates the depth and breadth of the interest. Collectively, these scholarly efforts involve scientists from *different disciplines* (e.g., sociology, psychology, medicine, public health, social work, and mental health); located in *different regions of the country* (e.g., New England, the upper Midwest, the Plains, the South, and the Far West); exploring many *different aspects of life* (e.g., loneliness, life satisfaction, fear of crime, family relations, social integration, and service delivery).

The above sampling of activities from three different arenas—legislative initiatives, community services, and scholarly research and publication—was presented to reinforce the assertion that there recently has been a surge in interest about the elderly in rural society. In the section that follows, we will examine some of the forces behind this intensification in concern.

Reasons for the Growing Interest in the Rural Elderly

It is reasonable to ask what forces were behind the resurgence of interest in the rural elderly, but it is more difficult to formulate a reasonable answer. The motivations behind the actions described earlier are multifaceted, sometimes difficult to discern, and often interwoven in a complex nexus of forces. Clearly, the intensification of interest in the *rural* elderly corresponded with, and benefited from, the dramatic mushrooming of attention to the plight of *all elders* in our nation. The "graying of America" (i.e., the increasing percentage of our total population that is over 65 years of age); the apparent hardship that many elders suffer in their later years; the economic burdens of health care for the elderly; and the sheer power of their numbers—each of these factors, singly and in combination, served to rivet the attention of America in the 1970s on its senior citizens. As a consequence, the lives of elders in all residential categories of our country came under greater scrutiny and profited from a more informed national consciousness.

There were some factors, however, distinctive to the rural sector of America, that served to enhance our focus on residents of those communities. The following sections briefly examine some of the most important forces. For a more in-depth discussion of these and other trends consult Ford (1978), Carlson, Lassey, and Lassey (1981), or Dillman and Hobbs (1982).

Community Characteristics

In general, data from the 1980 Census indicate that the proportion of the population that is elderly tends to increase as the size of a community declines (see Chapter 2 for more details). This high percentage of elders, combined with the distribution of other age

categories, results in higher dependency ratios for rural as compared to urban environments (Flax et al., 1979). The dependency
ratio is a measure of the percentage of people in a community who
are either over 65 or under 18 years of age as compared to the
number of individuals in all other age categories. It is referred to
as the "dependency" ratio because these two periods of the life span
are times when it is least likely that individuals will provide for
their own needs by active participation in the labor force.

As is the case with so many rural phenomena (Coward, 1979),
the distribution of the elderly varies considerably by region (see
Table 2.7 in Chapter 2 for greater details). Comparisons of all-
rural nonmetropolitan counties in 1980 indicated that the West
North Central States (Iowa, Kansas, Minnesota, Missouri, Nebraska, North Dakota, and South Dakota) had the highest mean
percentage of their populations (17.9%) over 65 years of age. In
contrast, the Pacific West States (Alaska, California, Hawaii, Oregon, and Washington) had the lowest mean percentage of their all
rural populations over the age of 65 (10.9%). Individual states
varied as well from a high in Kansas (19.9%) to a low in Alaska
(4.1%).

These demographic factors suggest that issues regarding aging
and the elderly may be more salient for smaller communities than
for urban areas. Rural town and county officials, researchers interested in rural communities, and rural service providers, prodded by
the rising national consciousness regarding the elderly, have begun to understand the prominence of this age population within
their own environments.

The Rural Renaissance

In the early 1970s, Calvin Beale (of the U.S. Department of Agriculture) began to describe a phenomenon that was almost entirely
unanticipated. He observed that hundreds of rural counties across
the country that had previously been declining in population were
unexpectedly indicating population gains via migration. This trend
was startling because it was contrary to the rural to urban migration pattern that had existed in the United States for well over a
century. The mid-census population survey of 1975 confirmed that,
indeed, more people had moved from metropolitan to nonmetropolitan counties than had made the opposite, more traditional, change
in residence (Beale, 1975; Tucker, 1976). This reversal of nonmetropolitan population trends—from declining to gaining—was the

result of two factors: (1) an increased movement away from cities; *and* (2) a decline in the movement away from rural communities (Wardwell, 1982). "Apparently in the eyes of some Americans, the appeal of major urban areas had diminished and the attractiveness of rural and small town communities had increased" (Coward, 1977, p. 2).

Data from the 1980 Census have demonstrated that this reversal has continued in all regions of the country except the South (Beale, 1981). For example, whereas the metropolitan areas of the Northeast experienced a modest 2 percent increase in their population between the 1970 and 1980 censuses, the nonmetropolitan areas of that region enjoyed a 12.4 percent increase over that time period. For the entire United States the percentage change in population was 9.1 and 15.4 for metropolitan and nonmetropolitan areas, respectively.

One astonishing aspect of this reversal is the prominence of the elderly. Previous research has indicated an inverse relationship between migration and age—i.e., that migrational streams are comprised primarily of younger adults and their families. Yet, in the reverse migration that formed the early rural renaissance, the elderly were *overrepresented*—a larger percentage of the migrants than of the general population was over age 65 (Fuguitt & Tordella, 1980). By restructuring data reported by Zuiches and Brown (1978), it can be demonstrated that individuals over the age of 65 accounted for 18.4 percent of the net metropolitan to nonmetropolitan migration between 1970 and 1975. Similarly, in a 1977 Midwestern sample described by Glasgow (1980), 32 percent of the metropolitan to nonmetropolitan migrants they interviewed were individuals 60 years of age and over. The prominence of elders in the migrational streams has also been reported by Tucker (1976) and Wang and Beegle (1977). Bowles (1978), however, has reported a distinctly different pattern using national data. Her analysis of data from the Current Population Survey indicated that 7 percent of the metropolitan to nonmetropolitan migrants were 55 to 64 years of age and an additional 6 percent were over 65 years of age. This discrepancy between the work of Bowles (1978) and others may be due to regional variations in the composition of streams or may be a reflection of the findings of Williams (1978) and DeLind (1978) that "early inmigrants in the turnaround flow were disproportionately retirement age persons" (Glasgow, 1980, p. 153).

Those elderly who comprise the stream moving to rural communities are significantly different, in some respects, from the resident elderly they join. Glasgow (1980), for example, found her sample of inmigrants to be better educated and more affluent. Clifford, Heaton, and Fuguitt (1982) have shown that elderly urban-to-rural migrants are disproportionately likely to live in "independent" households, while those with "dependent" living arrangements (living with relatives other than the spouse or with nonrelatives) are still more likely to move from rural to urban areas than the reverse. This suggests that elderly migrants to rural communities are not those most in need of community services, at least in the immediate future. The long-term needs of these elders are unknown, however, and the capacities of rural communities to satisfy these needs may be seriously challenged in later years.

The Rural Stake

The final major factor that enhanced awareness of the rural sector within our country was the resurgence of food and natural resources into the national consciousness. For decades Americans had become accustomed to, and complacent about, the power and influence of their food production capacity. Similarly, spurred by the prosperity and might of our industrial complex, we seemed unaware of the limits of our natural resources. In the 1970s we witnessed a shift in both of these trends. First, the economic and political power of our agricultural products began to be used on a more regular basis by our national leaders to influence the actions of foreign powers. Second, as a nation our consciousness was raised about the real limits of our natural resources and our responsibility for the stewardship of those nonrenewable products. Both issues served to direct attention toward the rural sector of our nation and to demonstrate the economic, political, and physical interrelatedness of this vast country.

Although the two issues described above did not focus attention directly on the elderly, the latter have benefited from an increased attention and commitment to the continued vitality and integrity of the rural sector. Legislative actions have been taken (see previous section) that were intended to preserve the strength and quality of life of rural America. When announcing his "Small Community and Rural Development Policy," President Carter noted that:

Rural and small town America is an integral part of the nation's economic and social fabric. Rural America provides our nation's food,

fiber and wood and accounts for most of our domestic mineral and
energy supply. It plays an increasingly important role in the nation's
manufacturing, trade and service economy. Earnings from rural ex-
ports make a vital contribution to our nation's trade balance. (Carter
Administration, 1979, p. 1)

Later in the presentation he continued this line of reasoning
when he asserted that:

Rural America's human and natural resources are a mainstay of the
nation's economy and contribute very significantly to the American
way of life. A conscious and sustained effort is needed to ensure the
wise use and continued productivity of these resources. (Carter Administration, 1979, p. 4)

Increased attention to the problems and potentials of rural
areas will ultimately help focus attention on issues involving the
rural elderly, since they constitute an increasingly important and
visible segment of the rural population.

Studying the Rural Elderly

In the preceding sections we have attempted to document the growing interest in the life circumstances of the rural elderly. We have
also described the major contextual forces that have facilitated this
escalating attention. Taken collectively these forces have created,
for the student of rural gerontology, the need to once again step
back (as Youmans and his colleagues did in 1967) and assess the
state of our knowledge regarding this population. This collection of
original manuscripts is an attempt to do just that—to bring together in one place a series of reviews and critiques of major areas
of research related to the quality of life of those elders who live in
the small towns, villages, hamlets, and open country of the United
States.

Increased attention to the elderly segment of the rural population is, in itself, however, insufficient to produce real advances in
our knowledge of their circumstances or in our ability to improve
the quality of their lives. Indeed, unless such attention is guided by
appropriate scientific standards, it may be self-defeating.

Researchers studying the elderly in rural society find themselves working at the intersection of two disciplines which have
traditionally been defined according to the populations they study.
Rural sociology is the study of rural residents, and social gerontol-

ogy is the study of older people. Rural gerontology, by logical extension, must be the study of the rural elderly. While this definition is a perfectly acceptable statement of the focus of our interests and concerns, its literal implementation in the research process would actually hinder scientific progress in understanding the lives of the rural elderly.

If we were so presumptuous as to formulate the objectives of rural gerontology, they would be as follows: to understand the implications of rural residence for the lives of the elderly and the implications of aging for the lives of rural residents. These objectives indicate an interest in the effects of two factors, residence and age, on human behavior. We are, in this context, most interested in the effects of *rural* residence and *old* age. To turn this interest into useful knowledge, however, we must be constantly aware of the fact that scientific knowledge is generated only by comparison. A study of the characteristics of the rural elderly, without data from other categories of the population, can give no clue to whether these characteristics are attributable to rural residence, old age, both, or neither.

Thus, we can learn very little about the rural elderly by studying only the rural elderly. The effects of rural residence and old age can be apprehended only by comparing rural with urban and old with young—in other words, by treating residence and age as variables rather than as boundary conditions which define the limits of our inquiries.

This is not meant to suggest that the rural elderly population is homogeneous in other respects; it certainly is not. There is great variation within this category on virtually all dimensions of interest to behavioral scientists (Coward, 1979). It is, of course, possible and often desirable to study relationships among other variables within this or any other population. But studies that focus exclusively on the rural elderly will not and cannot add to the knowledge base of the discipline of rural gerontology with respect to the effects of either rural residence or old age. Gerontologists must examine the entire spectrum of the life cycle in order to understand how age and aging affect human behavior, and rural sociologists must obtain and employ data from urban areas if they wish to observe and understand the effects of rural residence. If the emerging discipline of rural gerontology succumbs to the temptation to study only that category of the population specifically delineated by its label, it will ultimately prove to be of very little use.

The chapters that follow will review research documenting

many objective disadvantages associated with aging in rural environments. This list of disadvantages faced by many of the rural
elderly is depressingly long and raises serious questions about the
quality of life among the current generation of rural elderly, as
well as the quality of life to which future generations may aspire.
Yet most research on subjective measures of the quality of life
(emotional well-being, morale, and life satisfaction) has indicated
that there is a slight *advantage* in rural residence for the elderly
(Donnenwerth, Guy, & Norvell, 1978; Hynson, 1975; Sauer, Sheehan, & Boymel, 1976).

This is an interesting paradox. It suggests either that there
are some objective advantages to rural residence for the elderly
which counteract the effects of the factors mentioned above and
which are not yet well documented, or that the causal structure of
emotional well-being is different among the rural than the urban
elderly (Lee & Lassey, 1980, 1982). Our point here, however, is
that the knowledge that this paradox exists comes entirely from
rural–urban comparisons. No empirical generalizations about the
effects of rural residence or old age can be made, or even conceptualized, except in an explicitly comparative context.

The chapters which comprise this volume have all been written
with this comparative perspective in mind. The emphasis has not
been on describing characteristics of the rural elderly, but rather on
comparing their characteristics with those of the urban elderly and,
frequently, with those of other age groups. In this way, descriptions
are more meaningful and explanations are ultimately possible. We
hope that the synthesis of research and theory in these chapters will
promote a greater understanding of the ways in which aging affects
rural residents, and rural residence affects the aged.

References

Ahearn, M. C. *Health care in rural America.* Washington, D.C.: U.S. De-
    partment of Agriculture, Economics, Statistics and Cooperatives Ser-
    vice, Information Bulletin No. 428, 1979.
Ambrosius, R. *A report on National Rural Strategy Conference to improve
    service delivery to rural elderly.* Spencer, Iowa: Iowa Lakes Area
    Agency on Aging, February 1979.
Atchley, R. C., & Byerts, T. O. (Eds.). *Rural environments and aging.*
    Washington, D.C.: The Gerontological Society of America, 1975.
Atchley, R. C., & Miller, S. J. Housing and households of the rural aged.

In T. O. Byerts, S. C. Howell, & L. A. Pastalan (Eds.), *Environmental context of aging: Life-styles, environmental quality, and living arrangements.* New York: Garland STPM Press, 1979, pp. 62–79.

Bainton, B. Drinking patterns of the rural aged. In C. L. Fry (Ed.), *Dimensions: Aging, culture and health.* New York: J. F. Bergin Publishers, 1981, pp. 55–76.

Beale, C. L. *The revival of population growth in nonmetropolitan America.* Washington, D.C.: U.S. Department of Agriculture, Economic Development Division, Economic Research Service, 1975, ERS-605.

Beale, C. L. *Rural and small town population change: 1970–1980.* Washington, D.C.: U.S. Department of Agriculture, Economics and Statistics Service, February 1981, ESS-5.

Bowles, G. K. Contributions of recent metro-nonmetro migrants in the nonmetro population and labor force. *Agricultural Economics Research,* 1978, *30* (October), 15–22.

Carlson, J. E., Lassey, M. L., & Lassey, W. R. *Rural society and environment in America.* New York: McGraw-Hill Book Company, 1981.

Carter Administration. *Small community and rural development policy.* Washington, D.C.: The White House, December 20, 1979.

Christopherson, V.A. Alcohol use among the rural elderly in Arizona. In W. R. Lassey, M. L. Lassey, G. R. Lee, & N. Lee (Eds.), *Research and public service with the rural elderly.* Corvallis, Ore.: Western Rural Development Center, 1980, pp. 65–75.

Clifford, W., Heaton B. T., & Fuguitt, G. V. Residential mobility and living arrangements among the elderly: Changing patterns in metropolitan and nonmetropolitan areas. *International Journal of Aging and Human Development,* 1982, *14* (2), 139–156.

Coward, R. T. Delivering social services in small towns and rural communities. In R. T. Coward (Ed.), *Rural families across the life span: Implications for community programming.* West Lafayette, Ind.: Indiana Cooperative Extension Service, 1977, pp. 1–17.

Coward, R. T. Planning community services for the rural elderly: Implications from research. *The Gerontologist,* 1979, *19*(3), 275–282.

Coward, R. T., & Kerckhoff, R. K. *The rural elderly: Program planning guidelines.* Ames, Iowa: North Central Regional Center for Rural Development, 1978.

Coward, R. T., & Smith, W. M., Jr. (Eds.). *Family services: Issues and opportunities in contemporary rural America.* Lincoln: The University of Nebraska Press, 1983.

Davenport, J., & Davenport, J. A. Health-related social services for the rural elderly: Problems and opportunities. *Social Perspectives,* 1977, *5,* 36–41.

DeWeaver, K. L. Delivering rural services for developmentally disabled individuals and their families: Changing scenes. In R. T. Coward & W. M. Smith, Jr. (Eds.). *Family services: Issues and opportunities in contemporary rural America.* Lincoln: The University of Nebraska Press, 1983, pp. 150–170.

DeLind, L. B. *Leisureville: A developmental study of behavior and social organization within a rural U.S. county.* Unpublished dissertation, Michigan State University, 1978.

Dillman, D. A., & Hobbs, D. J. (Eds.). *Rural society in the U.S.: Issues for the 1980s.* Boulder, Colo.: Westview Press, 1982.

Donnenwerth, G. V., Guy, R. F., & Norvell, M. J. Life satisfaction among older persons: Rural-urban and racial comparisons. *Social Science Quarterly,* 1978, *59* (3), 578–583.

Ecosometrics, Inc. *Review of reported differences between the rural and urban elderly: Status, needs, services, and service costs.* Washington, D.C.: Administration on Aging (Contract No. 105-80-C-065), July 1981.

Flax, J. W., Wagenfeld, M. O., Ivens, R. E., & Weiss, R. J. *Mental health in rural America: An overview and annotated bibliography.* Washington, D.C.: National Institute of Mental Health, DHEW Publication No. (ADM) 78-753, U.S. Government Printing Office, 1979.

Ford, T. R. *Rural USA: Persistence and change.* Ames: Iowa State University Press, 1978.

Fuguitt, G. V., & Tordella, S. J. Elderly net migration: The new trend of nonmetropolitan population change. *Research on Aging,* 1980, *2,* 191–204.

Ginsberg, L. H. (Ed.). *Social work in rural communities: A book of readings.* New York: Council on Social Work Education, 1976.

Glasgow, N. The older metropolitan migrant as a factor in rural population growth. In A. J. Sofranko & J. D. Williams (Eds.), *Rebirth of rural America: Rural migration in the Midwest.* Ames, Iowa: North Central Regional Center for Rural Development, 1980, pp. 153–170.

Hassinger, E. W., & Whiting L. R. (Eds.). *Rural health services: Organization, delivery and use.* Ames: Iowa State University Press, 1976.

Hynson, L. M., Jr. Rural-urban differences in satisfaction among the elderly. *Rural Sociology,* 1975, *40,* 64–66.

Johnson, H. W. (Ed.) *Rural human services: A book of readings.* Itasca, Ill.: F. E. Peacock Publishers, 1980.

Keller, P. A., & Murray, J. D. (Eds.). *Handbook of rural community mental health.* New York: Human Sciences Press, 1982.

Keller, P. A., Zimbelman, K. K., Murray, J. D., & Feil, R. N. Geographic distribution of psychologists in the Northeastern United States. *Journal of Rural Community Psychology,* 1980, *1* (1), 18–24.

Kim, P. K. H. The low income rural elderly: Underserved victims of public inequity. In Community Services Administration, *Policy issues for the elderly poor.* Washington, D.C.: U.S. Government Printing Office, Community Services Administration Pamphlet 6172-8 (1981-341-509/2619), February 1981, pp. 87–94.

Kim, P. K. H, & Lamprey, H. A. *Bibliography on rural aging.* Lexington: Mental Health and Rural Gerontology Project, College of Social Professions, University of Kentucky, Publication Series No. 1979-1, 1979.

Kim, P. K. H, & Wilson, C. P. *Toward mental health of the rural elderly.* Washington, D.C.: University Press of America, 1981.

Kivett, V. R., & Learner, R. M. The rural elderly poor: Economic impacts and policy issues. In Community Services Administration, *Policy issues for the elderly poor.* Washington, D.C.: U.S. Government Printing Office, Community Services Administration Pamphlet 6172-8 (1981-341-509/2619), February 1981, pp. 103–114.

Kwan, U., & Bertrand, A. L. *Mortality and longevity in Louisiana: The relationship of rural residence to survival after age 65.* Baton Rouge: Center for Agricultural Sciences and Rural Development, Louisiana State University, Bulletin 707, 1978.

Lassey, M. L., Lassey, W. R., & Lee, G. R. Elderly people in rural America: A contemporary perspective. In W. R. Lassey, M. L. Lassey, G. R. Lee, & N. Lee (Eds.), *Research and public service with the rural elderly.* Corvallis, Ore.: Western Rural Development Center, 1980, pp. 21–38.

Lassey, W. R., Lassey, M. L., Lee, G. R., & Lee, N. (Eds.). *Research and public service with the rural elderly.* Corvallis, Ore.: Western Rural Development Center, 1980.

Lee, G. R., & Cassidy, M. L. Kinship systems and extended family ties. In R. T. Coward & W. M. Smith, Jr. (Eds.), *The family in rural society.* Boulder, Colo.: Westview Press, 1981, pp. 57–71.

Lee, G. R., & Lassey, M. L. Rural–urban differences among the elderly: Economic, social and subjective factors. *Journal of Social Issues,* 1980, *36* (2), 62–74.

Lee, G. R., & Lassey, M. L. The elderly. In D. A. Dillman & D. J. Hobbs (Eds.), *Rural society in the U.S.: Issues for the 1980s.* Boulder, Colo.: Westview Press, 1982, pp. 85–93.

Libertoff, K. Reflections on rural adolescent services. In R. T. Coward & W. M. Smith, Jr. (Eds.), *Family services: Issues and opportunities in contemporary rural America.* Lincoln: The University of Nebraska Press, 1983, pp. 171–185.

McCoy, J. L, & Brown, D. L. Health status among low income elderly persons: Rural–urban differences. *Social Security Bulletin,* 1978, *41* (6), 14–26.

McKelvey, D. J. Transportation issues and problems of the rural elderly. In S. M. Golant (Ed.), *Locations and environment of elderly population.* Washington, D.C.: V. H. Winston and Sons, 1979, pp. 135–140.

Miller, M. K. Health and medical care. In D. A. Dillman & D. J. Hobbs (Eds.), *Rural Society in the U.S.: Issues for the 1980s.* Boulder, Colo.: Westview Press, 1982, pp. 216–223.

Montgomery, J. E., Stubbs, A. C., & Savannah, S. The housing environment of the rural elderly. *The Gerontologist,* 1980, *20* (4), 444–451.

National Council on Aging. *NCOA public policy agenda: 1979–1980.* Washington, D.C.: National Council on Aging, 1979.

National Institute of Mental Health. *Federally funded community mental health centers.* Washington, D.C.: National Institute of Mental Health, Division of Mental Health Programs, 1973.

National Gerontology Resource Center. A review of the literature on rural aging. *Educational Gerontology: An International Quarterly,* 1980, *5* (4), 452–455.

Nelson, G. Social services to the urban and rural aged: The experience of area agencies on aging. *The Gerontologist,* 1980, *20* (2), 200–207.

New York State Senate Research Service. *Old age and ruralism: A case of double jeopardy.* Albany: New York State Senate Standing Committee on Aging, May 1980.

Patton, C. V. Age grouping and travel in a rural area. *Rural Sociology,* 1975, *40* (Spring), 55–63.

Rathbone-McCuan, E. E. A step toward integrated health and mental health planning for the rural elderly. In P. K. H. Kim & C. P. Wilson (Eds.), *Toward mental health of the rural elderly.* Washington, D.C.: University Press of America, 1981, pp. 257–273.

Sauer, W. J. The elderly: Challenges for the rural community. In R. T. Coward & W. M. Smith, Jr. (Eds.), *Family services: Issues and opportunities in contemporary rural America.* Lincoln: University of Nebraska Press, 1983, pp. 186–203.

Sauer, W. J., Sheehan, C., & Boymel, C. Rural–urban differences in satisfactions among the elderly: A reconsideration. *Rural Sociology,* 1976, *41*(2), 269–275.

Schoffner, S. M. Child care in rural areas: Needs, attitudes and preferences. *Family Economics Review,* 1979 (Fall), 187–195.

Stuetze, P. H. Some thoughts on rural transportation. *Generations,* 1977 (Fall), 11.

Taietz, P., & Milton, S. Rural–urban differences in the structure of services for the elderly in upstate New York counties. *Journal of Gerontology,* 1979, *34,* 429–437.

Tsutras, F. G. Congressional rural caucus. *Perspective on Aging,* 1978, 7 (1), 5–37.

Tucker, C. J. Changing patterns of migration between metropolitan and nonmetropolitan areas in the United States: Recent evidence. *Demography,* 1976, *13,* 435–443.

U.S. Department of Agriculture. *Welfare reforms, benefits and incentives in rural areas.* Washington, D.C.: U.S. Department of Agriculture, Economic Research Service, ERS 470, June 1971.

Wagenfeld, M. O. (Ed.). *Perspectives on rural mental health.* San Francisco, Calif. Jossey-Bass, 1981.

Wagenfeld, M. O., Wagenfeld, J. K. Values, culture, and delivery of mental health services. In M. O. Wagenfeld (Ed.), *Perspectives on rural mental health*. San Francisco, Calif. Jossey-Bass, 1981, pp. 1–12.

Wang, C., & Beegle, J. A. Impact of elderly migration on the revival of population growth in nonmetropolitan areas of the North Central region. Paper presented at the Annual Meetings of the Rural Sociological Society, Madison, Wis., 1977.

Wardwell, J. M. The reversal of nonmetropolitan migration loss. In D. A. Dillman & D. J. Hobbs (Eds.), *Rural society in the U.S.: Issues for the 1980s*. Boulder, Colo.: Westview Press, 1982, pp. 23–33.

Watkins, D. A., & Crawford, C. O. (Eds.). *Rural Gerontology in the Northeast*. Ithaca, N.Y.: Northeast Regional Center for Rural Development, 1978.

Weicher, J. C. *Housing: Federal policies and programs*. Washington, D.C.: American Enterprise Institute for Rural Policy Research, 1980.

Wilkinson, C. W. *The rural aged in America 1975–1978: An annotated bibliography*. Morgantown: Gerontology Center, West Virginia University, 1978.

Wilkinson, C. W. *Aging in rural America: A comprehensive annotated bibliography, 1975–1981*. Morgantown: Gerontology Center, West Virginia University, 1982.

Williams, J. D. *The changing causal and compositional structure of migration in the nonmetropolitan Midwest, 1955–1970*. Unpublished Ph.D. dissertation, University of Illinois, 1978.

Yenerall, J. D., & Hayes, S. F. *The rural aged in America: An annotated bibliography*. Albany, N.Y.: Institute for Public Policy Alternatives, State University of New York at Albany, 1975.

Youmans, E. G. *Older rural Americans: A sociological perspective*. Lexington: University of Kentucky Press, 1967.

Youmans, E. G. The rural aged. *Annals of the American Academy of Political and Social Science*, 1977, *429* (January), 81–90.

Zuiches, J. J., & Brown, D. L. The changing character of the nonmetro population: 1950–75. In T. R. Ford (Ed.), *Rural USA: Persistance and change*. Ames: Iowa State University Press, 1978, pp. 55–72.

2

The Rural Elderly
in Demographic Perspective

William B. Clifford, Tim B. Heaton, Paul R. Voss, and
Glenn V. Fuguitt

The 20th century has been marked by a rapid increase in the number and proportion of elderly persons in the United States. In 1900, the elderly population consisted of three million persons, representing only 4 percent of the total population. By 1980, the elderly population had increased eightfold to 25 million or 11.2 percent of the population. In different ways, all of the basic demographic processes—fertility, mortality, and migration—contributed to this expansion in the number and proportion of elderly. In the most general terms, however, the increasing accumulation of older persons is the result of the transition from high to low birth and death rates which has been associated with industrial development.

The large number of older persons today is due almost entirely to the high fertility of the late 19th and early 20th centuries. At the same time, advances in medicine and sanitation reduced death rates, allowing more of the population to survive past the age of 65. The size of the older population also was affected by the high level of immigration prior to World War I, although this effect has largely dissipated since the surviving immigrants of this period would now be well into their eighth or ninth decade.

The increase in the *proportion* of elderly, however, is due largely to declining fertility rather than lower death rates. A decline in fertility reduces the proportion of young persons and increases the proportion of adults and older persons. A decline in mortality generally increases the relative number of children, which would depress the proportion of elderly.

One of the features characteristic of contemporary American society is its concern with the needs and the quality of life of the elderly portion of the population. While the scope of this interest

25

has been broad, there is a real need to understand more about the nature and magnitude of the problems of the elderly in *rural* areas (see the opening chapter of this volume and also Lee & Lassey, 1982; Siegel, 1980). When studying rural elders, we must examine the extent to which their age structure reflects that of the total population and the extent to which its characteristics arise from the rural environment. The discussion that follows focuses on the age structure of the United States as a whole and of the rural population in particular. In the first section, definitions of urban and rural are reviewed. Next, characteristics of the rural elderly such as race, sex, and marital and family status are examined. Recent trends in the redistribution of the United States population prompt a discussion of the geographic distribution of the elderly, recent migration patterns, and factors associated with these changes.

Definitions of Urban and Rural

We must be careful not to oversimplify America society by dividing it into two distinct segments—urban and rural. American society is not sharply divided into two clearly differentiated parts; rather, considerable overlap and blurring exist. Nevertheless, it is generally agreed that for many statistical purposes, it is necessary to take some criterion (such as size of the community as measured by the number of inhabitants) as the basis for classifying the population into rural and urban categories. While acknowledging that the distinction is conceptually primitive, in this chapter we have followed the practice of the United States Bureau of the Census and defined the urban population to include anyone living in an urbanized area or in a place of 2,500 or more people and the rural population as that population living elsewhere. An urbanized area, as defined in the 1980 census, comprises an incorporated place and adjacent densely settled surrounding area that together have a minimum population of 50,000 or more residents.

Using this definition, the urban population is distributed across very diverse residential settings and is homogeneous only in terms of a minimum density criterion. The rural population has always been a residual, consisting of the nonurban population. As a result, it might be assumed to be homogeneous, but it, too, is made up of disparate parts such as the farm–nonfarm populations or persons living in villages and the balance dispersed across open country.

As a way of complementing the conventional rural–urban distinction, the U.S. Bureau of the Census employs the designation of Standard Metropolitan Statistical Area (SMSA). In the 1980 census, SMSAs consisted of counties (or townships in New England) which have either a city with a population of at least 50,000 or a Bureau of the Census urbanized area of at least 50,000 *and* a total metropolitan statistical area population of at least 100,000.

People living in an SMSA are designated by the Bureau of the Census as "metropolitan." Those living outside an SMSA constitute the "nonmetropolitan" population. While this distinction might reflect differences in settlement more accurately than the rural–urban dichotomy, substantial heterogeneity also exists within each of these categories. Both metropolitan and nonmetropolitan areas contain rural and urban populations—i.e., some farmers live in metropolitan areas while many nonmetropolitan cities contain services typically associated with urban population centers.

Older Populations in Urban and Rural Areas

In 1980, the proportion of the population 65 years old and older in urban and rural areas was 11.4 percent and 10.9 percent, respectively. This represents a shift from previous decades when the urban population was slightly lower in the proportion of elder persons (in 1970 the comparative figures were 9.8% for urban and 10.1% for rural). Over the decade, urban places, particularly those outside urbanized areas (see Table 2.1), generally increased the proportion of elderly more than the rural. The highest 1980 percentage (15.4 %), however, occurred in villages of 1,000 to 2,500 in rural territories, whereas the lowest, 10.0 percent, was in the urban fringe (i.e., that part of the urban population which may loosely be designated as suburban). This pattern was consistent with data from the 1970 census.

In general, 1980 data indicated that the proportion of the elderly population increased as the size of place declined. Outside urbanized areas, for example, 12.9 percent of the population of places 10,000 to 50,000 inhabitants were elderly; 14.7 percent of the populations of places 2,500 to 10,000; and 15.4 percent of the population of places 1,000 to 2,500. If age data for incorporated places under 1,000 had been tabulated, it is highly likely that they

Table 2.1. Total Population and Population Aged 65 and Over by Residence Areas for the United States, 1980

Residence areas	All ages	Number 65 and over	Percent
Total	226,472[a]	25,539	11.3
Urban	167,024	19,042	11.4
Inside urbanized areas	139,151	15,194	10.9
Central cities	67,029	8,014	12.0
Urban fringe	72,122	7,180	10.0
Outside urbanized areas	27,873	3,848	13.8
Places of 10,000 or more	13,480	1,736	12.9
Places of 2,500 to 10,000	14,393	2,112	14.7
Rural	59,448	6,497	10.9
Places 1,000 to 2,500	7,035	1,085	15.4
Other rural	52,413	5,412	10.3

[a]Numbers in thousands.
Source: Census of Population and Housing, 1980. Summary Tape File 1.

would have shown a still higher percentage of persons 65 and over than places of 1,000 to 2,500 (see Smith, 1954). If so, it would suggest that the residual open-country rural population would have had a somewhat lower concentration of older persons than the 10.3 percent figure shown in Table 2.1.

Despite the transformation of the United States from an essentially rural society to dominantly urban, it is still relatively true that villages and small towns are to a considerable extent America's "old folks' home" (Fuguitt & Johansen, 1975; Nelson, 1961; Smith, 1954). We must constantly remember, however, that in this urban society nearly three-quarters of the total population of the United States, and of the elderly population, live in urbanized areas.

While each of the demographic processes affect the above distribution, migration plays an especially important part (Cowgill, 1970; Sheldon, 1958). Migration affects the age structures of the populations of both origin and destination. Since migrants are most often young, migration tends to have a "younging" effect on the receiving population and, conversely, an "aging" effect upon the sending area. There is also a secondary and cumulative effect of migration. The outmigration of younger people tends to decrease the fertility of the population of sending areas and, hence, has a double effect in the direction of aging at population. In contrast, inmigration tends to have the opposite compounding effect. The effect of migration is evidenced in the high concentrations of elderly in central cities in contrast to the suburbs and the fact that many farm persons upon retirement move into nearby villages or small towns.

Differences in the Population by Race

Since blacks and "other races" have been characterized by somewhat higher fertility and mortality than whites, the concentration of older persons in these populations is less: in 1980, 7.6 percent of the total black population was over 65 years of age and 5.8 percent of "other races," as compared with 12.0 percent of the total white population. But the patterns of distribution across residential categories do not differ greatly between the racial groups. By far the largest proportion of the elderly in each racial group resided in urban areas (Table 2.2). There are some racial differences, however, in concentration of the elderly within urbanized areas. Over half of all elderly blacks (58%) and "other races" (51%) lived in central cities, whereas only 30 percent of the whites lived in central cities. A larger share of whites lived in the urban fringe and rural areas than either blacks or "other races."

Another way of analyzing these data is to examine the extent to which each residence category had more or less than its pro rata share of the aged population for each racial group (i.e., compare the distribution of the total population with the distribution of the over 65 years of age population). On this basis, a different pattern emerges. Table 2.2 indicates that central cities, smaller cities, and villages had more than their pro rata share of the white aged. The black elderly, meanwhile, tended to be concentrated in all places outside urbanized areas, especially in the "other rural" category. For the "other races," the elderly were most heavily concentrated in central cities and in rural areas. To a large extent these differences are the result of historical patterns of migration—e.g., the heavy migration of young adult blacks from the South to the central cities of the North and West, the movement to suburbs, and the location of immigrants in large metropolitan areas.

Table 2.2. Percent Distribution of Population Aged 65 and Over by Race and Residence Areas for the United States, 1980[a]

Residence areas	White		Black		Other	
	All ages	65 and over	All ages	65 and over	All ages	65 and over
Total	(172,944)[b] 100.0	(20,837) 100.0	(24,330) 100.0	(1,857) 100.0	(3,786) 100.0	(220) 100.0
Urban	73.9	76.4	86.9	82.6	84.7	82.7
Inside urbanized areas	60.9	61.0	77.9	70.1	75.9	73.2
Central cities	25.9	30.3	58.7	57.6	41.9	50.5
Urban fringe	34.9	30.5	19.0	13.0	34.0	23.0
Outside urbanized areas	13.0	15.6	9.2	12.5	8.8	9.5
Places of 10,000 or more	6.4	7.2	4.9	6.4	4.3	4.5
Places of 2,500 to 10,000	6.6	8.4	4.3	6.1	4.5	5.0
Rural	26.1	23.6	13.0	17.4	15.3	17.3
Places of 1,000 to 2,500	3.1	4.0	1.4	2.2	2.1	2.7
Other rural	23.0	19.6	11.6	15.2	13.2	14.5

[a] In order to maintain confidentiality, the Census Bureau suppresses tabulations of characteristics of very small groups of people. For example, on a record for an enumeration district with a population of 1 to 14 persons, population characteristics such as age are suppressed. Since the data in this table were obtained by aggregating across enumeration districts and block groups, the counts include only geographical areas with 15 or more persons.

[b] Numbers in parentheses are in thousands.

Source: Census of Population and Housing, 1980. Summary Tape File 1.

Differences in Male and Female Populations

It is generally recognized that the problems of old age in America are largely the problems of women. In 1980, 6 of 10 older Americans were women (Table 2.3). Women 65 years and over outnumbered their male counterparts by nearly five million; or put another way, for every 100 women aged 65 and over, there were only 68 men. This sex imbalance in the older population reflects higher male mortality at every age and is evident in each residence category. In addition, the sex imbalance among the aged has a very significant impact on the marital status and living arrangements of the elderly.

Most elderly, regardless of sex, resided in urban areas; but some residential differences in sex distribution did exist. It is evident that elderly women were more likely to be found in urban areas and less likely to reside in rural areas; for aged males, the opposite pattern held. The relatively high ratio of males among the elderly people in the "other rural" category reflects different patterns of migration for males and females. Elderly widowers were more likely to remain on farms, but farm widows most frequently moved to towns.

Differences in Marital and Family Status

In the remainder of the chapter we will use the metropolitan–nonmetropolitan distinction rather than the urban–rural categories. There is some basis to prefer this distinction because of the urban-like character of rural residents living within the boundaries of metropolitan areas. As previously noted, however, the two concepts are not synonymous. For marital and family status, 1980 Current Population Survey results are the only data currently available. These data cannot be tabulated by the urban–rural classification employed in the preceding tables. Instead, we have used 1980 metropolitan and nonmetropolitan categories with the latter subclassified by farm–nonfarm residence.

The marital distribution of the elderly noninstitutional population by sex and residence is shown in Table 2.4. For each residence category, most men 65 years and over were married and lived with their spouses; few lived alone. In contrast, women 65 years and over were much more likely to be widowed than married, except in the nonmetropolitan farm category where elderly widows have traditionally moved from farms to nearby villages and small towns at the time of the death of their spouse. Indeed, more of the elderly of both sexes were married and fewer widowed in nonmetropolitan farm areas than in metropolitan areas.

Table 2.3. Percent Distribution of the Male and Female Population Aged 65 and Over and Sex Ratios of the Elderly by Residence Areas for the United States, 1980[a]

Residence areas	Male		Female		Sex ratios
	All ages	65 and over	All ages	65 and over	
Total	(110,015)[b] 100.0	(10,300) 100.0	(116,457) 100.0	(15,239) 100.0	67.6
Urban	73.0	71.5	74.5	76.6	63.0
Inside urbanized areas	61.0	57.3	62.0	61.0	63.4
Central cities	29.0	29.5	30.2	32.7	60.9
Urban fringe	32.0	27.8	32.0	28.3	66.3
Outside urbanized areas	12.1	14.2	12.5	15.6	61.5
Places of 10,000 or more	6.0	6.3	6.0	7.1	60.1
Places of 2,500 to 10,000	6.2	7.9	6.5	8.5	62.6
Rural	27.0	28.5	25.5	23.4	82.5
Places 1,000 to 2,500	3.1	4.2	3.1	4.3	66.2
Other rural	24.0	24.3	22.4	19.1	86.2

[a]In order to maintain confidentiality, the Census Bureau suppresses tabulations of characteristics of very small groups of people. For example, on a record for an enumeration district with a population of 1 to 14 persons, population characteristics such as age are suppressed. Since the data in this table were obtained by aggregating across enumeration districts and block groups, the counts include only geographical areas with 15 or more persons.

[b]Numbers in parentheses in thousands.

Source: Census of Population and Housing, 1980. Summary Tape File 1.

Table 2.4. Marital Status of Persons Aged 65 and Over by Sex and Residence for the United States, 1980

Marital status	Metropolitan	Nonmetropolitan	Nonmetropolitan nonfarm	Nonmetropolitan farm
Total	(14,557)[a] 100.0	(7,703) 100.0	(7,146) 100.0	(557) 100.0
Married	52.0	57.3	56.1	73.3
Widowed	36.8	34.1	35.3	18.9
Divorced-separated	5.0	3.8	4.0	1.3
Never married	6.2	4.7	4.6	6.5
Males	(5,875) 100.0	(3,243) 100.0	(2,932) 100.0	(311) 100.0
Married	74.8	79.0	79.1	78.3
Widowed	14.9	11.5	11.6	11.3
Divorced-separated	4.8	5.0	5.2	2.3
Never married	5.5	4.5	4.1	8.1
Females	(8,682) 100.0	(4,460) 100.0	(4,214) 100.0	(246) 100.0
Married	36.7	41.6	40.1	67.0
Widowed	51.6	50.6	51.8	28.5
Divorced-separated	5.0	3.0	3.2	0.0
Never married	6.7	4.9	4.9	4.4

[a]Numbers in parentheses in thousands.
Source: March 1980 Current Population Survey.

While very few of the current cohort of elders of either sex were divorced or separated, men were more likely than women to report these statuses. Divorce and separation occurred least frequently in the nonmetropolitan farm population. Likewise, the proportions of elderly that were never married is quite small for both sexes. Females were more likely than males to have remained single, however, with metropolitan areas having the largest proportion and nonmetropolitan farms the smallest. In contrast, those few males that were never married were more likely to be found in nonmetropolitan farm category, followed by the metropolitan.

As we might expect based on the sex ratio and marital status data described above, the family statuses of males and females differed sharply. Table 2.5 reveals that a much greater proportion of older men were living in a family setting than older women regardless of residence category. For most of these men this family included their wives, but for women significantly fewer were living in families which included their husbands. Females were more often found living alone (about 4 out of 10 except for the farm category). It is also evident that "husband-wife families," for both elderly men and women, were more prevalent in the nonmetropolitan than in the metropolitan population. Within the nonmetropolitan population, there was little difference between the percentage of farm and nonfarm males that lived in "husband-wife" families; but for nonmetropolitan farm females, the proportion in husband-wife families was considerably above any other residence category. The largest proportion of elderly males living with "other relatives" were found in the nonmetropolitan farm population (25.3%), whereas for elderly females the largest proportion were located in the metropolitan population (25.2%).

While some of the residential differences in marital and family statuses between males and females are due to the tendency of married women to outlive their spouses and the low probability of women remarrying, migration certainly plays an important role. Clifford, Heaton, and Fuguitt (1982), for example, have reported a positive selection of dependent-type households in the nonmetropolitan to metropolitan migration stream. In contrast, there is a positive selection of independent households in those elders who migrated from metropolitan to nonmetropolitan areas. This selective migration is likely to increase the social and economic impact of elderly residential mobility in both metropolitan and nonmetropolitan areas.

Table 2.5. Family Status of Persons Aged 65 and Over by Sex and Residence for the United States, 1980

Family status	Metropolitan	Nonmetropolitan	Nonmetropolitan nonfarm	Nonmetropolitan farm
Total	(14,522)[a] 100.0	(7,695) 100.0	(7,138) 100.0	(557) 100.0
Husband-wife family	43.4	48.9	47.8	61.8
Other family	23.8	20.3	20.0	23.8
Living alone	30.9	29.4	30.5	14.3
Nonfamily	1.9	1.6	1.5	0.1
Males	(5,873) 100.0	(3,236) 100.0	(2,925) 100.0	(311) 100.0
Husband-wife family	60.7	66.3	66.5	64.7
Other family	21.8	18.7	18.0	25.3
Living alone	15.4	13.2	13.6	9.7
Nonfamily	2.1	1.8	2.0	0.3
Females	(8,649) 100.0	(4,459) 100.0	(4,213) 100.0	(246) 100.0
Husband-wife family	31.6	36.2	34.9	58.1
Other family	25.2	21.4	21.4	21.9
Living alone	41.4	41.1	42.3	20.0
Nonfamily	1.8	1.3	1.4	0.0

[a]Numbers in parentheses in thousands.
Source: March 1980 Current Population Survey.

Changes in Rural Age Structure:
1970–1980

The basic units of analysis in this section are all counties in the United States, with county equivalents designated for New England. The 1980 Census definition of metropolitan is used throughout the analysis. In order to distinguish different levels of urban development or possible metropolitan influence, nonmetropolitan counties are classified into subcategories as a function of their adjacency to metropolitan areas and the size of their largest place (Hines, Brown, & Zimmer, 1975). As a result, nonmetropolitan counties with no urban populations (i.e., no places larger than 2,500) may be regarded as the quintessence of rurality, especially those that are nonadjacent, because they are relatively free of urban contact.

Older Populations in Metropolitan–Nonmetropolitan Areas: 1970–1980

A cursory glance at the data presented in Table 2.6 reveals that metropolitan areas have a lower proportion of their populations over the age of 65 years than any nonmetropolitan category. The highest proportion of elderly was found in nonadjacent counties in which the size of the largest place was less than 2,500 persons (14.8%). It is also generally true that as the size of place increased and as the proximity to urban areas increased, the concentration of elderly decreased. For instance, 12.9 percent of the population in adjacent nonmetropolitan counties were aged 65 and over, whereas 13.3 percent were elderly in nonadjacent counties. Within the nonadjacent category, there was a definite gradient by size of largest place ranging from 11.9 percent for counties in which the largest place was 10,000 or more persons to 14.8 percent for those counties in which the largest place was less than 2,500. (Recall that data in Table 2.1, based on a different residence breakdown, also indicated a tendency for smaller-sized places to have a higher proportion of their population aged 65 years and over.)

The number of persons aged 65 and over increased in the decade of the 1970s in both metropolitan and nonmetropolitan areas. With the nonmetropolitan migration turnaround, the total population change for all age categories was higher in nonmetropolitan than metropolitan areas during the 1970–1980 period. This was not true, however, for the elderly population. The elderly popula-

Table 2.6. Percent 65 and Over of the Total Population 1980 and Decennial Percent Increase of the Total Population and the Elderly Population 1970 to 1980 by Metropolitan Status, Adjacency, and Size of Largest Place for the United States

Residence area	Percent 65 and over 1980	Percent change in elderly 1970–1980	Percent change in total 1970–1980
Total	11.3	27.9	11.4
Metropolitan	10.7	28.1	10.3
Nonmetropolitan	13.0	27.4	15.1
Adjacent	12.9	32.4	16.5
Less than 2,500	13.6	33.0	19.7
2,500–9,999	13.7	29.8	16.2
10,000 or more	12.1	34.5	16.1
Nonadjacent	13.3	22.9	12.8
Less than 2,500	14.8	16.4	12.1
2,500–9,999	14.0	22.8	11.9
10,000 or more	11.9	27.1	13.9

Source: Censuses of Population and Housing, 1970 and 1980. Summary Tape File 1.

tion in metropolitan areas increased by 28 percent during the decade while in nonmetropolitan areas the increase was 27 percent. In each of the nonmetropolitan adjacency categories, however, the rate of change exceeded the metropolitan rate. Moreover, in nonmetropolitan counties there was also a pattern of increase in the rate of growth as the size of the largest place increased. Thus, areas with low concentrations of the elderly (i.e., the most urban counties) had greater increases in the elderly population than did areas with high concentrations (i.e., the most rural counties).

Another striking feature of the data presented in Table 2.6 is that the rate of population growth among the elderly exceeded that of the total population in every category of counties. In many cases the rates were two to three times as high. The total national population increased by 11 percent over the decade of the 1970s, while the elderly population increased by 28 percent during this same period. In metropolitan areas, the total population increased by 10 percent and the elderly by 28 percent. In nonmetropolitan areas, the rates for the total population and the elderly were 15 percent and 27 percent, respectively. The smallest difference in the rates of growth between the total population and the aged population (12% versus 16%) occurred in nonadjacent counties in which the size of the largest place was less than 2,500 people.

The nonmetropolitan population reversal that has occurred since 1970 has included a net migration of the elderly that favored nonmetropolitan areas (Fuguitt & Tordella, 1980). Why, then, did the numbers of older persons increase more rapidly just in those areas with lower or negative elderly net migration rates? Evidently the answer lies in the nature of the turnaround. Many of the elderly have moved to areas which have a history of continuing migration loss of young people. These are areas, therefore, which had fewer residents present to move up to the age of 65 during the 1970s. The magnitude of this "aging in place" factor appears to be more important than elderly net migration in influencing the overall growth of the elderly in a locale.

Lichter, Fuguitt, Heaton, and Clifford (1981) have also examined recent shifts in the proportion of the elderly. In addition to the differentials in "aging in place" just discussed, metropolitan areas with a low proportion of their population over the age of 65 have seen this proportion increase in recent years (relative to nonmetropolitan areas) because of the net outmigration of the young. Similarly, although nonmetropolitan areas gained elderly migrants, they also gained younger migrants, which tended to cancel the effect of migration on the change in the proportion of the populated over 65 years of age.

State Variations: 1970–1980

Data in Table 2.7 demonstrate that in 1980 there was a definite gradient in the percentage of the population age 65 and over from metropolitan counties to the totally rural counties of the United States, ranging from 10.7 percent to 14.3 percent (for conciseness we have not distinguished adjacent and nonadjacent counties in these analyses). A similar gradient was found for (1) all census regions, (2) all divisions within regions except the Pacific, and (3) all states except Arizona, Colorado, Florida, Louisiana, Maryland, Nevada, Oregon, Rhode Island, Tennessee, Vermont, and West Virginia.

In Arizona and Rhode Island, which have no totally rural

Table 2.7. Percent 65 and Over of the Total Population 1980 and Decennial Percent Increase of the Elderly Population 1970 to 1980 by Residence Areas for Regions, Divisions, and States

Region, division, and state	Total		Metropolitan counties		Part-urban nonmetropolitan counties		All-rural nonmetropolitan counties	
	1980 Pct. 65+	1970–1980 Percent change	1980 Pct. 65+	1970–1980 Percent change	1980 Pct. 65+	1970–1980 Percent change	1980 Pct. 65+	1970–1980 Percent change
United States	11.3	27.9	10.7	28.1	12.8	31.4	14.3	7.9
Northeast	12.3	17.3	12.2	15.3	13.4	38.4	14.9	-3.2
New England	12.3	20.3	12.1	18.4	12.6	21.0	15.1	51.2
Connecticut	11.7	26.7	11.6	26.8	12.7	25.2	—	—
Massachusetts	12.7	14.8	12.4	12.7	—	—	18.5	63.1
Maine	12.5	13.5	12.1	23.7	12.7	20.4	13.6	30.0
New Hampshire	11.2	31.9	9.9	33.1	12.8	27.9	—	61.1
Rhode Island	13.4	22.2	13.6	21.3	11.3	35.5	—	—
Vermont	11.4	23.7	7.6	28.3	12.6	4.4	12.3	53.2
Middle Atlantic	12.4	16.3	12.2	14.3	13.6	43.7	13.6	-69.5
New Jersey	11.7	23.9	11.2	18.6	16.9	81.9	—	—
New York	12.3	10.7	12.2	10.0	12.7	34.1	13.3	-87.5
Pennsylvania	12.9	20.8	12.8	19.0	13.3	40.2	13.6	-52.2
North Central	11.4	17.3	10.2	19.3	13.7	17.8	17.1	-1.4
East North Central	10.8	18.4	10.2	20.2	12.8	20.4	15.4	-25.2
Illinois	11.0	15.9	10.2	24.4	14.4	10.0	16.2	-72.3
Indiana	10.7	19.0	10.1	20.2	12.0	16.7	12.1	17.1
Michigan	9.8	21.7	9.3	18.7	11.7	31.2	15.4	45.7
Ohio	10.8	17.8	10.6	17.7	11.6	32.0	13.9	-80.1
Wisconsin	12.0	19.9	10.8	18.5	14.0	20.6	16.9	30.2

Table 2.7. (cont.)

Region, division, and state	Total		Metropolitan counties		Part-urban nonmetropolitan counties		All-rural nonmetropolitan counties	
	1980 Pct. 65+	1970–1980 Percent change	1980 Pct. 65+	1970–1980 Percent change	1980 Pct. 65+	1970–1980 Percent change	1980 Pct. 65+	1970–1980 Percent change
West North Central	12.8	15.2	10.5	16.3	14.8	14.9	17.9	12.4
Iowa	13.3	11.0	10.2	12.9	15.0	10.3	18.3	8.7
Kansas	12.9	16.5	9.9	24.3	14.8	13.9	19.7	8.2
Minnesota	11.8	17.7	10.0	16.7	14.7	19.5	17.4	15.3
Missouri	13.2	15.7	11.6	14.2	15.3	17.9	18.7	17.8
Nebraska	13.1	12.6	9.5	16.3	14.9	12.7	18.8	7.1
North Dakota	12.3	21.6	9.0	23.2	12.7	22.4	15.9	19.7
South Dakota	13.2	13.4	9.6	25.5	13.8	12.1	15.6	8.9
South	11.3	41.1	11.3	45.8	12.8	36.6	13.2	19.8
South Atlantic	11.8	49.2	11.6	52.8	12.1	48.3	12.7	13.7
Delaware	10.0	35.6	9.4	29.8	11.1	46.7	—	—
District of Columbia	11.6	5.6	11.6	5.6	—	—	—	—
Florida	17.3	71.2	17.1	67.7	19.2	100.0	13.3	77.8
Georgia	9.4	45.4	8.0	53.0	11.4	38.9	12.6	35.0
Maryland	9.4	32.2	9.1	31.9	12.2	30.1	9.6	43.5
North Carolina	10.2	46.4	9.2	47.1	11.1	47.5	13.3	36.1
South Carolina	9.2	51.3	8.5	54.6	10.2	47.9	11.0	34.4
Virginia	9.5	34.2	8.4	49.6	11.4	40.7	12.9	+17.6
West Virginia	12.2	22.8	12.2	24.2	11.9	22.2	13.7	20.9

East South Central	11.3	30.9	10.2	33.0	12.3	30.4	12.8	23.3
Alabama	11.3	35.7	10.6	36.5	12.3	35.8	13.2	22.2
Kentucky	11.2	21.9	10.2	21.1	11.8	23.6	12.5	19.6
Mississippi	11.5	30.8	8.5	50.7	12.4	27.4	13.3	22.8
Tennessee	11.3	34.8	10.4	34.4	12.8	35.9	12.6	32.7
West South Central	10.4	35.0	8.7	39.7	14.3	28.9	15.0	27.8
Arkansas	13.7	32.0	11.2	34.3	14.9	29.1	17.5	44.0
Louisiana	9.6	32.5	9.0	33.61	10.8	30.7	9.2	33.5
Oklahoma	12.4	25.9	10.1	31.8	15.5	21.2	17.8	17.9
Texas	9.6	39.3	8.2	43.7	15.2	3.9	16.8	20.6
West	9.9	39.5	9.8	38.3	9.8	50.8	10.6	13.5
Mountain	9.3	53.3	8.9	61.1	10.0	55.9	10.9	−10.4
Arizona	113.	90.7	11.6	88.3	10.4	99.4	—	—
Colorado	8.6	32.1	8.0	35.6	11.5	24.2	9.3	14.2
Idaho	9.9	39.8	8.6	45.0	10.2	90.4	10.6	−66.3
Montana	10.7	23.5	9.4	32.2	10.5	22.4	13.8	18.0
Nevada	8.2	11.36	7.8	120.1	10.2	89.1	9.5	98.6
New Mexico	8.0	65.5	8.0	82.4	9.5	70.4	9.6	−35.1
Utah	7.5	42.9	7.0	41.6	9.0	48.1	10.3	39.7
Wyoming	7.9	23.6	6.3	19.4	7.9	23.8	12.3	27.5
Pacific	10.2	35.4	10.0	34.1	11.4	45.4	10.4	56.2
Alaska	2.9	67.9	2.0	103.6	3.3	55.4	4.1	56.9
California	10.2	34.7	10.1	33.7	11.5	52.7	13.3	66.5
Hawaii	7.9	73.1	7.3	76.9	—	—	10.3	63.7
Oregon	11.5	34.4	11.3	29.5	12.0	44.0	11.6	38.4
Washington	10.4	34.6	10.0	33.8	12.4	37.3	12.4	37.6

Source: Censuses of Population and Housing, 1970 and 1980. Summary Tape File 1.

counties, and in West Virginia, the concentration of older persons
in the metropolitan areas exceeded that in the part-urban nonmetropolitan counties. For the remaining states (Colorado, Florida,
Louisiana, Maryland, Nevada, Oregan, Tennessee, and Vermont),
the percentage of persons 65 years and over in the totally rural
counties was lower than that in the part-urban counties.

Among the states in 1980, the highest concentrations of persons age 65 and over in totally rural counties were found in Kansas, Iowa, Massachusetts, Missouri, and Nebraska (18.0–19.7%).
With the exception of Massachusetts, each of these states is located
in the West North Central division where there has been a history
of outmigration of the young coupled with a greater practice of
formal retirement to villages and small towns. Those having the
lowest concentrations—ranging from 4.1 to 9.6%—were Alaska,
Colorado, Louisiana, Maryland, Nevada, and New Mexico.

In general, the states with high concentrations of elderly persons were those in which the level of fertility had been moderate
and from which there had been a rather consistent pattern of general outmigration for most of the 20th century. Those with low
concentrations were states with relatively high levels of fertility
and/or a heavy inmigration of young persons. As was seen for the
nation as a whole in Table 2.6, some of the states which had the
greatest increases in their rural aged population since 1970 were
states with relatively low proportions of the rural aged. Likewise,
some of the states with the highest proportions of the rural aged in
1980 were those which evidenced the least increase during the
previous decade. Recent shifts in the patterns of redistribution for
nonmetropolitan areas and the ability of these areas to retain their
populations are associated with this situation, but the exact mix of
demographic components underlying absolute and proportional elderly growth is complex and difficult to determine.

Within states, also, the totally rural counties which contained
the heaviest concentration of elderly in 1980 usually had the slow-
est rate of decennial change in the elderly population. In the decade 1970 to 1980, the percent change in the elderly population in
the United States was 28 percent for metropolitan counties, 31
percent for part-urban nonmetropolitan counties, and 8 percent for
totally rural counties. Of the 45 states with all-rural counties, only
14 had rates of change in their elderly populations who lived in
all-rural counties which exceeded the state rate for metropolitan
counties. In those states with no all-rural counties (i.e., Arizona,
Connecticut, Delaware, New Jersey, and Rhode Island), the rate of

growth in the part-urban counties exceeded that of the metropolitan counties (with the exception of Connecticut).

For the period of 1970 to 1980, the totally rural population aged 65 and over in Michigan, Nebraska, New Mexico, New York, Pennsylvania, and Virginia grew at rates less than for the nation as a whole. In absolute numbers, these states experienced a less than 8 percent growth since 1970. Indeed, with the exception of Nebraska, there was a percentage decrease in the all-rural elderly population in each of these states. All other states had rates of growth in their all-rural populations which exceeded the national average. A large number of states had rapid growth (defined as 30% or more of the comparable 1970 figure) in their all-rural elderly population during this period. Indeed, the rural elderly populations in California, Florida, Hawaii, Massachusetts, and Nevada grew more than 60 percent between 1970 and 1980 and several other states that registered high growth rates included Alaska (57%), Arkansas (44%), Maryland (44%), Michigan (46%), and Vermont (53%).

Of the four geographic regions of the nation, the South had the highest rate of growth in the elderly population (41.1%) followed by the West (39.1%), Northeast (28.7%), and North Central (22.4%) regions. The greatest change in the metropolitan elderly populations occurred in the South (45.8%), and the smallest change occurred in the Northeast (27.9%). In the West, the rate of change for this category exceeded the national average, whereas in the North Central region it was less than the average for the entire country. The greatest change in the part-urban nonmetropolitan population occurred in the West, followed by the Northeast, South, and the North Central regions. The completely rural counties in the South had by far the highest rates of growth among regions. In the Northeast and the North Central regions there was a percent decrease in the all-rural elderly populations primarily because of the Middle Atlantic states of New York and Pennsylvania and the East North Central states of Illinois and Ohio. For the most part the regions with the lowest concentrations of elderly in each of these categories of counties are the fastest growing and vice versa.

Given these varying and changing patterns of distribution, it is important not to assume that the highest percentages and the highest rates of growth are synonymous with the greatest numbers of the aged. The patterns of distribution of the elderly in terms of absolute numbers approximates that of the total population. The primary concentration of the elderly is in cities and small towns rather than in wide-open spaces. When planning services and assessing markets, absolute numbers may be more significant than percentages.

Migration of the Elderly to Nonmetropolitan Areas

At several points in the preceding analysis the impact of migration on the distribution of the elderly population has been evident. In the decade of the 1970s the United States witnessed a new pattern of migration marked by deconcentration away from large cities and the Northeast, and corresponding growth in suburbs, smaller SMSAs, and nonmetropolitan areas. The elderly were an important part of this movement, and their movement to nonmetropolitan areas often preceded that of the general population. Several authors documented this change up through 1975 (Bowles, 1978; Fuguitt & Tordella, 1980; Golant, 1979; Tucker, 1976).

Between 1950 and 1960 there was a small net outmigration of the elderly from nonmetropolitan counties matched by a small net inmigration for metropolitan areas. In nonadjacent nonmetropolitan counties the net migration was almost zero for counties which had a city with more than 10,000 people but was almost minus 10 per 1,000 population per year for completely rural counties. Between 1960 and 1970 the metropolitan–nonmetropolitan rates reversed, with a very slight net loss for metropolitan counties and a net gain in migration for nonmetropolitan counties. For nonadjacent counties the differential by size of largest place almost disappeared and also reversed: completely rural counties had a slightly higher net gain in migration than did the more urbanized counties. The nonmetropolitan net gains for the period 1970 to 1975 were systematically above those for 1960–1970, reflecting an intensification of the process that began in the previous decade (Fuguitt & Tordella, 1980). It was not until 1970–1975 that the under-65 and total nonmetropolitan net migration rates exceeded the metropolitan rates, although this was true for the elderly in 1960–1970. These results suggest that at least part of the more recent nonmetropolitan migration gain for the younger ages may be in response to opportunities made possible by the earlier movement of the elderly which brought to rural areas the incomes of the elderly and their demands for construction, trade, and services.

Unfortunately, net migration figures for the period 1970–1980 are not yet available. The March 1980 Current Population Survey does provide some insights, however, into the metropolitan–nonmetropolitan migration and characteristics of movers between 1975 and 1980. Table 2.8 demonstrates that the net flow of persons age 65 and over to nonmetropolitan areas persisted through the last half of the 1970s. Both young and old experienced a net inmigration to nonmetropolitan areas, but the elderly population grew at a slightly higher rate due to migration (2.7%) than did the younger age categories (2.3%). Because the young and elderly rates are similar and migration was small relative to the nonmigrant population, migration had only a minuscule effect on the changing percentage of the nonmetropolitan population that was aged 65 or more.

Attempts to explain the moving patterns of the elderly have found inadequate the dominant migration theories which emphasize potential economic gains. Quality of life and family ties appear to be more appropriate explanations for moves (Cebula, 1979; Long & Hansen, 1979). The greatest gains of elderly migrants in nonmetropolitan counties occurred in areas with mild climates and developed recreation sectors (Heaton, Clifford & Fuguitt, 1981). Migration to nonmetropolitan areas has also been associated with retirement (Heaton, Clifford & Fuguitt, 1980) and, thus, implies that job opportunities are not as salient in the decision to move for those in the later years of life.

Table 2.8. Comparison of Young and Elderly Migration Between Metropolitan and Nonmetropolitan Areas, 1975–1980

	0–64	65+
1. Metropolitan residents	113,284[a]	14,752
2. Metropolitan to nonmetropolitan migrants	6,856	481
3. Nonmetropolitan residents	48,873	8,165
4. Nonmetropolitan to metropolitan migrants	5,736	257
5. Net exchange(#2, above, minus #4)	1,120	224
6. Net impact on nonmetropolitan areas (#5, above, divided by #3)	2.3	2.7

[a]Numbers in thousands, except #6.
Source: March 1980 Current Population Survey.

The typology developed by Wiseman and Roseman (1979) helps to place elderly migration in perspective. They present three types of elderly migration:

1. *Amenity migration* generally occurs in the early retirement period, although the selection of the place to live may have been made earlier based on vacation experience or property ownerships.
2. In *return migration* the loss of a spouse or deteriorating health may be more salient in the decision to move, and the choice of a destination is conditioned by prior residential experience.
3. *Kinship migration,* like return migration, may be precipitated by the loss of independence but the destination is constrained to the area in which the children are employed.

The frequency of these various types of migration in nonmetropolitan areas remains to be documented.

Presumably, migration occurs when the perceived benefits for an individual exceed the costs. Individual costs and benefits, however, may not parallel the costs and benefits for the community as a whole—particularly with respect to the elderly. For the community, the costs and benefits will depend to a large extent on the characteristic of the migrants. For example, the migration of the poor to areas with a lower cost of living creates a different impact than does the migration of the rich in search of amenity-endowed environments.

Results from the March 1980 Current Population Survey (see Table 2.9) reveal several interesting contrasts between migrants to and from nonmetropolitan areas. Migrants to metropolitan areas, male and female, were less likely to be married with a spouse present than nonmetropolitan migrants. As a result, nonmetropolitan areas experienced a relative gain in elderly married couples vis-à-vis those without a spouse. Migrants were more educated than the overall nonmetropolitan population, particularly those who moved *into* nonmetropolitan areas. Thus, migrational patterns have resulted in a net educational gain for the nonmetropolitan elderly. Among males, there was little difference between the two migrant groups in the proportion not in the labor force. Among females, however, those coming to nonmetropolitan areas were more likely to be employed than those in the counterstream. As a

Table 2.9. Characteristics of Elderly Migrants to and from Nonmetropolitan Areas, 1975–1980

Characteristics	Total nonmetro population		Nonmetro to metro		Metro to nonmetro	
	No.	Percent	No.	Percent	No.	Percent
Marital status						
Males						
Married, spouse present	2,874[a]	78.1	78	72.2	157	77.0
Other	806	21.9	30	27.8	47	23.0
Females						
Married, spouse present	2,058	41.3	51	34.5	111	40.1
Other	2,920	58.7	97	65.5	166	59.9
Education						
Males						
0–11	2,517	68.4	54	49.5	101	49.8
12	651	17.7	37	33.9	44	21.7
13+	511	13.9	18	16.5	58	28.6
Females						
0–11	3,066	61.6	77	52.0	135	48.7
12	1,110	22.3	40	27.0	66	23.8
13+	802	16.1	31	20.9	76	27.4
Labor force participation						
Males						
Not in labor force	2,984	81.1	96	88.1	179	87.7
In labor force	696	18.9	13	11.9	25	12.3
Females						
Not in labor force	4,542	91.2	146	98.6	257	92.4
In labor force	436	8.8	2	1.4	21	7.6

Table 2.9. (cont.)

Characteristics	Total nonmetro population		Nonmetro to metro		Metro to nonmetro	
	No.	Percent	No.	Percent	No.	Percent
Income						
Males						
0–2,999	726	19.7	13	11.9	20	9.8
3,000–4,999	880	23.9	22	20.2	43	21.1
5,000–6,999	703	19.1	27	24.8	49	24.0
7,000–9,999	612	16.6	25	22.9	38	18.6
10,000+	758	20.6	22	20.2	54	26.5
Females						
0–2,999	2,248	45.2	58	40.6	106	42.2
3,000–4,999	1,289	25.9	58	40.6	65	25.9
5,000–6,999	606	12.2	17	11.9	41	16.3
7,000–9,999	430	8.6	9	6.3	26	10.4
10,000+	405	8.1	1	0.7	13	5.2
Public assistance						
No	3,025	98.9	74	97.4	161	100.0
Yes	34	1.1	2	2.6	0	0.0
Poverty level						
Above	2,892	86.2	75	92.6	162	95.9
Below	463	13.8	6	7.4	7	4.1

[a] Numbers in thousands.

Source: March 1980 Current Population Survey.

consequence, nonmetropolitan areas appear to have benefited economically from the migration exchange. Migrants to nonmetropolitan areas had higher incomes and were less likely to be on public assistance or below the poverty level than either the total nonmetropolitan population or migrants to metropolitan areas. In fact, the migration of those on public assistance into nonmetropolitan areas was virtually nil.

In sum, elderly migration relocates into nonmetropolitan areas people who are positively selected on the basis of income, education, and marital status. Since migration tends to flow to certain areas, the impact in these areas is greater than is the impact on the aggregate nonmetropolitan population. Thus, elderly migration may be beneficial to receiving areas. Whether or not this benefit persists as the migrants reach older ages remains to be seen.

Reviewing Survey Data

So far, this consideration of elderly migration has been based on the limited kinds of data available from the Current Population Survey of the U.S. Bureau of the Census. Another, much richer source of information lies in sample surveys of migrants to specific nonmetropolitan areas that have witnessed unusually high rates of growth in recent years. Studies from which some information on elderly migrants can be gleaned include interview surveys of the Upper Midwest (Sofranko & Williams, 1980; Sofranko, Williams, & Fliegel, 1981), the Ozarks (Roseman, 1977), the Upper Great Lakes region (Voss & Fuguitt, 1979; Koebernick & Beegle, 1977), and Central New York State (Scholvinck, 1979).

Although these studies are useful in illuminating the dynamics of elderly nonmetropolitan migration, they often are based on a detailed examination of only one or a small number of counties. Consequently, generalizations to substate regions—and certainly to larger regions of the country—are drawn with some peril. Nevertheless, certain major findings appear to be repeated in enough studies of widely separated nonmetropolitan areas of the country that the beginning of some general comments can be made. And, once again, these can be associated with elements of the Wiseman and Roseman typology (1979).

The first relates to retirement. Just as with the migration streams of migrants to selected portions of the metropolitan sunbelt (see Biggar, 1980), retirees—many of them below the customary retirement ages of 62 to 65 years—are a major component of

the migration to many of the nation's nonmetropolitan areas. Social factors, rather than economic causes, underly much of this
migration, although economic motivations, including living costs
and size of housing, probably are present (see Murphy, 1979). Ties
to an area that often have developed over a period of many years
appear to play a major role in this process. For some migrants
(although a clear minority) this represents returning to an earlier,
sometimes childhood, place of residence. Longino (1979), for example, has studied return migration (as defined by migration to
one's state of birth) and concluded that it constitutes a major part
of the migration of the elderly. Other sample survey data reveal,
nevertheless, that migration back to state of birth is only a relatively small part of what more broadly can be considered as migration to a familiar area. For example, Ploch (1979) reported that as
many as 40 percent of the migrants to Maine between 1970 and
1975 were "returnees," but only half of these in fact were born in
Maine. For the remainder, more recent prior residence or simply
vacations in Maine provided the crucial link to the area. This is
similar to the findings of Voss and Fuguitt (1979) for recent migrants to the Upper Great Lakes region. While older metropolitan-
origin migrants to nonmetropolitan counties in northern Minnesota, Wisconsin, and Michigan were the *least* likely to be return
migrants (using several different measures of prior residence in
defining "return"), they were also the *most* likely to cite "ties to
this place" as the main reason for choosing their present place of
residence. More than 75 percent of the recent metro-origin older
migrants had vacationed in the area prior to moving, and over 60
percent owned a home and/or land in the area before migrating.
Similar findings were reported by Koebernick and Beegle (1977) in
their study of the characteristics of elderly households who migrated between 1960 and 1972 to Clare County in the central part
of Michigan's Lower Peninsula. Corroborative evidence is also
available for the Ozark region (Hoffman, 1976; Roseman, 1977),
northern New England (Roseman, 1977), and central northern
New York State (Scholvinck, 1979).

The selection by retirees to nonmetropolitan areas of locations
that have been favorite vacation areas is hardly surprising. It not
only is consistent with the theoretical notion that persons seek to
minimize the uncertainty associated with a move (Wolpert, 1965), it
also is a rational strategy. Murphy (1979) interprets much of the
relocation after retirement as a delayed decision to move (delayed
because of work-place ties) in response to changing household needs.

The discussion of vacations and second home ownership in a rural area prior to moving is related to another general conclusion that can be drawn concerning retiring migrants to nonmetropolitan communities. Because second homes are used for recreational purposes, it stands to reason that migration to nonmetropolitan areas at the time of retirement generally is not a long distance move, i.e., not more than a day's drive from one's prior permanent residence. In fact, nearly all studies of such migration have indicated that rapidly growing nonmetropolitan areas are being fed predominantly by nearby large metropolitan areas. This was shown in considerable detail by Voss and Fuguitt (1979) for the Upper Great Lakes region and has been found in several other studies (Koebernick & Beegle, 1977; Roseman, 1977; Scholvinck, 1979). Hoffman's (1976) anecdotal account of moving to the Arkansas Ozarks is a useful illustration of this phenomenon.

As a consequence of amenity seeking, the settlement pattern of nonmetropolitan migrants—and especially the elderly—is more dispersed than that of the existing local population (Voss & Fuguitt, 1979; Scholvinck, 1979). Residence in the open country, or on lakes or rivers, or at other scenic sites is consistent with the trend toward taking up primary occupancy in what once was a second home. It also is consistent with the conception that somehow this migration represents a "back to the land" phenomenon in the form of country living. Several studies have shown, however, that this is not the case in the sense that migrants have not entered agriculture except in token numbers (Scholvinck, 1979; Sofranko et al., 1981; Voss and Fuguitt, 1979).

Summary

We have considered some demographic aspects of the elderly, with particular attention to those living in rural and/or nonmetropolitan areas. The United States is an urban and metropolitan society, so it is not surprising that only about one-fourth of the elderly (those 65 and over) and one-fourth of those below that age live in rural areas, with similar proportions living in nonmetropolitan areas. Nevertheless, the concentration of the elderly is somewhat higher in smaller places, with the highest proportion in villages. Remote rural nonmetropolitan areas also have high elderly proportions.

During the decade of the 1970s, the number of older people increased in every residential category. There have been variations in this absolute increase, and in the proportion over 65, however, with more urban and metropolitan settings generally experiencing greater increases. Since these are the areas with lower proportions, the differentials in concentration among residence types declined in the period between 1970 and 1980.

Absolute increases in the elderly population are largely due to "aging in place," although the migration of this age group is also important. Relative increases depend, in addition, on natural increases and the migration of the younger population. The recent muting of residential differences in elderly proportions may be attributed in large part to the nonmetropolitan turnaround in growth (i.e., in the most recent decade the loss of younger people to metropolitan areas was reversed). State and regional trends generally reflected those of the nation, with variations in the concentration and magnitude of change in the elderly population mirroring the history of population growth in the area.

The elderly experienced a net migration gain in nonmetropolitan areas in the 1960s, 10 years before this became the case for those below that age. It is easy to exaggerate the magnitude of the elderly migration, however, as the proportion moving is generally considerably less than for the younger population. Nevertheless, in terms of the characteristics of those who do migrate, nonmetropolitan areas have generally benefited in regard to higher economic and social statuses.

Surveys of migrants in a variety of nonmetropolitan settings are beginning to provide information on the local impacts of such movement. Among other findings, these studies have indicated that in some areas older people are a relatively large proportion of the newcomers, and most of these appear to prefer dispersed settlement. Return migration is important in some situations, and most migrants have had previous experience or ties with the areas in which they settle.

We considered also differentials in race, sex, and marital and family status. Overall, populations of blacks and other races have lower proportions of the elderly, with blacks more concentrated outside urbanized areas, and "other races" more concentrated in central cities. The elderly are much more likely to be women than men, and women are found more in urban and metropolitan areas. Men, being the smaller proportion, are more likely to be married and to be living with their spouse than women. Here a major difference by residence is that women are unlikely to be found on farms unless they are married, i.e., in husband-wife families.

Because most 1980 census data have not yet been released, we could not compare the social and economic characteristics of the elderly by residence. We would expect some important differences, however, based on analyses for earlier periods. For example, a residence comparison based on 1970 data (Fuguitt & Johansen, 1975) demonstrated that the percent of those 65 and over in poverty was highest in the metropolitan village category, which had the highest proportion of the elderly as well.

In addition to characteristics such as education, employment, income, and poverty status, future research needs to give more attention to subgroups of the elderly population. Not only has the population aged, it has aged within the elderly category. The "old-old" should have characteristics that are rather different from those of the "young-old," and redistribution, particularly through migration, may also be quite different (Wiseman, 1980).

The most important gap in our knowledge is a comprehensive understanding of the impacts of these trends and differentials. Although national-level differences by residence need to be considered, they are by and large small in size and, therefore, do not in themselves justify separate consideration for older persons in rural and nonmetropolitan areas. Issues such as the ease of access to services or low density service provision seem to be more critical when considering the special circumstances of the rural elderly, as will be noted elsewhere in this volume.

Nevertheless, these relatively small differences cover up much larger variations at the substate level. Some local communities have faced rapid growth of the elderly through migration, possibly along with growth in the younger age categories. Other communities have experienced growth in numbers and proportions of elderly—but with total population stagnation or decline through the out-migration of the young. A more systematic understanding of the social and economic consequences of population changes in the elderly is now needed, set within the context of shifting patterns of population redistribution and recent changes in the underlying demographic components that generate growth in elders.

References

Biggar, J. C. Reassessing elderly sunbelt migration. *Research on Aging*, 1980, *2*, 177–190.
Bowles, G. K. Contributions of recent metro–nonmetro migrants to the

nonmetro population and labor force. *Agricultural Economics Research*, 1978, *30*, 15–22.

Cebula, R. J. *The determinants of human migration*. Lexington, Mass.: D.C. Heath and Company, 1979.

Clifford, W. B., Heaton, T. B., & Fuguitt, G. V. Residential mobility and living arrangements among the elderly: Changing patterns in metropolitan and nonmetropolitan areas. *International Journal of Aging and Human Development*, 1982, *14*, 139–156.

Cowgill, D. O. The demography of aging. In A. M. Hoffman (Ed.), *The daily needs and interests of older people*. Springfield, Ill.: Charles C. Thomas, 1970, pp. 27–69.

Fuguitt, G. V., & Johansen, H. E. *The social characteristics of villages in the United States*. Madison: University of Wisconsin, Center for Demography and Ecology, Working Paper 75-79, 1975.

Fuguitt, G. V., & Tordella, S. J. Elderly net migration: The new trend of nonmetropolitan population change. *Research on Aging*, 1980, *2*, 191–204.

Golant, S. M. Central city, suburban and nonmetropolitan area migration patterns of the elderly. In S. M. Goland (Ed.), *The location and environment of elderly population*. New York: Wiley, 1979, pp. 37–54.

Heaton, T. B., Clifford, W. B., & Fuguitt, G. V. Changing patterns of retirement migration. *Research on Aging*, 1980, *2*, 93–104.

Heaton, T. B., Clifford, W. B., & Fuguitt, G. V. Temporal shifts in the determinants of young and elderly migration in nonmetropolitan areas. *Social Forces*, 1981, *60*, 41–60.

Hines, F. K., Brown, D. L., & Zimmer, J. M. *Social and economic characteristics of the population in metro and nonmetro counties*. Washington, D.C.: U.S. Department of Agriculture, Economic Research Service, Agricultural Economic Report No. 272, 1975.

Hoffman, A. C. A migration from Chicago to Bull Shoals—Some demographic observations. *American Journal of Agricultural Economics*, 1976, *58*, 967–970.

Koebernick, T., & Beegle, J. A. Migration of the elderly to rural areas: A case study in Michigan. In *Patterns of migrations and population change in America's heartland*. East Lansing: Michigan State University Agricultural Experiment Station, North Central Regional Research Publication No. 238, 1977, pp. 86–104.

Lee, G. R. & Lassey, M. L. The elderly. In D. A. Dillman & D. J. Hobbs (Eds.), *Rural society in the U.S.: Issues for the 1980s*. Boulder, Colo.: Westview Press, 1982, pp. 85–93.

Lichter, D. T., Fuguitt, G. V., Heaton, T. B., & Clifford, W. B. Components of change in residential concentration of the elderly population: 1950–1975. *Journal of Gerontology*, 1981, *36*, 480–489.

Long, L. H., & Hansen, K. A. Reasons for interstate migration. *Population Reports*, Series P-23, No. 81, 1979.

Longino, C. F. Going home: Aged return migration in the U.S., 1965–1970. *Journal of Gerontology*, 1979, *34*, 736–745.

Murphy, P. A. Migration of the elderly: A review. *Town Planning Review*, 1979, *50*, 84–93.

Nelson, L. Farm retirement in the United States. *Geriatrics*, 1961, *16*, 465–470.

Ploch, L. A. The inmigrants: Some are returning home. *Update*, University of Maine, 1979, *7*, unpaginated.

Roseman, C. C. *Changing migration patterns within the United States, resource papers for college geography No. 77-2*. Washington, D.C.: Association of American Geographics, 1977.

Scholvinck, J. W. W. *Migration and population growth in rural areas in New York State*. Ithaca, N.Y.: Cornell University, Department of Agricultural Economics, 1979.

Sheldon, H. D. *The older population of the United States*. New York: Wiley, 1958.

Siegel, J. S. On the demography of aging. *Demography*, 1980, *17*, 345–364.

Smith, T. L. The distribution and movements of the aged population. *The Journal of Business*, 1954, *27*, 108–118.

Sofranko, A. J., & Williams, J. D. (Eds.). *The rebirth of rural America: Rural migration in the Midwest*. Ames: North Central Regional Center for Rural Development, Iowa State University, 1980.

Sofranko, A. J., Williams, J. D., & Fliegel, F. C. Urban migrants to the rural Midwest: Some understandings and misunderstandings. In C. C. Roseman, A. J. Sofranko, & J. D. Williams (Eds.), *Population redistribution in the Midwest*. Ames: North Central Regional Center for Rural Development, Iowa State University, 1981, pp. 97–127.

Tucker, C. J. Changing patterns of migration between metropolitan and nonmetropolitan areas of the United States: Recent evidence. *Demography*, 1976, *13*, 435–443.

Voss, D. R., & Fuguitt, G. V. *Turnaround migration in the Upper Great Lakes region*. Madison: Applied Population Laboratory, Department of Rural Sociology, University of Wisconsin–Madison, Population Series 70-12, August 1979.

Wiseman, R. F. Why older people move: Theoretical issues. *Research on Aging*, 1980, *2*, 144–154.

Wiseman, R. F., & Roseman, C. C. A typology of elderly migration based on the decision-making process. *Economic Geography*, 1979, *55*, 324–337.

Wolpert, J. Behavioral aspects of the decision to migrate. *The Regional Science Association*, 1965, *15*, 159–169.

3

Work, Retirement, and Financial Situations of the Rural Elderly

Willis J. Goudy and Cynthia Dobson

Great diversity exists among the rural elderly in the areas of work, retirement, and financial status. Some general trends have emerged, however, including the tendency of rural workers—and those employed on farms in particular—to remain in the labor force longer than their urban counterparts and the tendency of the urban elderly to have higher incomes than the rural elderly. Yet there are few current studies of financial status or work and retirement among the rural elderly. This is in marked contrast to the flurry of activity that occurred in the 1950s and early 1960s. Much of the early research was in response to the original Social Security Act and the later amendments that covered farm laborers, farm operators, and farm landlords. Today, national studies tend to ignore rural residents in their reports, frequently indicating that farmers and other rural residents have been excluded from the analysis. This lack of current information limits the depth of our understanding of the situation of today's rural elderly and provides an area of clear need for future research.

This chapter is divided into three sections. The first will examine work and retirement. Then the financial situation of the rural elderly will be reviewed in terms of income levels, poverty status, sources of income, and perceptions of income adequacy. In the final section, we will suggest that future research be more comparative in nature, include females, and examine more clearly the economics of aging.

Work and Retirement

This section will rely more heavily on data from farmers and includes less information from the more general rural population than we would like. Over recent decades the United States has experienced increasing diversity in rural employment patterns. By 1978, less than 10 percent of the total *rural* population was engaged in agricultural pursuits (U.S. Bureau of the Census, 1979) and the March 1980 Current Population Survey indicated that less than 3 percent of the total elderly population lived on farms (see Table 2.4 in Chapter 2). Nevertheless, few studies of retirement have been completed among the general rural elderly population and, therefore, in some instances we are forced to rely on detailed data representing a small segment of the overall rural population. This represents a severe limitation on our knowledge which at this point is unavoidable.

Labor Force Participation

Rural residents, and especially farmers, continue to work at ages when many others have retired. Among those employed, male farmers and farm managers had the highest median age (50.8) of the 10 broad occupational categories reported by the U.S. Bureau of the Census (1973). The average age of all employed males was 40.2; for females, it was 39.2, with female farmers and farm managers averaging 49.8 years of age. Nearly 40 percent of all farmers and farm managers were 55 years or older.

Males residing on farms were least likely to leave the labor force as they aged from 55 through the years normally associated with retirement (Table 3.1). In contrast, males living in rural nonfarm areas consistently showed the smallest proportions continuing in the labor force. For females, however, the trends were quite different. For all but those 75 or older, rural farm females were far less likely to be counted in the labor force than were other females.[1] Such statistics, however, do not reflect the very active roles that many rural farm females take in the operation of farms (Hill, 1981).

The later life work patterns of farmers are quite different from those of other occupational groups. Palmore (1964, 1965), Pampel

[1]Results based on a classification system using metropolitan and nonmetropolitan dimensions are relatively similar to those reported here (U.S. Bureau of the Census, 1978; U.S. Bureau of Labor Statistics, 1980).

Table 3.1. Percent of Specified Age Categories in the Labor Force, by Sex and Place of Residence, 1970

Age	Total		Urban		Rural nonfarm[a]		Rural farm	
	% Males	% Females	% Males	% Females	% Males	% Females	% Males	% Females
40–44	94.6	52.1	95.1	53.5	92.9	49.9	94.9	38.8
45–49	93.5	53.0	94.2	54.9	90.9	49.3	94.1	37.6
50–54	91.4	52.0	92.4	54.4	88.0	47.0	92.0	35.7
55–59	86.8	47.4	88.1	50.2	81.9	41.4	88.6	30.9
60–64	73.0	36.1	75.0	38.9	65.2	29.5	78.5	22.6
65–69	39.0	17.2	39.8	18.5	32.3	13.7	56.3	11.0
70–74	22.4	9.1	22.4	9.8	17.9	7.3	41.7	6.3
75–79	14.2	5.5	14.1	5.8	10.9	4.5	30.8	4.8
80–84	9.1	3.5	9.0	3.7	6.8	3.0	21.3	3.5
85 or older	10.2	4.6	11.0	4.9	6.9	3.6	16.9	3.9

[a]The number of individuals in the rural nonfarm category is much larger than that in the rural farm category. For example, whereas there were 7,716,362 males over age 40 years in the rural nonfarm category, there were only 1,871,141 males these ages in the rural farm population. Comparable figures for women were 8,225,552 and 1,750,201.

Source: U.S. Bureau of the Census, Census of the Population: 1970, Detailed Characteristics, U.S. Summary, Table 215. Washington, D.C.: U.S. Government Printing Office, 1973.

(1981), Pihlblad and Rosencranz (1968), Rones (1978), and Simpson (1973) have all noted that farmers are overrepresented among members of the labor force in older age groups. The data reported by Pampel (1981) indicated that this overrepresentation increased from 1952 through 1978. Rones (1978) found that farmers and farm managers in the 65 and over age group were included in the labor force at a rate more than five times the average for all occupations; for farm laborers and foremen, the rate was nearly twice the average. But Schwab (1974) more recently indicated that farm laborers were more likely to take early retirement than were members of some other occupational categories. While most studies indicate longer labor force participation among rural residents, an early study of McKain (1957) found that rural and urban residents did not differ markedly in their employment status after they reached the age of 65. Apparently farm operators tend to remain in the labor force beyond the years normally associated with retirement; but when all rural residents are included, this tendency for farmers is counterbalanced by opposite trends for others living in rural areas.

Bauder and Doerflinger (1967) have argued that rural–urban differences in the labor force participation of older persons reflect occupational rather than residential influences, being primarily differences between farmers and others. Rones (1978) identified several factors explaining the overrepresentation of older farmers in the labor force:

> Most important is the decline in the size of the farming industry. As few new workers have entered agriculture, the age structure has risen over time. Other factors are also important. Older workers, particularly those in the farmer and farm manager occupations, are often able to continue working because of the flexibility that self-employment affords them. Also, the low rate of attrition from farming reflects, to some extent, older farmers' lower incomes and, hence, their ability to work and still pass the social security income test. On the other hand, their low career earnings and lack of pension coverage force many farmers to keep working well into old age. Finally, although farming is still physically demanding work, the infusion of mechanization into a field that was once heavily labor intensive has made farmers able to stay on the job longer. (p. 9)

Orientation to Retirement

The early research on expectations regarding retirement suggested that many rural residents would remain in the work force beyond the ages of 62 to 65, the usual years when the transition occurs.

For example, in a study of several villages and the surrounding open country in New York, Taietz, Streib, and Barron (1956) noted that only 10 percent of the farm operators expected to retire. Of those engaged in other occupations, 20 percent thought they would voluntarily stop work, and another 13 percent believed that they would be forced to retire. Although most disliked the idea of retirement, the farmers (81%) were even more likely to be opposed than were those employed in other occupations (64%). The authors added that there also was a negative component among the few who looked forward to retirement since this favorable orientation often resulted from difficulties with work rather than a positive anticipation of retirement. Donahue, Orbach, and Pollak (1960) concluded that negative forces often were the key factors:

> ... both reasons for retiring and reasons for continuing to work are of a negative character. Retirement because of health is often viewed as a release from an unpleasant situation, not a passage into a pleasant one. Similarly, continuing to work is often the result of a desire to avoid passing into what is viewed as a more unpleasant position rather than a positive attachment to one's work. (p. 358)

The study in New York by Taietz and his colleagues was one of several conducted by Agricultural Experiment Stations in various states in collaboration with the U.S. Department of Agriculture. The results of all of these studies showed that few farmers expected to retire. Studies in Connecticut, Kentucky, Minnesota, Texas, and Wisconsin indicated that from 15 to 35 percent of the farmers interviewed expected to retire; the remainder either did not expect to retire or were uncertain (see Baill, 1955, for a summary of these studies).[2] In addition, tenants and hired farm workers were even less likely to expect to retire in those studies for which data for them were reported separately. Another Kentucky study (Youmans, 1968) reported rural–urban comparisons indicating that a slightly larger proportion of city residents (56%) than of rural inhabitants (49%) expected to retire sometime.

Twenty years after these studies, little had changed. In the Social Security Administration's Retirement History Study, for example, 62 percent of those employed as farmers/farm managers and as farm laborers/foremen claimed that they never expected to retire (Goudy 1982b). The respondents were from 60 to 65 years of

---

[2]For a study with a significantly higher proportion with definite retirement plans (25%) or expecting to retire (60%), see Sauer, Bauder, and Biggar (1964).

age when they were first interviewed. In contrast, only 39 percent
of those employed in all other occupations made a similar claim.
Moreover, both categories of farm employees were less likely to
have retired when contacted two and four years later. Thus, not
only do farmers *stay* in the labor force longer than others, but they
also *plan* to do so.

A substantial proportion of those not expecting to retire in fact
do so in the next few years; these have been called "unexpected
retirees" (Goudy, 1981, 1982a, 1982b). For example, 14 percent of
the farmers and farm managers who had said that they would not
stop working in a 1971 interview had retired by a 1973 reinter-
view. By 1975, this had increased to 29 percent. The same figures
for farm laborers and foremen were 8 percent and 33 percent respectively. These percentages were approaching those for both
farm groups who consistently said that they never expected to stop
working (40% of the farmers/farm managers, 42% of the farm la-
borers/foremen).

Rural people frequently report that they retire because of
health concerns (Bauder & Doerflinger, 1967; Kivett, 1976; Kivett
& Scott, 1979; Nelson, 1947, 1961; Parnes & Nestel, 1981; Pihlblad
& Rosencranz, 1968; Samson & Mather, 1950). For example,
Parnes and Nestel (1981) reported that 71 percent of those formerly employed in farm occupations had retired because of health
reasons, a figure nearly identical to that found much earlier by
Samson and Mather (1950). Youmans (1963) pointed out that poor
health was given as a reason for retirement more frequently by
rural (83%) than by urban (40%) workers. Because the differences
in actual health status between urban and rural workers were not
as great, Youmans (1963) wrote that:

> Perhaps the arduous demands of farm occupations play an important
> role. It is generally recognized that agricultural work requires
> greater physical exertion than most urban occupations. With the
> normal decline in physical vigor and the consequent inability to
> perform as well as in the past, the rural male probably is more
> aware of his physical incapacities than the urban male, and he tends
> to attribute this incapacity to poor health. (p. 10)

This suggests caution in interpreting "reasons" given for retirement, a position which Campbell and Campbell (1976) strongly
support. They believe that the potential receipt of Social Security
retirement benefits plays a much greater role than individuals
recognize (see also Bauder, 1960).

Adjustment to Retirement

Many rural residents have found retirement to be better than they had anticipated, and adjustment has been discovered to be relatively good among the rural retired. Taietz et al. (1956) found that less than one-third of their respondents answered negatively on six items measuring attitudes toward adjustment to retirement. Although working farm operators were more negative in their evaluations of future retirement than were men employed in other occupations, retired farm operators were better adjusted than were other retirees. Subsequent studies of rural groups (Atchley, 1975; Goudy, Keith, & Powers, 1977; Stone & Slocum, 1957; Taves & Hansen, 1963) have also reported that fewer than one-third of the respondents were poorly adjusted to retirement.

Bauder and Doerflinger (1967) acknowledged that income and health differences could cause retirement adjustment to be more difficult for the rural than for the urban aged. They concluded, however, that there were few rural–urban differences because of broader changes in the national culture. Morrison and Kristjanson (1958) predicted that retired men in rural areas would be less well adjusted than were urban men, but found no difference. Goudy et al. (1977) noted that the actual adjustment of retired men to the loss of the work role was relatively positive, but men who had not retired anticipated far greater difficulties with adjusting to retirement. Anticipation of the event was far more negative than was the event itself.

Many of these studies, as well as others that have suggested that retirement is worse in anticipation than in actuality (Kivett, 1976; Kivett & Scott, 1979; Loeb, Pincus, & Mueller, 1963; Thompson, 1973; Warren, 1952; Youmans, 1963), were conducted when significant changes were occurring in the societal perceptions of the meaning of retirement. Writing in 1969, Back noted that many individuals had spent much of their work lives during a period when there was no guaranteed national retirement plan. Thus, it was difficult for many workers even to imagine retirement. Back (1969) continued:

In consequence [the worker] is a victim of change, caught between two patterns of work and retirement. Members of today's [1969] labor force, the retirees of the future, can give new meaning to work and leisure, and plan for a new pattern of life which includes placing a positive value on retirement. (pp. 111–112)

Similarly, Bauder (1967) found that the definitions that farmers held of retirement were a mixture of traditional agricultural and newer urban conceptions of the term.[3] Thus, as changes continue to take place in the meaning of work and leisure within American society as a whole, differences within and among rural occupational groups should be expected in labor force participation, orientation to retirement, and adjustment to retirement.

The Financial Situation of the Rural Elderly

Income Level

The double handicap of age and location of residence is evident when financial variables are examined (Kreps, 1967; Lee & Lassey, 1980; Youmans, 1963, 1977). In a study reported by the U.S. Bureau of the Census (1981a), the lowest median income ($12,881) was among families in which the householder was 65 years of age or older. For those 55 through 64, the median was $23,531; it was $27,256 for those 45 through 54, the highest for any (by Census definition) age group. For unrelated individuals (by Census definition those persons not living in families), of course, the figures were substantially lower, but the pattern was identical. Urban families had higher incomes than rural families, regardless of whether the comparison was between farm ($15,755) and nonfarm ($21,151) families or between nonmetropolitan ($18,069) and metropolitan ($22,590) families.[4]

The impacts of sex and employment status upon median income also were great (U.S. Bureau of the Census, 1981a). The median income for all men was $12,530; but for men 65 years old and older the median was $7,342. The disparity for women was lower, but then the medians were also substantially lower ($4,920 for all females, $4,226 for females 65 years old and older). The effect of age was much less important, however, when only those fully employed were considered. For this group, the median income figures were as follows: all males, $19,173; males age 65 years and older, $17,307; all females, $11,591; females age 65 years and older, $12,342.

---

[3]See Taylor (1958) for a study of farmers' definitions of partial and full retirement.
[4]Unfortunately, these urban/rural figures were not cross-tabulated with age categories of householders.

These recent data for income were not reported for both age and place of residence, but earlier findings can be used to obtain more detailed comparisons (Table 3.2). The interacting handicaps of age and rural location were apparent in 1969 for both families and unrelated individuals, and the disadvantaged position of older rural nonfarm residents was particularly evident (U.S. Bureau of the Census, 1973). For example, regardless of residential location, the median income of families with heads aged 65 and over was approximately half that for all families. The rural elderly in general had lower incomes than the urban elderly, with the median income of older farm families being 71 percent and that of older nonfarm families being 65 percent of the median income of older urban families. Rural–urban differences were similar for unrelated individuals, although the median income levels were much lower.

Poverty Status

The elderly make up a disproportionate share of those whose incomes fall below the poverty guidelines. Income levels determining poverty differ by residence and by age of householder. The standard for farm families is approximately 85% of that for nonfarm families and the cutoff for older families is about 90% of that for families with the householder below age 65. The differentials reflect assumptions about lower costs of living for older farm residents, primarily lower housing costs and the opportunity to produce food on the farm (Jackson & Velten, 1969; Kreps, 1967; MacDonald, 1965), notions at least partially debunked by Clawson (1967), Coward (1980), and Ford (1969).

In 1980, the overall poverty rate was 13.0%, but the rate for all persons 65 years and older was 15.7% (U.S. Bureau of the Census, 1981a). The relationship between age and poverty was affected by sex. For women, old age was associated with a higher level of poverty (women 65 years and older, 19.0%; all women, 14.7%), but for men the rates were 11.2% for all and 10.9% for those 65 and over. The position of the elderly improved somewhat from 1970 and 1980, especially in the first years of the decade. The proportion in poverty declined from 24.0% in 1970 to 15.7% in 1974; it remained relatively stable through 1980. The percentages for the total population below the poverty level varied between 11% and 13% for persons of all ages during this period.

The poverty rate also varied by place of residence. In 1979, for example, the rate for metropolitan residents was 10.7% while

Table 3.2. Median Income of Families and Unrelated Individuals, by Age and Place of Residence, 1969

Place of residence	Families				Unrelated individuals			
	Total	45–59	60–64	65 or older	Total	45–59	60–64	65 or older
Urban	$10,226	$12,020	$10,230	$5,718	$2,649	$4,420	$3,589	$1,907
Rural nonfarm	$8,244	$9,001	$6,994	$3,615	$1,820	$2,878	$2,176	$1,499
Rural farm	$7,082	$7,625	$6,103	$4,066	$1,908	$2,668	$2,359	$1,765

Source: U.S. Bureau of the Census, *Census of the Population: 1970, Detailed Characteristics, U.S. Summary, Table 250.* Washington, D.C.: U.S. Government Printing Office, 1973.

it was 13.7% for those living in nonmetropolitan areas (U.S. Bureau of the Census, 1981b). Using an alternative classification system, poverty was experienced by 11.6% of the nonfarm population and 13.2% of those on farms. The differences for those 65 years and over were much more striking. In metropolitan areas, 12.0% of the elderly fell below the poverty guidelines; in nonmetropolitan areas, the figure was 20.5%. Again, using the alternative classification system, the poverty rate for those 65 and over was 7.5% in farm areas and 15.4% in nonfarm areas. Thus, the problem of insufficient income for the elderly was greatest in rural nonfarm localities.

Sources of Income

Four sources currently provide the vast majority of the total money income of persons aged 65 and older (Allan & Brotman, 1981). These sources include employment earnings (23%), Social Security benefits (38%), other retirement income and pensions (16%), and income from assets (19%). Public assistance accounted for only 2% of the income of older persons. In 1977, those families with both earnings and other sources of income were the least likely to be poor, with only 4% falling below the poverty guidelines (U.S. Bureau of the Census, 1979). In the same year, about 31% of those families whose only source of income was Social Security and 49% of those with both Social Security and Supplemental Security income were below the poverty level.

Rural–urban residence affected the proportion of income coming from various sources. Based on 1969 data, a higher percentage of older rural farm families had income from earnings than either urban or rural nonfarm families (Table 3.3). Rural nonfarm residents received a higher proportion of their income from Social Security. Those living in urban areas received greater proportions of their incomes from other sources, including pensions, which are available less frequently to those employed in agriculture (Thompson, 1978, 1979). The highest proportion of older families receiving public assistance lived in rural nonfarm areas and the lowest lived on farms (U.S. Bureau of the Census, 1973).

In a study comparing older rural persons living in southern Illinois with those in Chicago, Auerbach (1976) reported that more older persons received Social Security benefits in rural (82%) than

Table 3.3. Source of Income of Families With Head Aged 65 and Over, by Location of Residence, 1969

Source of income	Total	Urban	Rural nonfarm	Rural farm
Percent of aggregate family income from:				
Earnings (wage and salary and self-employed income)	52.3%	52.5%	48.7%	61.0%
Social Security income	20.5	19.1	26.5	21.1
Public assistance income	1.2	1.0	2.4	1.0
Other income	26.0	27.4	22.5	16.9
Total	100.0%	100.0%	100.1%	100.0%
Percent of families receiving specific type of income:				
Earnings (wage and salary and self-employed income)	56.8%	57.1%	51.1%	76.2%
Social Security income	83.4%	82.8%	84.7%	85.6%
Public assistance income	9.0%	7.8%	13.0%	6.6%
Other income	57.2%	61.8%	46.9%	45.7%

Source: U.S. Bureau of the Census, *Census of the Population: 1970, Detailed Characteristics, U.S. Summary, Table 264.* Washington, D.C.: U.S. Government Printing Office, 1973.

in urban (74%) areas. But far more urban (70%) than rural (30%) elderly had income from savings and investments; and more urban (10%) than rural (2%) aged received financial aid from relatives.[5] In a study of older men living in and around Iowa cities of 2,500 to 10,000, Dobson (1977) noted that income was more dependent upon occupation and employment status than on age. Of those 65 and older, about half of the retired reported an income of less than $8,000 in 1974, while two-thirds of those employed full-time had incomes in excess of $15,000. The partially employed were similar to the retired, although they reported somewhat higher incomes. The income of farmers had increased most dramatically from 1964 to 1974 among the five occupational categories studied, although blue-collar workers also gained during this period. Only minor changes occurred among small businessmen and salaried and self-employed professionals. Net worth increased for all occupational categories during the study period, although the gains were very modest for blue-collar workers and small businessmen; indeed, gains tended to be offset by inflation and some lost ground in terms of income and net worth.

Income Adequacy

Many early studies found that rural respondents were satisfied with their situations no matter what their income. More recently in an Iowa study (Dobson, 1977), nearly all respondents (84%) reported that they had more than enough to live on or were at least living comfortably. Persons working full time were most likely to feel their situations were adequate, but men who continued to work part time did not perceive their financial situations to be any more or less precarious than those who had fully retired.

Kivett (1976) found that 27% of a sample of older rural North Carolina residents felt that they did not have enough money to meet their needs; the comparable figure in a subsequent study was 24% (Kivett & Scott, 1979). In the latter study, the feeling that one's income was adequate tended to increase with age. Youmans (1963) noted that slightly fewer rural residents (22%) in his sample cited finances as their most important problem than did those liv-

---

[5]The economic status of the elderly is also influenced by noncash benefit programs; Allan and Brotman (1981) noted that 93 percent of the households headed by a person aged 65 or older were covered by Medicare, 16 percent were under Medicaid, 6 percent were receiving food stamps, and 5 percent were living in subsidized housing in 1979.

ing in an urban area (25%); but Monahan and Marshall (1968) found that residents of two rural Wisconsin communities were more likely to state that they did not have enough money to live on than were the residents of an urban area. Thus, although rural residence is associated with substantially lower incomes for the elderly, there do not appear to be large or consistent rural–urban differences in older individuals' evaluations of their financial situations.

Research Issues

It is crucial to recognize the diversity within rural America on work, retirement, and financial issues. In each instance, there are far greater differences within rural areas than between rural and urban areas. These variations occur across regions but, more importantly, they exist within neighboring communities thought to be homogeneous in common mythology. Myths concerning the rural elderly have not been obliterated even though research suggests that they should be (Coward, 1980; Powers, Keith, & Goudy, 1981). Thus, we strongly encourage research of a comparative nature—in sites selected for examination, in theoretical and methodological treatments, in subgroups included in a sample, and in time. The series of studies completed in the 1950s and early 1960s on farmers' attitudes toward Old Age and Survivors Insurance provides an example of a starting point; several states conducted these studies, with a few asking some of the same questions (Baill, 1955). Data from these studies allow for some comparisons among various groups of respondents within a state as well as comparisons between states.

Abeles and Riley (1976) suggested that the dimension of time is important:

> [I]n respect to social change and the life course, economic fluctuations result in sharp distinctions in the subsequent life histories of workers starting out in periods of prosperity as opposed to economic depression. Workers are set apart not only in career trajectories, but also in opportunities to accumulate assets and in the development of living styles and consumption aspirations with which they enter into retirement. (p. 12)

Those entering retirement several years ago probably did not anticipate inflation of the magnitude occurring in recent years. Those that will enter in the next few years may be faced with changes in Social Security programs that they could not have anticipated.

Panel studies, especially those including multiple age groups, would enable the researcher to examine retirement orientations and experiences among several cohorts. Census data provide useful cross-sectional perspectives, but they cannot answer questions concerning the sequence of events, such as what forces create "unexpected retirees." Few panel studies of work and retirement among the rural elderly exist; an exception is the work of Goudy et al. (1977), but only two interviews have been held with their sample of older Iowa males.

Females are infrequently included in studies of older workers or retirees, especially in rural areas, but we strongly advocate their inclusion in future studies. Their contribution to work on the farm, which is seldom counted officially among labor statistics, has not been tallied as effectively as it should be. In addition, women have joined the labor force in increasing proportions in the last few decades; the extent to which women in general (Rogers & Goudy, 1981) and older women in particular have entered into traditional work roles in rural areas needs attention. Male farmers were studied so extensively in the 1950s and early 1960s that Doerflinger and Bauder (1967) and Friedmann and Orbach (1974) believed that more was known about their orientations toward retirement than those of any other occupational category. But other occupations have tended to be ignored in rural areas. Further comparative work among various occupations for both sexes is needed.

One of the components of the transition from work to retirement is the decision on residential location. For many farmers, a move to a nearby small town has been the answer (Cowles, 1956; Smith, 1950). Some retirees, however, have reversed the procedure by changing from other occupations to farming, usually on a very limited basis (Alleger, 1955; Heffernan, Green, Lasley, & Nolan, 1982). Whether rural life has certain advantages preferred by retirees or whether an urban environment repels retirees remains to be documented (Lee & Lassey, 1980).

Currently, this country is debating various changes in the Social Security program (see Clark & Spengler, 1980, for example). The impact of such changes is seldom considered in terms of rural areas. The feasibility of early retirement (62–64), which occurs more frequently for wage workers having had some farm employment (Epstein, 1966), probably contributes to the migration turnaround now occurring. If the age at which full retirement benefits can be earned were raised from 65 to 68, older people might delay—or possibly give up—their plans to migrate to rural areas. Other inducements to remain in the labor force (e.g., increased benefits for each year worked beyond a certain age) might also work to slow migration. These and other issues should be studied before legislation is enacted, unlike the studies of attitudes toward Old Age and Survivors Insurance that were completed well after laws effecting farmers went into effect.

Lee and Lassey (1982) have stated that "much more research is needed on the economics of aging in rural areas" (p. 89). With the changing economic and employment patterns of rural America, more rural people may have the financial stability to retire at the usual time—or even earlier—than in the past. Incomes do tend to be lower in rural than in urban areas, but great variation exists among older people in both areas. The particularly disadvantaged position of rural nonfarm groups calls for further study. Research on how the wealth of some older people in rural areas is used needs to be completed, as do investigations about those rural elderly who function on low incomes. Lee and Lassey (1982) listed several issues that must be examined:

> Are there opportunities unique to rural communities that allow the elderly to remain reasonably independent and self-supporting even on low incomes? . . . What are the consequences of low income in terms of health, nutrition, access to services, transportation, and housing for the rural elderly? How can these consequences be most effectively ameliorated? . . . How do the expenditures of the low-income elderly differ from those with higher incomes? (pp. 89–90)

There is also the question of what retirement really means to farmers. Terminating labor but retaining ownership of the land and, therefore, decision-making authority may not constitute retirement as generally defined. For farm laborers and foremen, however, retirement may be similar to that of salary and wage earners in other occupations. The availability of part-time employment in rural areas may change with shifts in the structure of American agriculture, and this too may influence retirement decisions. The meaning of retirement in rural areas may be a profitable issue to investigate as part of the effort to understand the frequent expectation of farmers that they will never retire and the lower probability that they will indeed retire.

For professionals engaged in counseling people as they go through the transition from work to retirement, little material specifically geared to rural circumstances is available. Thus, the development of applied publications, slide/tape presentations, and video programs should be encouraged. Programs for retirement preparation were called for long ago (McKain, 1957), and the expansion of these to include continued counseling before, during, and after the event has been advocated (Goudy, 1982b; Trent, 1981) but seldom put into practice.

The study of work, retirement, and financial situations of the rural elderly has been neglected in recent years. This cannot be allowed to continue. A substantial proportion (37%) of older persons now live in nonmetropolitan areas (Allan & Brotman, 1981) and greater proportions of the population will be in the elderly category in the forthcoming decades. Some rural nonfarm areas, indeed, are likely to have majorities of older people. Without the information and understanding essential for wise planning for the needs of the rural elderly, the quality of life of this large group of older Americans could be severely damaged.

References

Abeles, R. P., & Riley, M. W. A life-course perspective on the later years of life: Some implications for research. *Social Science Research Council, Annual Report*. Washington, D.C.: Social Science Research Council, 1976, pp. 1–16.

Allan, C., & Brotman, H. (Compilers). *Chartbook on aging in America: The 1981 White House Conference on Aging*. Washington, D.C.: U.S. Government, Printing Office, 1981.

Alleger, D. E. The role of agriculture in retirement adjustment: A study in five Florida counties. *Rural Sociology*, 1955, *20*, 124–131.

Atchley, R. C. Adjustment to loss of job at retirement. *International Journal of Aging and Human Development*, 1975, *6*, 17–27.

Auerbach, A. J. The elderly in rural areas: Differences in urban areas and implications for practice. In L. H. Ginsberg (Ed.), *Social work in rural communities: A book of readings*. New York: Council on Social Work Education, 1976, pp. 99–107.

Back, K. W. The ambiguity of retirement. In E. Busse & E. Pfeiffer (Eds.), *Behavior and adaption in late life*. Boston: Little, Brown, 1969, pp. 93–114.

Baill, I. M. *The farmer and old-age security: A summary analysis of four studies*. Washington, D.C.: U.S. Department of Agriculture, Agriculture Information Bulletin 151, 1955.

Bauder, W. W. Farmers' definitions of retirement. *The Gerontologist*, 1967, *7*, 207–212.

Bauder, W. W. *Iowa farm operators' and farm landlords' knowledge of, participation in, and acceptance of the Old Age and Survivors Insurance Program.* Ames: Iowa State University, Agricultural Experiment Station, Research Bulletin 479, 1960.

Bauder, W. W., & Doerflinger, J. Work roles among the rural aged. In E. G. Youmans (Ed.), *Older rural Americans: A sociological perspective.* Lexington: University of Kentucky Press, 1967, pp. 22–43.

Campbell, C. D., & Campbell, R. G. Conflicting views on the effect of Old-Age and Survivors Insurance on retirement. *Economic Inquiry,* 1976, *14,* 369–388.

Clark, R. L., & Spengler, J. Economic responses to population aging with special emphasis on retirement policy. In R. Clark (Ed.), *Retirement policy in an aging society.* Durham, N.C.: Duke University Press, 1980, pp. 156–166.

Clawson, M. Rural poverty in the United States. *Journal of Farm Economics,* 1967, *49,* 1227–1233.

Coward, R. T. Research-based programs for the rural elderly. In W. R. Lassey, M. L. Lassey, G. R. Lee, & N. Lee (Eds.), *Research and public service with the rural elderly.* Corvallis, Ore.: Western Rural Development Center, 1980, pp. 39–56.

Cowles, M. L. Housing and associated problems of the rural farm aged population in two Wisconsion counties. *Rural Sociology,* 1956, *21,* 239–248.

Dobson, C. Income and net worth. In E. A. Powers, P. M. Keith, & W. J. Goudy, *Later life transitions: Older males in rural America.* Ames: Iowa State University, Department of Sociology and Anthropology, Sociology Report 139, 1977, pp. 65–85.

Doerflinger, J., & Bauder, W. W. Work and the older person in rural Iowa. *Iowa Farm Science,* 1967, *22,* 110–113.

Donahue, W., Orbach, H. L., & Pollak, O. Retirement: The emerging social pattern. In C. Tibbitts (Ed.), *Handbook of social gerontology.* Chicago: University of Chicago Press, 1960, pp. 330–406.

Epstein, L. A. Early retirement and work-life experience. *Social Security Bulletin,* 1966, *29*(3) 3–10.

Ford, T. R. Rural poverty in the United States. In Task Force on Economic Growth and Opportunity, *Rural poverty and regional progress in an urban society.* Washington, D.C.: Chamber of Commerce of the United States, 1969, pp. 153–176.

Friedmann, E. A., & Orbach, H. L. Adjustment to retirement. In S. Arieti (Ed.), *American handbook of psychiatry* (2nd ed.). New York: Basic Books, 1974, pp. 609–645.

Goudy, W. J. Changing work expectations: Findings from the retirement history study. *The Gerontologist,* 1981, *21,* 644–649.

Goudy, W. J. Antecedent factors related to changing work expectations: Evidence from the retirement history study. *Research on Aging,* 1982, *4,* 139–157. (a)

Goudy, W. J. Farmers, too, must plan for retirement. *Journal of Extension,* 1982, *20, 9–14. (b)*

Goudy, W. J., Keith, P. M., & Powers, E. A. *Older workers in small towns: Occupational involvement and adaptation.* Ames: Iowa State University, Department of Sociology and Anthropology, Sociology Report, 140, 1977.

Heffernan, W. D., Green, G., Lasley, P., & Nolan, M. F. Small farms: A heterogenous category. *The Rural Sociologist,* 1982, *2,* 62–70.

Hill, F. Farm women: Challenge to scholarship. *The Rural Sociologist,* 1981, *1,* 370–382.

Jackson, C., & Velten, T. Residence, race, and age of poor families in 1966. *Social Security Bulletin,* 1969, *32* (6), 3–11.

Kivett, V. R. *The aged in North Carolina: Physical, social and environmental characteristics and sources of assistance.* Raleigh: North Carolina State University, Agricultural Experiment Station, Technical Bulletin 237, 1976.

Kivett, V. R., & Scott, J. P. *The rural by-passed elderly: Perspectives on status and needs.* Raleigh: North Carolina State University, Agricultural Experiment Station, Technical Bulletin 260, 1979.

Kreps, J. M. Economic status of the rural aged. In E. G. Youmans (Ed.), *Older rural Americans: A sociological perspective.* Lexington: University of Kentucky Press, 1967, pp. 144–168.

Lee, G. R., & Lassey, M. L. Rural–urban differences among the elderly: Economic, social and subjective factors. *Journal of Social Issues,* 1980, *36* (2), 62–74.

Lee, G. R., & Lassey, M. L. The elderly. In D. A. Dillman & D. J. Hobbs (Eds.), *Rural society in the U.S.: Issues for the 1980s.* Boulder, Colo.: Westview Press, 1982, pp. 85–93.

Loeb, M. B., Pincus, A., & Mueller, J. *Growing old in rural Wisconsin.* Madison: University of Wisconsin, School of Social Work, Project on Aging, 1963.

MacDonald, D. Our invisible poor. In L. Ferman, J. Kornbluh, & A. Haber (Eds.), *Poverty in America: A book of readings.* Ann Arbor: University of Michigan Press, 1965, pp. 6–24.

McKain, W. C., Jr. Aging and rural life. In W. Donahue & C. Tibbitts (Eds.), *The new frontiers of aging.* Ann Arbor: University of Michigan Press, 1957, pp. 118–128.

Monahan, W., & Marshall, D. G. *Retirement and migration in the north central states: Retired persons in three Wisconsin communities.* Madison: University of Wisconsin, Department of Rural Sociology, Population Series No. 14, 1968.

Morrison, D. E., & Kristjanson, C. A. *Personal adjustment among older persons.* Brookings: South Dakota State University, Agricultural Experiment Station, Technical Bulletin 21, 1958.

Nelson, L. *Farm retirement in Minnesota.* St. Paul: University of Minnesota, Agricultural Experiment Station Bulletin 394, 1947.

Nelson, L. Farmers retirement in the United States. *Geriatrics,* 1961, *16,* 465–470.

Palmore, E. Retirement patterns among aged men: Findings of the 1963 survey of the aged. *Social Security Bulletin,* 1964, *27*(8), 3–10.

Palmore, E. Differences in the retirement patterns of men and women. *The Gerontologist,* 1965, *5,* 4–8.

Pampel, F. C. *Social change and the aged: Recent trends in the United States.* Lexington, Mass.: Lexington Books, 1981.

Parnes, H. S., & Nestel, G. The retirement experience. In H. Parnes (Ed.), *Work and Retirement: A longitudinal study of men.* Cambridge, Mass.: MIT Press, 1981, pp. 155–197.

Pihlblad, C. T., & Rosencranz, H. A. *Retirement status of older people in the small town: An interim report.* Columbia: University of Missouri, Department of Sociology, 1968, Vol. 3, No. 1.

Powers, E. A., Keith, P. M., & Goudy, W. J. Family networks of the rural aged. In R. T. Coward & W. M. Smith, Jr. (Eds.), *The family in rural society.* Boulder, Colo.: Westview Press, 1981, pp. 199–217.

Rogers, D. L., & Goudy, W. J. Community structure and occupational segregation, 1960 and 1970. *Rural Sociology,* 1981, *46,* 263–281.

Rones, P. L. Older men—the choice between work and retirement. *Monthly Labor Review,* 1978, *101* (11), 3–10.

Samson, A., & Mather, W. G. *Personal and social adjustments of 49 retired rural men.* University Park: Pennsylvania State University, Agricultural Experiment Station, Progress Report 19, 1950.

Sauer, H. M., Bauder, W. W., & Biggar, J. C. *Retirement plans, concepts and attitudes of farm operators in three eastern South Dakota counties.* Brookings: South Dakota State University, Agricultural Experiment Station, Bulletin 515, 1964.

Schwab, K. Early labor-force withdrawal of men: Participants and nonparticipants aged 58–63. *Social Security Bulletin,* 1974, *37* (8), 24–38.

Simpson, I. H. Problems of the aging in work and retirement. In R. Boyd & C. Oakes (Eds.), *Foundations of practical gerontology* (2nd ed.). Columbia: University of South Carolina Press, 1973, pp. 157–172.

Smith, T. L. The aged in rural society. In Industrial Relations Research Association, *The aged and society.* Champaign, Ill.: Industrial Relations Research Association, 1950, pp. 40–53.

Stone, C. L., & Slocum, W. *A look at Thurston County's older people.* Pullman: Washington State University, Agricultural Experiment Station, Bulletin 573, 1957.

Taietz, P., Streib, G. F., & Barron, M. L. *Adjustment to retirement in rural New York State.* Ithaca: Cornell University, Agricultural Experiment Station, Bulletin 919, 1956.

Taves, M. J., & Hansen, G. D. *Minnesota farmers and social security.* St. Paul: University of Minnesota, Agricultural Experiment Station, Bulletin 467, 1963.

Taylor, J. S. Farmers' view of retirement in relation to post retirement work activity. *Northwest Missouri State College Bulletin,* 1958, *52* (22), 3–30.

Thompson, G. B. Work versus leisure roles: An investigation of morale among employed and retired men. *Journal of Gerontology,* 1973, *28,* 339–344.

Thompson, G. B. Pension coverage and benefits, 1972: Findings from the retirement history study. *Social Security Bulletin,* 1978, *41* (2), 3–17.

Thompson, G. B. Black–white differences in private pensions: Findings from the retirement history study. *Social Security Bulletin,* 1979, *42* (2), 15–22.

Trent, C. The elderly: A priority clientele. *Journal of Extension,* 1981, *19* (3), 34–38.

U.S. Bureau of the Census. *Census of the population: 1970, detailed characteristics, United States summary, final report* PC(1)-D1. Washington, D.C.: U.S. Government Printing Office, 1973.

U.S. Bureau of the Census. *Social and economic characteristics of the metropolitan and nonmetropolitan population: 1977 and 1970.* Current Population Reports, Special Studies, Series P-23, No. 75. Washington, D.C.: U.S. Government Printing Office, 1978.

U.S. Bureau of the Census. Social and Economic Characteristics of the Older Population: 1978. *Current population reports,* Special Studies, Series P-23, No. 85. Washington, D.C.: U.S. Government Printing Office, 1979.

U.S. Bureau of the Census. Money income and poverty status of families and persons in the United States: 1980. *Current population reports,* Consumer Income, Series P–60, No. 127. Washington, D.C.: U.S. Government Printing Office, 1981.(a)

U.S. Bureau of the Census. Characteristics of the population below the poverty level: 1979. *Current population reports,* Consumer Income, Series P-60, No. 130. Washington, D.C.: U.S. Government Printing Office, 1981.(b)

U.S. Bureau of Labor Statistics. *Handbook of labor statistics: Bulletin 2070.* Washington, D.C.: U.S. Government Printing Office, 1980.

Warren, R. L. Old age in a rural township. In New York State Legislature, *Age is no barrier.* Albany: New York State Legislature, Joint Committee on Problems of the Aging, Document 35, 1952, pp. 155–166.

Youmans, E. G. *Aging patterns in a rural and an urban area of Kentucky.* Lexington: University of Kentucky, Agricultural Experiment Station, Bulletin 681, 1963.

Youmans, E. G. *Plans and expectations for older age: A study of middle-aged persons in a Kentucky county.* Lexington: University of Kentucky, Agricultural Experiment Station, Bulletin 708, 1968.

Youmans, E. G. The rural aged. *Annals of the American Academy of Political and Social Science,* 1977, *429,* 81–90.

Part II

Life Conditions of the Elderly in Rural Society

This section contains five chapters, each of which documents and analyzes rural–urban differences in a dimension of life considered important for the elderly. The chapters deal successively with physical health, mental health, housing, family and kin, and relations with non-relatives. Each, in its own way, serves to disabuse us of some widely held stereotypes or myths about the lives of the rural elderly.

One such myth is that people living in rural environments, including particularly the elderly, are healthier than their urban counterparts. Lassey and Lassey, in Chapter 4, demonstrate that this generalization is clearly contrary to fact. On virtually every dimension of health, the rural elderly are disadvantaged. Some of the difference is attributable to factors such as lifelong income and education differentials between the rural and urban elderly; a lower standard of living in rural areas; less widespread knowledge of sound nutritional practices; and less positive orientations toward health care systems among the elderly. But part of the difference may also be due to the lesser availability of quality health care in rural areas, the greater distances involved in obtaining access to health care, and the difficulty of supporting medical specialists in areas of low population density. As in the case of many specialized services, the rural elderly must often travel considerable distances to obtain medical care and, thus, there are many financial and other disincentives. The increased expense and difficulty involved result in the rural elderly more frequently doing without health care, especially care of a preventive nature. As a consequence, the rural elderly tend to have somewhat more, and more severe, health problems than do the urban elderly.

In Chapter 5, Scheidt demolishes the myth that mental health problems, among the elderly at least, stem from the exigencies of urban life.

Although much of the data he reviews indicate minimal differences in the occurrence of mental health problems between the rural and the urban elderly, it is clear that the rural elderly are by no means advantaged in this regard. A number of studies have shown that the rural elderly tend to score slightly higher than the urban on measures of emotional adjustment such as morale and life satisfaction—despite the "objective" disadvantages on socioeconomic and health-related dimensions with which they live. But this advantage apparently does not extend to more specific measures of mental health status and functioning. Once again, part of the problem may stem from the lesser availability of mental health services in rural areas. The causal structures of most problems of mental functioning remain largely unknown. Scheidt, however, makes it clear that the rural elderly are not at all immune from these causes and that they are afflicted by mental difficulties at least as frequently as the urban elderly. Furthermore, when such problems do occur among the elderly, rural residents are less likely to receive treatment.

The housing situation of the rural elderly is also not particularly encouraging, as Bylund reports in Chapter 6. Compared to the urban elderly, older rural people do have the twin advantages of higher rates of homeownership and lower housing costs. Yet the quality of their housing is much lower according to virtually any commonly accepted indicator. The houses of the rural elderly are older, in much poorer condition, and more likely to lack plumbing, electrical, and other features than those of the urban elderly. Furthermore, a disproportionate share of the federal funds available for housing programs and improvements are channeled to urban areas, either by design or by default. Many of the rural elderly may own their homes not because it represents the best or most desired option for them, but because they have very limited options due to the scarcity of rental property in rural areas. However, in spite of the many objective deficiencies of their homes, the rural elderly appear to be unusually well satisfied with their housing and express little interest in programs directed toward housing improvement. This paradox raises many important issues for both explanatory theory and policy development.

In Chapter 7, by Lee and Cassidy, the common belief that rural people in general, and the rural elderly in particular, have stronger and more viable family and kinship networks than urban residents is compared to relevant data. It does not appear that the rural elderly are especially advantaged in this regard, at least in any general sense. They do not tend to live closer to children or other relatives, or to interact with them more frequently, than do the urban elderly. Furthermore, marriages among the rural elderly do not appear to be any happier or more satisfying, even though divorce rates are indeed notably lower for rural residents. This does not mean that the rural elderly benefit less from marital and familial ties than do others, but rather that they are not uniquely advantaged in this regard.

The same may be true of friendship, neighborhood, and community relations, as Kivett shows in Chapter 8, although the data on this issue are somewhat more equivocal. Residents of rural areas, though, are not necessarily embedded in supportive networks of friends, neighbors, or other associates, and social isolation is not an exclusively urban phenomenon. Patterns of social and civic participation evidence some differences in kind between urban and rural elderly populations, but few differences of degree. Evidence supporting the stereotype that the rural elderly have more or better friends, are more active in community affairs, or are less likely to be lonely or isolated than the urban elderly is very limited.

The primary message conveyed by each of these chapters is that the rural elderly are not generally blessed by the benefits which common stereotypes bestow on them and are in fact substantially disadvantaged in many tangible and not-so-tangible ways. Life in the country is not nearly so idyllic, peaceful, or comfortable for the elderly as some believe. Instead, many of the privations of old age are exacerbated by rural residence, and many of the privations of rural residence are exacerbated by old age.

4

The Physical Health Status of the Rural Elderly[1]

William R. Lassey and Marie L. Lassey

As compared to the total U.S. population, elderly people have nearly two and one-half times as many restricted activity days because of illness; this includes twice as many days in bed at home or in hospitals and an average of seven visits to physicians' offices annually compared to four for children and five for people 25 to 64 (McCoy & Brown, 1978). The number of restricted activity days is greater for rural than urban older people. Furthermore, 87 percent of the rural elderly have a chronic illness of some type—although this does not necessarily always imply serious functional impairment (Nelson, 1980).

In the United States, 30 percent of the national health care costs are attributable to older people. Elders occupy up to 75 percent of all available hospital beds in some communities (Rowe, 1982). If health care costs continue to rise at the rate of 15 percent annually (as they did in 1981) while Medicare and Medicaid are cut back (as they were in 1982), an increased share of community resources will be required to provide equal-to-present health care for the elderly (Quinn, 1982).

Several statewide surveys have indicated that the rural el-

[1]We wish to thank Drs. Michael K. Miller, Raymond T. Coward, and Gary R. Lee for their very helpful reviews and comments on earlier versions of this chapter. The Department of Sociology, Louisiana State University, provided various forms of critical and very helpful support while the manuscript was in preparation, while the Louisiana State University Medical Center, New Orleans (Dr. Henry Rothschild, in particular) helped us learn at first hand about health and aging, while we were on professional leave during 1981–1982 at Louisiana State University. The Department of Rural Sociology and the Agricultural Research Center, Washington State University, supported final preparation of the chapter.

derly, as compared to the urban elderly, feel that they do not have adequate access to health services, physicians, and other health personnel (Maurer, Christenson, & Warner, 1980). As a consequence, some policymakers believe that the rural elderly's feelings of optimism, well-being, and economic security could be improved by programs which would provide greater access to health knowledge and health care services.

The relative geographical isolation of the rural elderly, as compared to their urban counterparts, puts them at greater risk of remaining undiscovered for considerable periods after suffering acute, immobilizing illnesses or trauma such as strokes or disabling accidents. Yet resources for in-home care, to help prevent premature institutionalization, are considerably less abundant in rural areas (Greene, 1982; Taietz & Milton, 1979). This may be one of the causes of earlier entry into skilled nursing facilities by rural elderly, as compared to urban elderly, in one state (Greene, 1982). Moreover, research findings presented in earlier chapters of this volume indicate that the elderly population of rural America is growing rapidly, thus potentially magnifying the already existing pressures on rural health maintenance systems.

It is clear that health status is among the most prominent concerns of older people as they evaluate their quality of life (American Healthcare Corporation, 1980). Good physical health is central to life satisfaction, the ability to function independently, participation in enjoyable social activities, and conserving income—all factors contributing to an overall sense of well-being (Coward & Kerchoff, 1978). Physical health status is therefore a crucial issue for the elderly population, their relatives, and for professionals concerned with the general well-being of rural older people.

The first section of this chapter focuses upon verified differences in the physical health of the rural and urban elderly, with particular emphasis given to the underlying factors which contribute to these differences. Second, rural–urban differences in the delivery of health care services to the elderly are examined. Special reference is made to different health care models as they apply to the rural and urban elderly—these alternative models reflect differing requirements for health care financing. Finally, the gaps in our present base of knowledge are employed as a basis for defining future research needs.

Health Status:
Rural–Urban Contrasts

Studies of health status among the elderly, based on national samples, suggest rather clearly that the relative advantage or disadvantage of rural, urban, or suburban residence is not constant across all health measures. Rural older people tend to suffer more chronic illnesses than urbanites, while in other respects they are no less healthy (Paringer, Bluck, Feder, & Holahan, 1979).

Male farm residents aged 65 to 74 experience the greatest number of restricted activity days, as compared to females or other residential categories, but the same group also has the fewest indications of disability requiring days in bed. As age increases beyond 75 years, farm men and women exhibit both more restricted days and more bed days than nonfarm residents (Paringer et al., 1979).

The prevalence of chronic illness among older rural people may be partially attributable to rural nonwhite ethnic groups (especially black males) who experience much higher chronic illness rates than rural white older people (McCoy & Brown, 1978). The incidence of chronic illness among older people also varies considerably by geographic region. For example, the highest rates for white males are in the Southeast and in selected mining regions. Chronic illness rates for older males are consistently higher than for older females in both rural and urban regions. Death rates from chronic diseases are now higher in rural than urban areas for both males and females—although this was not the case in earlier decades of this century (Sauer, 1976). The incidence of chronic disease in elderly populations is related to characteristics of the specific environments, lifestyles, income levels, and exposure to hazardous conditions as well as rural–urban residence (Paringer et al., 1979).

The Income Factor

Multivariate analysis of morbidity rates (an index including incidence of acute illness, prevalence of chronic disease, restricted activities because of these conditions, bed disability, utilization of medical services, and functional limitations) suggests that rural–urban differences arise from several specific intervening factors such as income levels (see Chapter 3 for a discussion of rural–urban comparisons on income). Lower-income rural regions tend to have poorer health services and often have a higher incidence of occupational or environmental hazards, especially in lumbering and mining regions. Chronic diseases—defined as any illness lasting more than three months, such as cancer, hypertension, stroke, heart disease, and diabetes—are clearly associated with poverty as well as rural residence (Paringer et al., 1979).

The influence of income is illustrated particularly well in a study of low-income and disabled persons undertaken in 1973 (McCoy & Brown, 1978). The sample included elderly persons (n = 17,551) receiving Old Age Assistance (OAA) and a comparison group of older individuals with incomes of $5,000 or less or couples with an income up to $6,500 who did not receive any form of public assistance.

Recipients of OAA were more likely than the comparison group to have evaluated their health as "poor" (50% vs. 22%), reported more health disorders, and indicated more severe activity limitations. Furthermore, rural members of the sample had a poorer health profile than did their urban counterparts. Rural residents exhibited a higher prevalence of chronic disease than urban residents, even with age, sex, and race controlled (Paringer et al., 1979). Musculoskeletal, digestive, and genitourinary conditions were more prevalent in rural than urban areas. The rural respondents in the sample demonstrated a lower prevalence of circulatory problems, and fewer hearing, visual, back, or extremities impairments. Rural black men were particularly subject to musculoskeletal disorders (63%, as compared to 36% for urban black men).

These results suggest, as of 1973, that poor rural older people suffer from what might be referred to as a "poverty-illness syndrome"—that is, they are poor, which causes them to suffer from a series of lifestyle characteristics; this limits their access to medical services while subjecting them to many of the risk factors associated with a higher incidence of chronic disease. Because of these chronic diseases they are often unable to improve their incomes. Geographic and social isolation limit their abilities to escape from either poverty or poor health (McCoy & Brown, 1978).

Self-evaluation of Health Status

Older people tend to accurately perceive their health status. That is, their personal evaluations of health conditions coincide with physician assessment roughly two-thirds of the time, as illustrated in controlled studies of self-assessment versus professional assessment (Kane & Kane, 1981). While both rural and urban older people generally consider themselves to be in "good" health (on a scale with "good," "fair," and "poor" as the choices), older rural residents are more likely than urbanites to rate their health as "poor" or "fair" (Paringer et al., 1979).

Nutrition

Direct relationships have been established between dietary patterns and some of the chronic illnesses of older age (Hickey, 1980). In some instances dietary pattern is a contributing factor to illness (e.g., diabetes), while in other instances a state of illness contributes to the need for a specific dietary pattern (e.g., heart disease). Regardless of the causal relationship, it is clear that nutrition contributes to health status regardless of age or place of residence (Natow & Heslin, 1980).

Differences between rural and urban elderly with respect to nutrition have not been established. Research dealing with nutrition has generally neglected rural–urban variation (Posner, 1979) or has focused on either the rural or the urban end of the continuum (Rawson, Weinberg, Herold, & Holtz, 1978; Timmreck, 1977).

There is little evidence that aging brings a marked decrease in the ability to consume most foods, although protein digestion has been shown to be somewhat less efficient among the elderly (Natow & Heslin, 1980). Calcium deficiencies, which are associated with weaknesses of bone and joint structure, have often been reported among older people (Franz, 1981). Deficiencies of iron, vitamins A and C, protein, and niacin have also been regularly detected and associated with the aggravation of chronic diseases (Posner, 1979).

Delivery of Health Services

Physician Services

Illness prevention and health maintenance services are less accessible to the rural elderly than to their urban counterparts. For example, approximately five times as many physicians are available per capita in cities over five million as compared with towns of less than 10,000 and open country, rural regions (Wallack & Kretz, 1981). While the physician-to-population distribution has been improving steadily in recent decades (Newhouse, Williams, Bennett,

& Schwartz, 1982), the uneven geographical distribution of primary care and, particularly, specialized physician services continues to present obstacles to ready access for older people.

Younger physicians remain disinclined to establish new practices in underserved rural areas heavily populated with older people (Harris & Cole, 1980). Major public and private efforts to help establish permanent and self-sufficient medical practices in areas defined by the U.S. Public Health Service as "underserved" have been notably unsuccessful (Wallack & Kretz, 1981).

Efforts to achieve improved physician distribution continue, however. For example, the School of Medicine at the University of North Carolina has developed physician practice models (initially subsidized with funds from the Robert Wood Johnson Foundation) which have been judged as "successful" on the basis of continuing physician practice in the target region through the trial period (Madison, 1980). Geriatric medicine was a major component of each practice "model" although no special emphasis was given to training in geriatrics or serving older people.

The University of Washington Medical School and the University of Utah Medical School have also focused on training of health care professionals to serve in rural areas. However, special emphasis on the unique medical and health maintenance problems of older people has not been characteristic of these efforts (Rowe, 1982; Schwartz, 1978).

The lack of emphasis on geriatric medicine appears to remain a problem despite reports from the 1980 census and earlier that nonmetropolitan counties in the United States without a physician in residence tend to have a higher than average proportion of residents aged 65 and older—13.3 percent, as compared to 11.3 percent for all nonmetro counties (Getz, 1982). The new data seem to suggest, but do not necessarily confirm, that older rural people continue to have less access to specialized physician services than the urban elderly *despite* the growth in number of physicians relative to the total population.

Although the preceding data might suggest that physicians show a lack of interest in serving rural people in general and older people in particular, there is recent evidence that the practice of medicine in many rural areas is not economically feasible on a fee-for-service basis—even if physicians receive only modest incomes (Wallack & Kretz, 1981). This appears to be especially the case in locations where a substantial proportion of the population is low income and/or elderly. The reimbursement rates from Medicaid, Medicare, and other forms of insurance are decidedly lower than in urban areas and extra physician costs are involved in distance and time of travel for serving hospitalized patients.

Physician Utilization

Elderly people living in counties not adjacent to a metropolitan county indicate fewer visits to physicians annually than older citizens who live adjacent to urban centers, even when income levels are controlled (Paringer et al., 1979). Travel time to a regular source of health care takes more time, and waiting time upon arrival at the health care unit averages somewhat longer for rural older people, particularly among farm residents. Much of the national rural–urban discrepancy in physician utilization, however, is accounted for by older people who live in the southern region of the United States. For example, elderly southern blacks visit physicians roughly one-half as often as do other older people.

A study in rural Minnesota revealed that older people utilized physicians and other medical services at a higher rate than did younger members of the population; the elderly also reported higher satisfaction with physician services than did their younger counterparts (Chaska, Krishan, Smoldt, Ilstrup, Weidman, & Nobrega, 1980). Although the study contained no urban comparisons, the relatively higher levels of utilization and satisfaction were attributed to a greater concern with geriatric medicine among physicians located in this rural region, compared to less interest in the medical problems of older people among urban physicians.

Physician Attitudes

Physicians without specific training in geriatric medicine often have little understanding of the special physiological, nutritional, mental, and other attributes arising from the normal aging process (Rowe, 1982). The assumption is made that illnesses of old age are a necessary part of life which leads to diminished provision of treatment for illnesses that might readily be cured. Symptoms that are normally treatable in younger people are disregarded or undiagnosed in older patients. Furthermore, the orientation of a substantial proportion of physicians is toward the treatment of acute illnesses rather than chronic illnesses, which predominantly afflict older people (Harris & Cole, 1980).

Hospital Services

The National Health Survey indicates that rates of hospitalization are only slightly lower for older people in rural areas compared to urban elderly, although farm residents exhibit higher rates than either nonfarm rural people or urbanites (Paringer et al., 1979). Hospital beds per 1,000 population are now distributed similarly in rural and urban regions, providing approximately equal access (all other utilization factors assumed equal) for all residential categories. The quality and technological completeness of hospital facilities are highly variable, but the most comprehensive and specialized treatment centers are largely located in urban centers—where the most highly trained and specialized physicians are also concentrated (Hickey, 1980).

Hospital admissions of older people are somewhat lower in urban areas, where the supply of physicians is highest, than in rural areas (Davis & Reynolds, 1976). Physician visits are apparently substituted for hospitalization if accessibility for office calls is adequate. The average length of hospitalization is roughly comparable for older people in rural and urban areas (Paringer et al., 1979).

Emergency Medical Services

Although emergency medical service (EMS) is obviously an important resource for older rural people, no research results which specifically compare rural and urban EMS could be located. Such services have been discussed in various settings (e.g., the 1982 Annual Institute of the American Rural Health Association, held in Jeffersonville, Vermont, included several research sessions on rural EMS systems), but studies which control for age and place of residence have yet to be published.

Transportation for Health Care

/Transportation has been consistently defined as a problem for older rural people, particularly as age advances (McKelvey, 1979; Patton, 1975). Public transportation systems are generally little developed, although special buses for the aged and disabled are now available in many rural areas. Nonetheless, as the ability to drive decreases, older people become more dependent on relatives, friends, and neighbors for assistance in securing medical services (Harris & Cole, 1980). This situation is especially problematic for older women.

Many elderly people have, however, found methods to compensate for their lower access to private, personal transportation. For example, a study of nonemergency health transportation in one Texas county indicated that 82 percent of a small but randomly selected sample of older people ($n = 99$) owned their own cars, which they either drove or allowed others to drive (Gombeski & Smolensky, 1980). Another 13 percent had ready access to an automobile. Only 6 percent reported serious transportation problems for securing medical care.

Another study, in southwest Virginia, indicated that less than 10 percent of the rural elderly ($n = 103$) felt any dependence on public forms of transportation (Notess, 1978a). Fifty percent of the sample were able to drive themselves to secure medical services an average of 1.3 times per month. Slightly more than 40 percent were readily able to secure rides with other people. The same study reported a much higher dependency on public transporation in an urban setting (San Antonio, Texas). Sixty percent of the urban sample drove themselves or rode with friends, relatives, or neighbors, while the comparable proportion in the rural location was 98 percent. The inference drawn from the data was that no more than 20 to 35 percent of the elderly in rural areas would use special elderly oriented public transportation if it were available (Notess, 1978b).

Long-term Care

The population of rural elderly residents is increasing dramatically, as is the length of life (see Chapter 2 of this collection). This implies that an increased number of accommodations for long-term care may be needed if alternatives to institutionalization are not considerably increased. At present, approximately 5 percent of the over-65 population reside in such settings (Hickey, 1980).

It is difficult to be precise about the relative tendency toward institutionalization of elderly people in rural as compared to urban locations. Some rural people move to urban long-term care units when they are diagnosed as no longer able to care for their own needs in the rural setting. There is evidence, however, that many rural elderly may enter such institutions "prematurely" (Greene, 1982). The scarcity of rural community home care and medical care resources may be driving the rural elderly into long-term care homes at younger ages than their functional impairments would require. The mean age at entry into long-term care institutions in the study by Greene (1982) in Arizona was 77.6 years for rural patients and 79.5 years for urban patients ($n = 292$). Perhaps more important, the rural patients were also found to be less functionally impaired than urban patients.

The problem may be particularly serious for older rural women who outlive their spouses and are less able to manage transportation and medical costs than older rural men (Krauss, Spasoff, Beattie, Holden, Lawson, & Rodenburg, 1976). In 1977, 71 percent of the residents in long-term care facilities nationally were women (Hickey, 1980).

Long-term care has become a major industry in both rural and urban areas. A 1977 National Nursing Home Study counted 18,300 institutions with 1,287,400 patients, employing 635,000 people (Hickey, 1980). The average charge per patient per month was $700, much of which was paid from Medicaid and Medicare funds. Both Medicaid and Medicare have been considered of greater benefit to rural than to urban older people because of the generally lower incomes of the rural elderly and the lower incidence of other forms of medical insurance (Roemer, 1976b). A study in Minnesota indicated that the "quality of care" in rural long-term care facilities was higher than in urban areas. The criteria used for evaluation, however, and the limited range of the sample provide little basis for generalizations to the national level (Kart & Manard, 1976).

Health Care Financing

Financing health care for older rural people represents a major challenge. It is likely that medical costs will continue to increase, while Medicare and Medicaid are being cut back (Quinn, 1982). Cuts in those programs will be damaging to physician service access, hospitalization, and long-term care. The acquisition of needed prescription drugs is a perpetual problem. Drugs represent the largest per capita outlay by older people for health services; but except in long-term care or hospital situations, drug costs are not covered by either Medicaid or Medicare (Harris & Cole, 1980; Kart, Metress, & Metress, 1978).

Collectively, Medicare and Medicaid have had a dramatic impact on the utilization of medical services by the rural elderly (Roemer, 1976a). Admissions to hospitals, visits to physicians, and admissions to long-term care facilities have each risen more rapidly than population growth since the initiation of the Medicare and

Medicaid programs (Harris & Cole, 1980). Enrollment in Part B of Medicare (physician services) requires the payment of a fee, which was generally lower in rural areas as compared to urban centers, thus enabling lower income rural people to enroll who might otherwise have found participation difficult (Roemer, 1976b). This has also meant that physician reimbursement rates and hospital payments are lower in rural areas, and the lower fee scale has made private medical practice difficult since older people constitute a high proportion of the patient load (Wallack & Kretz, 1981).

Medicaid requires state participation. This has tended to cause wide variation in medical benefits to the rural elderly since many of the poorer and most rural states either chose not to participate or provide levels of reimbursement so minimal that the costs for health care are far above Medicaid payments. Many doctors, hospitals, and long-term care institutions therefore refuse to accept Medicaid patients (Hickey, 1980). A survey of physicians in one state revealed that their failure to participate in Medicaid was based on inadequate reimbursement, excessive paperwork, patient abuses of the program, and bureaucratic complexity, among other factors (Garner, Liad, & Sharpe, 1979). Regardless of these problematic circumstances, older rural people have benefited substantially more than the urban elderly as a consequence of the federal initiatives. The flow of assured fees has also added appreciably to the income of rural doctors and health care institutions (Roemer, 1976b).

The issue of financing adequate health services for the rural elderly is likely to be a subject of continuing policy discussion at local, state, and national levels in the years ahead—in part because of diminishing federal support and also because of the increased proportion of rural populations who are beyond 65 years of age. Medicare and Medicaid relieve much of the pressure on financial resources for the dependent elderly, their families, and local health care institutions. If publicly supported health insurance diminishes, the health status of the rural elderly may decline while the pressure on family and community resources may increase (Quinn, 1982).

Remote rural counties may feel the impact most dramatically, because the proportions of older people are highest in these locations and growth in the numbers of elderly citizens is continuing (Lichter, Fuguitt, Heaton, & Clifford, 1981). Numerical growth creates increased needs for health services as well as other social adjustments to fit the needs of older people. When growth in the proportion and numbers of older people is coupled with the declining death rate (a 25 percent decline in the decade 1968–1978), the implications for increases in health care costs are clear—unless an alternative lower-cost health care system can be implemented (Quinn, 1982).

Alternative Health Care Systems

The inadequacies of health status among older rural people are undoubtedly based in part on personal socioeconomic circumstances, environmental conditions, personal lifestyles, response to opportunities for care of illness, as well as the complex nature of the "system" of medical care and health services (W. K. Kellogg Foundation, 1981). The Center for Disease Control (Atlanta) has estimated that "lifestyle" contributes approximately 48 percent to the leading cause of death in the United States, while "hereditary" (biological) factors contribute 26 percent, environmental conditions 16 percent, and the medical care system 10 percent (W. K. Kellogg Foundation, 1981). This implies that the costs of maintaining health would be substantially lowered if individuals would alter their lifestyles to a healthier mode, while measures are taken to improve environmental conditions (particularly the various forms of pollution). The medical system would then have a less difficult and less costly task in moderating the negative effects of hereditary factors while also managing disease once it is contracted. Although the needed changes in lifestyle and environment would be most beneficial to people at younger ages, older people can also diminish the problems of illness and disease by modifying their behavior (Hickey, 1980).

Recent data on the antecedents of longevity suggest that medical service improvements have contributed less to lower mortality rates than has usually been assumed (Miller, 1982). It is therefore quite likely that health education and preventive health measures could serve to diminish costs and increase the health status of many older people. The need for the present extraordinarily high, and increasing, costs of advanced medical technology, professional health care personnel, and physical facilities might therefore be diminished (Miller, Voth, & Danforth, 1982; Schwartz, 1978).

The *medical-* or *disease-oriented* model of health care remains generally predominant, however, (Miller, 1982). It is best suited to acute and occasional illnesses by helping the older patient through a crisis to a state of at least temporary recovery. The model is graphically outlined in Figure 4.1.

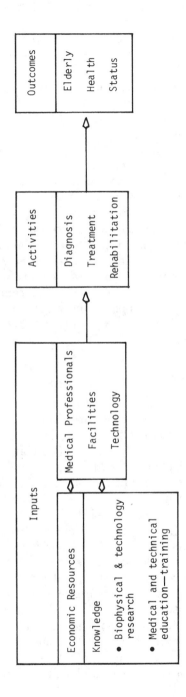

Figure 4.1. Structure of the predominant medical care system.

Adapted from: Miller, M. K. Health systems vs. sickness systems: Implications for the physical well-being of Americans. In R. F. Morgan (Ed.). *The Iatrogenics Handbook.* Toronto, Ontario: IPI Publishing, Ltd., 1983, pp. 59–77.

The more comprehensive *disease prevention/health maintenance* model places greater emphasis on long-term health care
over the life span (W. K. Kellogg Foundation, 1981). Rather than
focusing on the treatment of acute crisis arising from disease, the
model would encourage the older people (as well as the remainder
of the population) to avoid disease through "preventive" behavior
and a health-maintaining lifestyle (House Select Committee on
Aging, 1977). Because of the greater access to preventive health
care opportunities, the urban elderly generally find this model
more available to them than do the rural elderly (Wallack &
Kretz, 1981). The more comprehensive model is summarized in
Figure 4.2.

The crucial additions to the more comprehensive model include: much greater emphasis on health education and preventive
(as opposed to curative) medicine; a focus on the role of health-
producing behavior; emphasis on improvement of the environmental conditions encouraging good health (such as control of air and
water pollution); and social support from professional health care
personnel as well as friends and family for healthy behavior
(Miller & Stokes, 1978).

Basis for Preventive Health
Behavior in Old Age

The major illnesses of both rural and urban older people are heart
disease (which causes 38% of all deaths), cancer (20% of deaths),
and stroke (10% of deaths) (W. K. Kellogg Foundation, 1981). Control of these illnesses depends in major parts on eating and living
habits throughout a lifetime, but adjustments in lifestyle during
old age can modify the likelihood of disease, prolong life, and increase optimism about life. As noted earlier, self-perceived good
health exerts a major influence on an older person's feelings of
well-being and lack of economic stress (American Healthcare Corporation, 1980). The available evidence suggests that the financing
and delivery of health services to the rural elderly would be enhanced by a more comprehensive approach as represented by the
disease prevention/health maintenance model—while also decidedly improving their physical health status. It seems unlikely,
meanwhile, that the conventional medical model will be either
plausible for or affordable by individuals, localities, states, or the
nation, at future cost projection levels (Knowles, 1977; Wallack &
Kretz, 1981).

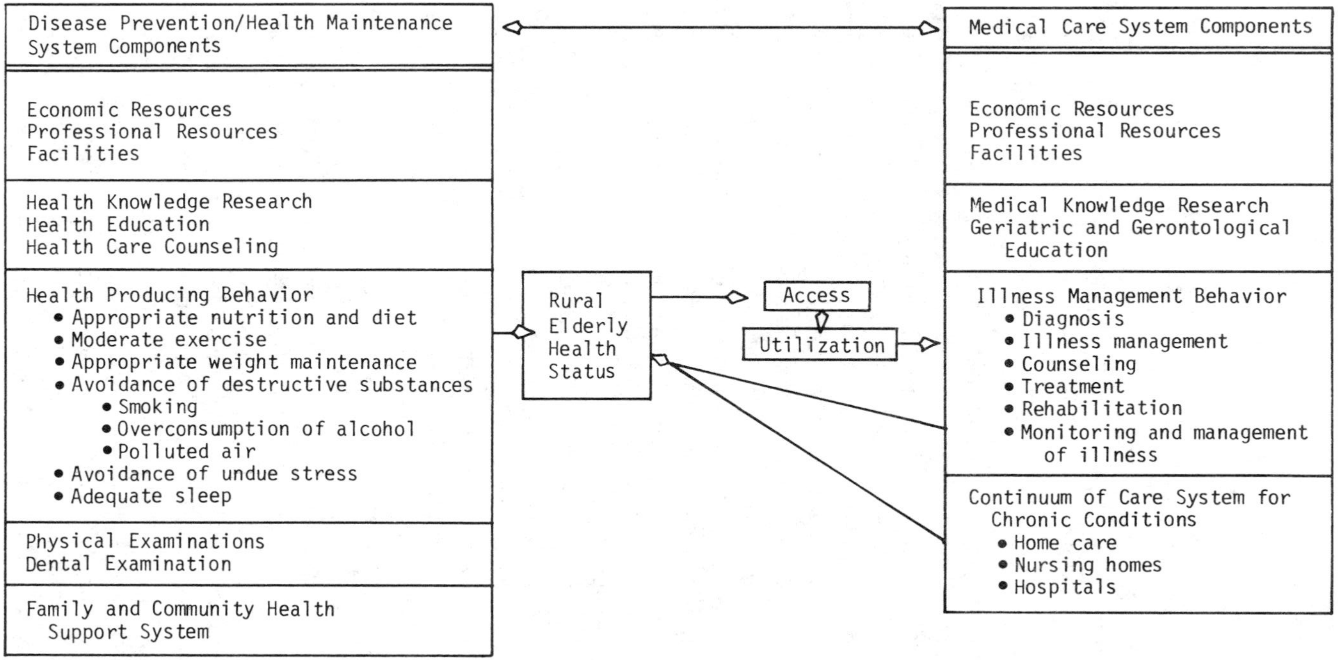

Figure 4.2. Disease prevention/health maintenance model integrated with the medical system model.

Future Needs in Research

The preceding sections illustrate the substantial gaps in knowledge about the physical health status of the rural elderly. The National Health Survey and studies limited to one state or parts of states provide the basis for rural–urban comparisons on selected issues, but few findings can be confidently generalized to the national level. Most research focuses either on health conditions, health service delivery, or financing, for the population of all elderly people without controls for rural–urban variation (Copp, 1976).

To gain a more thorough understanding of the complex of factors related to the health status of the rural elderly, research is needed which specifically compares randomly selected rural and urban samples of elderly people. Multivariate analysis potential can be provided by the measurement (at minimum) of age, sex, residential characteristics, socioeconomic status, ethnicity, and region of the United States. It is clear that each of these variables affects health status, but it remains unclear precisely how they interact or collectively "cause" elderly health conditions—particularly higher death rates from chronic diseases among the rural elderly. Outcome variables of clear importance include functional abilities to perform activities of daily living at various levels of health or illness status (Bangerter & Smith, 1981).

Rural–urban comparisons are needed on elderly hospital admissions and care, access to or delivery of emergency medical services, and the relative adequacy of long-term care facilities. These are each critical components of the needed continuum of care for the ill, elderly person. At present there is little basis for distinguishing how the adequacy of these components directly affects the health status of the rural elderly.

Although near universal agreement is evident among physicians and nutritionists that diet and general nutritional patterns play key roles in health status, little data are available on the specific characteristics of diet and nutrition as they are practiced by or affect the health of the rural elderly. It is only clear that many rural people probably do not understand the specific relationships between nutrition and health, nor do they likely practice health-maintaining dietary patterns (Purtle, 1982).

The financing of rural health services is clearly entering a new phase, as Medicare and Medicaid are cut back while the costs of health care continue to increase. Careful studies are needed of alternative financing schemes, accompanied by examinations of the potential impact of adopting a more comprehensive disease prevention and health maintenance approach. Major field experimental studies may be needed to develop appropriate health maintenance alternatives in a sample of representative communities and states (W. K. Kellogg Foundation, 1981).

Additional research is needed on the stereotypes and attitudes of rural elderly populations and professional health service providers. There is some evidence that part of the health care problems of older people are a direct consequence of the prejudices or negative attitudes of physicians, nurses, and other health professionals responsible for the care of older people (Ciliberto, Levin, & Arluke, 1981). Such predisposing factors, as well as health-producing factors, can be interrelated in multivariate analyses (Shortell, Richardson, Logerfo, Diehr, Weaver, & Green, 1977; Ward, 1977). Causal models are needed which link social-psychological variables, structural variables, organizational characteristics of provider units, and behavioral variables such as the utilization patterns of older people and the quality of professional provider performance. The causal model approach, using data from randomly selected comparative samples, would overcome many of the shortcomings of existing nonpredictive data (Miller, 1982; Shortell et al., 1977).

The comparative literature on the rural and urban elderly suggests a curious paradox: although health care services and health status are less adequate in rural locations, the morale and satisfaction with life appear to be consistently higher among rural older people as compared to urbanites (refer to Chapter 1 for a discussion of this seeming contradiction). Research is needed which explains this paradox with specific respect to health status (Lee & Lassey, 1980). The explanation may or may not be a function of community, neighborhood, friendship or family relations, or interdependencies between any of these factors, which are variously used as explanations without thorough documentation.

An assortment of studies indicates that the rural and urban elderly hold differential values, beliefs, and attitudes with respect to health; generally rural older people are found to be more conservative and are less likely to trust sophisticated medical care. However, the relationships are not clear and need further explanation (Miller, 1982).

A wide variety of experiments or demonstrations has been attempted for the provision of health care to the rural elderly. Evaluations have been undertaken, but are of widely varying comprehensiveness and quality. The results of demonstrations and experiments, whether publicly or privately sponsored, deserve to be vigorously evaluated. Findings should then be integrated to allow comprehensive and scientific judgments about which efforts appear to be most effective.

Other nations maintain rural elderly health care programs which are sometimes judged to be more effective than the U.S. pattern. Further evaluation and articulation of the policy implications of such programs would be helpful in improving American health programs that reflect the special needs of this population (Miller, 1982; Roemer & Roemer, 1981).

Summary

The evidence is clear that rural older people are less physically healthy than their urban counterparts. Health services are less accessible and the quality of health care facilities is inferior in certain respects; i.e., advanced technologies for dealing with heart disease, cancer, and cardiovascular diseases are less available in rural hospitals. Although general practice physicians are accessible in most rural regions, specialists are concentrated in urban medical centers. Both physicians and nurses are in demand for location in rural counties and communities which tend to have a disproportionately large population of older people. Lower compensation rates through Medicare and Medicaid, compared with other insurance programs, as well as the complexity of filing claims, are regarded as partially responsible for the lack of interest of many medical practitioners in establishing practices in rural areas with high proportions of elderly patients (Somers, 1980). This lack of interest may also be partially traceable to the medical model of health care which focuses on curing disease, often an impossible goal among older patients with chronic long-term health problems.

Although there are clearly rural–urban differences in elderly health status, service delivery, and health service financing—all to the disadvantage of rural areas—the primary contributing factor to each "difference" appears to be socioeconomic level. Rural areas contain higher proportions of poor older people than urban areas and it is the deprived elderly population which suffers from the poorest health status and has the greatest difficulty in securing and paying for health services.

The most recent national studies, however, suggest that there is relatively little relationship between longevity (one measure of the incidence of chronic disease) and ready access to health care. Rather, lifestyle characteristics, biological factors, and environmental conditions bear greater relationship to long life than access to, or utilization of, medical services (Miller, 1982). These findings suggest that the improved health status of rural older people can best be achieved by strategies involving health promotion and health maintenance, rather than greater investments in the curative components of the health care system associated with advanced medical skills, technology, and high-cost facilities.

Such conclusions, however, must be based partially on inference or speculation. The research evidence is by no means definitive. Carefully constructed longitudinal and comparative studies are needed to assess the predictors of functional health among older people in both rural and urban America.

References

American Healthcare Corporation. *Aging in America: Trials and triumphs.* Monticello, Ill., 1980.

Bangerter, R., & Smith, L. Assessing functional abilities of elderly outpatients. *Health and Social Work,* 1981, *6,* 33–40.

Chaska, N., Krishan, I., Smoldt, R., Ilstrup, D., Weidman, K., & Nobrega, F. Use of medical services and satisfaction with ambulatory care among a rural Minnesota population. *Public Health Reports,* 1980, *95* (1), 44–52.

Ciliberto, D., Levin, J., & Arluke, A. Nurses' diagnostic stereotyping of the elderly. *Research on Aging,* 1981, *3* (3), 299–310.

Copp, J. Diversity of rural society and health needs. In E. W. Hassinger & L. R. Whiting (Eds.), *Rural Health Services: Organization, delivery, and use.* Ames: Iowa State University Press, 1976, pp. 26–37.

Coward, R. T., & Kerckhoff, R. K. *The rural elderly: Program planning guidelines.* Ames, Iowa: North Central Regional Center for Rural Development, 1978.

Davis, K., & Reynolds, R. The impact of medicare and medicaid on access to medical care. In R. N. Rosett (Ed.), *The role of health insurance in the health services sector.* New York: National Bureau of Economic Research, 1976, pp. 414–425.

Franz, M. Nutritional requirements of the elderly. *Journal of Nutrition for the Elderly,* 1981, *1* (2), 39–56.

Garner, D. D., Liad, W. C., & Sharpe, T. R. Factors affecting physician participation in a state medicaid program. *Medical Care,* 1979, *17* (1), 43–58.

Getz, V. *Counties without a physician.* Washington, D.C.: U.S. Department of Agriculture, Economic Development Division, Economic Research Services, ERS Staff Report No. AGES811229, 1982.

Gombeski, W. R., Jr., & Smolensky, M. H. Non-emergency health transportation needs of the rural Texas elderly. *The Gerontologist,* 1980, *20* (4), 452–456.

Greene, V. L. *Premature institutionalization among the rural elderly.* Paper presented at the Sixth Annual Institute on the Delivery of Human Services to Rural People, Jeffersonville, Vermont, Sponsored by the American Rural Health Association, 1982.

Harris, D. K., & Cole, W. E. *Sociology of aging.* Boston: Houghton-Mifflin, 1980.

Hickey, T. *Health and aging.* Belmont, Calif.: Wadsworth, 1980.

House Select Committee on Aging, Sub-Committe on Health and Long-Term Care, United States Congress, *Sourcebook on aging.* Chicago: Marquis Who's Who, 1977.

Kane, R., & Kane, R. *Assessing the elderly: A practical guide to measurement.* Washington, D.C.: United States Government Printing Office, 1981.

Kart, C. S., & Manard, B. B. Quality of care in old age institutions. *The Gerontologist,* 1976, *16,* 250–256.

Kart, C. S., Metress, E. S., & Metress, J. F. *Aging and health: Biologic and social perspectives.* Menlo Park, Calif.: Addison-Wesley, 1978.

Knowles, J. H. (Ed.). *Doing better and feeling worse.* New York: W. W. Norton, 1977.

Kraus, A. S., Spasoff, R. H., Beattie, E. J., Holden, D. E., Lawson, J. S., Rodenburg, M., & Woodcock, J. M. Elderly applicants to long-term care institutions. *Journal of the American Geriatric Society,* 1976, *24,* 165–172.

Lee, G. R., & Lassey, M. L. Rural–urban residence and aging: Directions for future research. In W. R. Lassey, M. L. Lassey, G. R. Lee, & N. Lee, (Eds.), *Research and public service with the rural elderly.* Corvallis, Ore.: Western Rural Development Center, 1980, pp. 79–87.

Lichter, D., Fuguitt, G. V., Heaton, T. B., & Clifford, W. B. Components of change in the residential concentration of the elderly population. *Journal of Gerontology,* 1981, *36* (4), 480–489.

Madison, D. L. *Starting out in rural practice.* Chapel Hill: School of Medicine, University of North Carolina, 1980.

Maurer, R. C., Christenson, J. A., & Warner, P. D. *Perspectives of community service among rural and urban elderly.* Paper presented at the Annual Meetings of the Rural Sociological Society, Ithaca, N.Y., 1980.

McCoy, J. L., & Brown, D. L. Health status among low-income elderly persons: Rural–urban differences. *Social Security Bulletin,* 1978, *41,* 14–25.

McKelvey, D. J. Transportation issues and problems of the rural elderly. In S. M. Golant (Ed.), *Location and environment of elderly population.* Washington, D.C.: J. H. Winston and Sons, 1979, pp. 135–140.

Miller, M. K. Health systems vs. sickness systems: Implications for the physical well-being of Americans. In R. F. Morgan (Ed.), *The iatrogenics handbook.* Toronto, Ontario: IPI Publishing, Ltd., 1983, pp. 59–77.

Miller, M. K., & Stokes, C. S. Health status, health resources, and consolidated structural parameters: Implications for public health care policy. *Journal of Health and Social Behavior,* 1978, *19,* 263–279.

Miller, M. K., Voth, D. E., & Danforth, D. M. *The medical care system and community malady: Rural, urban, and suburban variations in impact.* Revision of a paper presented at the Annual Meetings of the Rural Sociological Society, Ithaca, N.Y., 1982.

Natow, A. B., & Heslin, J. A. *Geriatric nutrition.* Boston: CBI Publishing, 1980.

Nelson, G. Social services to the urban and rural aged: The experience of area agencies on aging. *The Gerontologist,* 1980, *20* (2), 200–207.

Newhouse, J. P., Williams, A. P., Bennett, B. W., & Schwartz, W. B. Where have all the doctors gone? *Journal of the American Medical Association,* 1982, *247* (17), 2392–2396.

Notess, C. B. *Transit needs of the rural elderly.* Paper presented at the Annual Meetings of the Rural Sociology Section, Southern Association of Agricultural Scientists, Houston, Tex., 1978. (a)

Notess, C. B. Rural elderly transit markets. *American Institute for Planners Journal,* 1978, *44,* 328–334. (b)

Paringer, L., Bluck, J., Feder, J., & Holahan, J. *Health status and use of medical services.* Washington, D.C.: The Urban Institute, 1979.

Patton, C. W. Age groupings and travel in a rural area. *Rural Sociology,* 1975, *40* (1), 55–63.

Posner, B. M. *Nutrition and the elderly.* Lexington, Mass.: D. C. Heath, 1979.

Purtle, V. S. Food and nutrition. In D. A. Dillman & D. J. Hobbs (Eds.), *Rural society in the U.S.: Issues for the 1980s.* Boulder, Colo.: Westview Press, 1982, pp. 224–233.

Quinn, J. B. Shopping for health care. *Newsweek,* 1982, February 1, p. 58.

Rawson, I. G., Weinberg, E. I., Herold, J. A., & Holtz, J. Nutrition of rural elderly in southwestern Pennsylvania. *The Gerontologist,* 1978, *18* (1), 24–29.

Roemer, M. I. *Rural health care.* St. Louis: C. V. Mosby Co., 1976. (a)

Roemer, M. I. Historical perspective of health services in rural America. In E. W. Hassinger & L. R. Whiting (Eds.), *Rural health services: Organization, delivery, and use.* Ames: Iowa State Press, 1976, pp. 3–25. (b)

Roemer, M. I., & Roemer, X. *Health care systems and comparative manpower policies.* New York: Dekker Press, 1981.

Rowe, J. R. *The status of geriatric medicine.* Paper presented to the Faculty and Students of Louisiana State University Medical School, New Orleans, La., 1982.

Sauer, H. I. Risk of illness and death in metropolitan and nonmetropolitan areas. In E. W. Hassinger & L. R. Whiting (Eds.), *Rural health services: Organization, delivery and use.* Ames: Iowa State University Press, 1976, pp. 38–55.

Schwarz, M. R. Medical education and rural health in the Pacific Northwest and Alaska. *Biosciences Communications,* 1978, *4,* 59–66.

Shortell, S. M., Richardson, W., Logerfo, J. P., Diehr, P., Weaver, B., & Green, K. E. The relationships among dimensions of health services in two provider systems: A causal model approach. *Journal of Health and Social Behavior,* 1977, *18,* 139–159.

Somers, A. R. Rethinking health policy for the elderly: A six-point program. *Inquiry* (a publication of Blue Cross Insurance Corporation), 1980, *17* (1), 3–17.

Taietz, P., & Milton, S. Rural–urban differences in the structure of services for the elderly in upstate New York counties. *Journal of Gerontology,* 1979, *34* (3), 429–437.

Timmreck, T. C. Nutrition problems: A survey of the rural elderly. *Geriatrics,* 1977, *32* (10), 137–140.

Wallack, S. S., & Kretz, S. E. *Rural medicine: Obstacles and solutions for self-sufficiency.* Lexington, Mass.: D. C. Health, 1981.

Ward, R. A. Services for older people: An integrated framework for research. *Journal of Health and Social Behavior,* 1977, *18* (1), 61–70.

W. K. Kellogg Foundation. *Viewpoint: Toward a healthier America.* Battle Creek, Mich.: W. K. Kellogg Foundation, 1981.

5

The Mental Health
of the Aged
in Rural Environments

Rick J. Scheidt

This chapter offers a selective, evaluative review of information pertaining to the mental health of older rural Americans. It attempts to assess the knowledge and issues pertaining to the prevalence and treatment of mental disorder in this population, drawing upon rural–urban comparisons where possible. This chapter attempts to identify problems and gaps in the existing base of knowledge, and to recommend strategies for improving future research in this area. Finally, the relevance of current research for mental health service providers working with rural elderly populations is discussed.

To gain a fuller appreciation of the meaning of research and intervention pertaining to the mental health of rural aged populations, however, it is necessary to briefly consider some major and more general issues in the field of aging and mental health. These are issues which particularly influence the conduct, conceptualization, and interpretation of research.

First, recent reviews of the concept of mental health as it relates to aging underscore the ambiguity of the term (Birren & Renner, 1981); this continues to be a source of dismay for researchers and applied professionals (Kaplan, 1976; Rosow, 1981). There is general agreement among professionals that "single criterion" definitions of mental health are problematic, based on elusive evaluative standards. Examples include attempts to define normality via statistical or cultural standards, to define "good" adjustment in the context of conforming behavior, or to judge competent functioning against similar criteria. Though most agree that multiple criteria should be sought, there is continuing disagreement among leading gerontologists about the usefulness of developing "old-age"-specific criteria of mental health. Birren and Renner (1981), for instance, hold that professionals should seek multiple criteria sensitive to the changes in meaning of *positive* mental health across the life span. They have suggested the inclusion of self-evaluation, reflection or life review, and reconciliation of past and present experiences as evaluative criteria of mental health in old age. On the other hand, Rosow (1981) has argued that such criteria should be general rather than age-specific, recommending the development of independent definitions for the ambiguous criteria which now exist. He has suggested that the criteria for positive mental health necessarily invite idealization and disagreement and that "mental health is not yet ready for useful scientific discourse" (Rosow, 1981, p. 258). He advised professionals to channel their energies into refining the existing criteria of mental illness or *pathology,* which he believed possesses greater consensus. The tractability of these criteria, in his view, makes them more useful to theory, research, and treatment. (The present chapter follows this basic approach, attempting to distinguish older rural Americans "at risk" or displaying assessed psychopathology.) Thus, at a conceptual level, the least controversial yet practical approach is to view mental disorder essentially as a failure to adapt, that is, "as a failure to meet the individual's basic needs, or meeting them only at the expense of pain, suffering, and disorder within the individual or within the environment" (Pfeiffer, 1977, p. 650). This approach carries its own problems and ambiguities, as will be noted below. The point to be emphasized, however, is that these doubts and laments about the meaning of mental health provide the context within which research and intervention proceed.

Second, these controversies and ambiguities affect the interpretability and comparability of research studies on older populations, making generalizations difficult. Gerontologically focused research on mental health and mental disorder encompasses a wide range of emotional and behavioral domains. Much of this research falls under the rubric of "subjective well-being" and includes both social epidemiological studies of mental health and gerontological studies of the factors affecting the quality of later life (George, 1981). Thus, mental health or well-being is used as a second-order construct, encompassing such concepts as life satisfaction, happiness, morale, positive self-image, and psychological pathology or disorder. Many of these concepts are semantically and empirically related, with measurement techniques ranging from observational to self-report indices (Adams, 1971). Evidence pertaining to the construct, or to the predictive and concurrent validity of the indices, is sparse and has only recently emerged (Lawton, 1977). There is currently a sore need to examine the conceptual and psychometric distinctions among these measures (George, 1981). Further, assessments of subjective well-being and its personal and situational correlates yield results of greater predictive and explanatory value on the aggregate level than the individual level (Larson, 1978). We also "have little idea how the construct [well-being] permeates ongoing daily experience" (Larson, 1978, p. 112). In summary, inferences and data about mental disorder must inevitably be drawn from relevant but heterogeneous research spanning a variety of concepts and measures.

Third, it is generally recognized that community studies to detect mental disorder among the elderly suffer from a variety of problems (Pfeiffer, 1977). Epidemiological studies, which typically analyze the distribution of morbidity in place and time, as well as factors influencing this distribution, are subject to several cautions (Kay & Bergmann, 1980). Most studies lack standardization in several critical respects, including criteria of rurality (Ansello, 1981), definitions of "case," diagnostic criteria, sources of data, sampling strategies, and assessment devices (Flax, Ivens, Wagenfeld, & Weiss, 1978; Kay & Bergmann, 1980; Mueller, 1981; Wagenfeld, 1982).

In addition, there are few studies which examine or report interactions between age and rural–urban status. Field studies attempting to identify "true" and "treated" morbidity rates tend to focus rather exclusively on rural–urban differences or adult age differences in mental disorder, but rarely consider cross-classified rates for those two dimensions. Extrapolations performed to compare divergent field studies largely focus upon rural–urban or age-group dimensions alone (Dohrenwend & Dohrenwend, 1969; Dohrenwend, Dohrenwend, Gould, Link, Neugebauer, & Wunsch-Hitzig, 1980; Summers, Seiler & Hough, 1971). Further, national data on treatment rates for various types of mental disorder across all types of mental health facilities are more readily available for various age-groups than for rural–urban service areas (Redick & Taube, 1980; Taube, 1982).

Despite this discouraging set of caveats, data gathered over the past two decades have been of some value in depicting the conditions of mental disorder for aged populations. The following section includes (1) a broad overview of estimates of psychopathology in rural–urban locales, as well as among the general population of older Americans; (2) an evaluation of studies which specifically examine mental disorders among older persons in both urban and rural settings; and (3) suggestions that emerge from this evaluation which might serve to improve future field research on aging and mental disorders.

Aging and Mental Disorder: An Overview of Community Studies

Community studies which attempt to detect the "true" incidence of mental disorder among older Americans fall into two categories. In one group are studies which seek to identify individuals exhibiting psychiatric disorders which may be classified by traditional diagnostic criteria, i.e., psychoses, neuroses, or personality disorders. These diagnoses are more easily determined by professionals in clinical settings than through household field surveys. Thus, these studies tend to define "true" cases as those receiving *treatment* on an inpatient or outpatient basis in mental health facilities or general practitioner care.

The second category of studies attempts to assess the existence of mental disorder among older community residents who may or may not be receiving treatment, and thus includes the possibility of identifying "true" but *untreated* cases. These studies focus more on assessed degree of impairment (mild, moderate, or severe), employing "batteries of symptom questions with fixed alternative response formats," which tap "a variety of physical and psychological symptoms thought to be related to psychiatric disorders" (Link & Dohrenwend, 1980a, p. 114). Studies of these field measures reveal that they are imperfectly and often only indirectly related to clinical psychiatric disorders, promptimg Link and Dohrenwend (1980a) to note that they may actually be measuring something akin to Frank's (1973) concept of "demoralization," e.g., poor self-esteem, helplessness-hopelessness, sadness, anxiety, and confused thinking. This conditon may or may not manifest itself in clinical disorder, but certainly is a "common property of the conditions which psychotherapy attempts to relieve" (Frank, 1973, p. 278). Demoralization is associated with a variety of problems most likely to be experienced by elderly individuals, including chronic illness, social marginality, and stressful life events.

Estimates of the incidence of mental disorder are available

from research in both of the above categories, though, again, researchers usually report only age-group estimates or rural–urban estimates with little or no consideration of the way in which these dimensions interact. We will briefly review this research, however, as it provides a useful context for evaluating findings of research which does examine age/residence interactions.

Rural–Urban Estimates

At present, rural–urban comparisons of the prevalence of mental disorder are made at great risk and with considerable difficulty. Indeed, Dohrenwend (1977) has stated that "given the differences in concepts and methods used in identifying cases in the true prevalence studies, comparisons of rate differences across studies done in rural and urban settings by different investigators is an exercise in futility" (p. 58). For instance, Dohrenwend and Dohrenwend (1965) compared several short-term prevalence studies of treated and untreated mental disorder assessed with field measures across several geopolitical areas in rural and urban sites. Rates for North American studies conducted in this century varied considerably within both urban (1.8% to 32%) and rural (1.7% to 64%) locales. These wide ranges of psychopathology are attributed largely to methodological discrepancies between studies.

A more helpful approach is to examine data from studies employing both urban and rural settings, which may aid the search for trends (Dohrenwend, 1977). Recent estimates which qualify by this criterion are reported by Link and Dohrenwend (1980b), who evaluated studies of treated versus untreated status of mental disorder within the same design. These authors report that one investigation, using the Health Opinion Survey screening scale in both urban and rural sites in Florida in 1977, found higher true rates in rural areas (33.3%) compared to urban areas (25.9%) but lower rural treatment (5.3%) compared to urban treatment rates (9.3%) among these cases. A National Opinion Research Center study (Link & Dohrenwend, 1980b) employing the Langner Psychiatric Index reported highly comparable true prevalence rates for rural and urban residents (32.9% and 32.1%, respectively), with slightly lower reported "ever in treatment" rates for rural compared to urban residents (18.9% and 23.1%) who were identified as true cases.

In a more extensive and recent review, Mueller (1981) concluded that regional field studies, as well as national surveys using symptom surveys (e.g., The Langner Psychiatric Screening Index, the Health Opinion Survey, or the General Well-Being Scale), yield inconsistent results regarding the prevalence of rural–urban mental disorder. Metropolitan prevalence rates across eight studies reviewed by Mueller ranged from 7.8 to 37.1 percent, while those from small towns and rural areas ranged from 10.5 to 45 percent. Some studies report higher urban than rural prevalence rates (e.g., Manis, Brawer, Hunt, & Kercher, 1963), while others report higher rural rates (Schwab, Warheit, & Holzer, 1974; Srole, 1978). Interestingly, when Mueller (1981) controlled for a variety of sociodemographic variables, he found little difference between six categories of rural–urban residents on General Well-Being scores obtained from a National Health and Nutrition Examination Survey conducted from 1971 to 1975. This is consistent with the national survey reported by Gurin, Veroff, and Feld, (1960), which also found little relationship between place of residence and adjustment measures.

Age Estimates

In a careful review of studies conducted since 1950, Neugebauer (1980) provided estimates of the "true" prevalence (including institutionalized cases) of functional and organic disorders among the U.S. elderly. Unfortunately, he found only two U.S. research programs reporting prevalence rates (New York State Department of Mental Hygiene, 1959; Pasamanick, 1962), both of which were conducted in urban areas. He concluded that 3.5 to 5.5 percent of adults 60 years and older display severe forms of senile and arteriosclerotic organic psychoses, 3.5 percent display severe functional psychoses (depression, schizophrenia), 6.0 to 10.5 percent exhibit neuroses, while 5.0 percent display personality disorders. In these samples, older women exhibited higher rates of neuroses, with men showing higher rates of personality disorder. The rates across disorders total 18.0 to 24.5 percent; again, these are estimates obtained from urban samples.

Age estimates of the prevalence of demoralization provided by epidemiological field studies are provided by Link and Dohrenwend (1980b). These authors reviewed true prevalence studies in an attempt to estimate the number of untreated to treated cases exhibiting functional psychiatric disorders in the United States. Three of these studies provide useful age estimates. Myers and Weismann (see Link & Dohrenwend, 1980b) reported that while 27.3 percent of older (66 years plus) residents of urban New Haven,

Connecticut reported evidence of a disorder in their lifetime (using Research Diagnostic Criteria developed to parallel the new *Diagnostic and Statistical Manual III* of the American Pyschological Association), only 26.7 percent of this group had ever received treatment. Warheit (see Link & Dohrenwend, 1980b), using the Health Opinion Survey screening scale, reported that about 40 percent of his older (60 years plus) rural–urban Florida sample were classified as true cases, with only 1.6 percent of these reporting ever having been in treatment. Finally, a National Opinion Research Center survey reported that in a national sample, 31.5 percent of the respondents who were 61 to 70 years of age and 37.7 percent of those over 70 years of age reported psychological distress interpretable as demoralization. In contrast, the treatment rates ranged from 10.9 percent in the 61 to 70 years of age group to 12.8 percent for those past 70 years. Compared to younger age-groups, the numbers of true cases ever in treatment were dramatically lower for older adults in each of the three studies; overall, true rates did not show a consistent relation with age across studies. The implications of such low treatment rates are examined below.

Mental Disorder Among Older
Rural–Urban Residents

The above studies provide a limited context for understanding mental disorder among older Americans across urban and rural sites. In this section, selected studies conducted in the United States in the last 20 years which analyze in more direct fashion the conditions of mental disorder for older urban community residents will be examined. These include studies in which rural–urban comparisons of older adults are incorporated within the same design, as well as studies focusing solely upon older rural residents.

One of the more relevant studies of this period was a national interview survey of 3,996 community-based residents 65 years of age or older, conducted in 1968 by Schooler (1975). Schooler also completed a follow-up study, three years later, on a subsample of 521 members of the original group. The primary focus of the study was to examine the relationships between residential environment, health, the formation and maintenance of social relationships, and morale (Schooler, 1975). This is one of the few national surveys to examine rural–urban differences among older persons. Using the Census Bureau definition of urban (towns 2,500 and greater) and rural (towns of less than 2,500), Schooler reported that the rural elderly (n = 960), compared to their urban counterparts (n = 3,038), exhibited significantly greater alienation (Srole Anomie Scale) and lower morale on a factor called "attitude toward own aging" (Philadelphia Geriatric Center Morale Scale). No differences existed, however, for "agitated depression" or for "lonely dissatisfaction," both akin to depression factors. A control for demographic differences did not, by and large, change the directions of these differences in morale. Furthermore, there was no difference between the amount of aggregate change in morale between the rural and urban elderly over a three-year period. Within-sample analyses relating changes in morale to changes in physical health status showed that, overall, changes in morale were associated with changes in health to a much greater extent among the urban than the rural elderly. Applying controls for social relations factors (contact with family and friends) and environmental factors (rated condition of dwellings) showed that only *improved* social relations among the rural elderly served to maintain the weak association between change in morale and change in health. Improved social relations among the urban elderly actually increased the association between morale and health. That is, the rural buffering effect "may be due to the maintenance and improvement of social relations in the rural environment" (Schooler, 1975, p. 37). The specific reasons for these associated changes in morale and health among the urban elderly and the lack of associated changes among the rural elderly remain unknown, though Schooler believed that they may have reflected differences in the aging process among urban and rural populations. The process-focused approach of Schooler should lead to a better understanding of the factors that affect "at risk" older populations as well as suggesting variables of interest to interventionists.

Using a portion of the data generated from a 1973 national probability survey conducted by the National Opinion Research Center, Hynson (1975) examined the extent of satisfaction which 319 rural and urban elderly (60 years plus) expressed with their families, communities, and current life situation. The latter was assessed with a standard "happiness" item (Campbell, Converse, & Rodgers, 1976): "Taken all together, how would you say things are these days—would you say that you are very happy, pretty happy, or not too happy?" A three-category rural–urban variable was constructed using the place of residence of respondents (rural = areas under 2,500 in population; intermediate zone = areas between 2,500 and 250,000; large city = areas over 250,000). Hynson reported that a greater percentage of the rural elderly were "generally happy" (47.1%) as compared with the elderly living in intermediate zones (39.6%) and the urban elderly (29.3%). Rural elderly also expressed higher community satisfaction and less fear of crime than elderly in the other two residential categories. No differences emerged for satisfaction with family. Hynson concluded that these rural–urban differences supported the premise that city life related negatively to feelings of community satisfaction, happiness, and fearfulness among older persons.

Using the same data and a more comprehensive measure of life-satisfaction, Sauer, Shehan, and Boymel (1976) demonstrated that rural–urban residence disappeared as a significant predictor of general happiness when control variables such as health, marital status, race, and income were taken into account. In fact, the latter were significantly stronger predictors. Though features of this reanalysis have come under some criticism (Lee & Lassey, 1980), the broad advice offered by Sauer and his associates (1976) is still instructive. They suggested that future research would do better to more closely examine the "differential import the predictors of satisfaction may have for rural and urban aged," rather than by "emphasizing only differences in levels of satisfaction between rural and urban elderly" (Sauer et al., 1976, p. 273).

In 1968 a major epidemiological study of the mental health needs of community residents of a southeastern Florida county was initiated by Schwab et al. (1974). Randomly selected urban and rural farm and small-town residents were interviewed with a protocol that included several standard measures—among them Leighton's Health Opinion Survey (H.O.S.). Using H.O.S. scores of 30 and higher to identify possible and probable "caseness" (psychiatric disorder), and controlling for age, sex, race, and income, these investigators reported that the highest percentages of caseness included men over 60 who grew up and resided in rural areas (45.8%) and rural women (50%) over 45 years of age who were raised in villages (2,500 and under) or small cities. The lowest caseness (less than 10%) occurred among rural and urban males between 18 and 44 years of age and women aged 30 to 44 who resided in rural areas and grew up in villages or small cities (less than 10% cases in both groups). Overall, 25.5 percent of the total population exhibited H.O.S. caseness, with age positively related to the proportion of reported cases (36.8% among those 60 and over). Regardless of rural–urban residence and place of origin, more than 50 percent of the sample with annual incomes of less than $3,000 exhibited scores within the range defined as caseness. The authors concluded that "simple rural–urban comparisons of mental illness rates are relatively meaningless in view of evidence which shows clearly that 'caseness' is associated with low incomes and deprivation while health is associated with relative affluence and opportunity" (Schwab et al., 1974, p. 274). The authors also caution that high H.O.S. scores among the elderly in particular may be due to the endorsement of H.O.S. items assessing physical symptomatology which may be unrelated to mental illness. Moreover, the accelerated social change within the county makes it difficult to compare these results to other urban and rural regions experiencing less change.

In an effort to identify the major mental health needs of the residents of three rural counties in North Carolina, Edgerton, Bentz, and Hollister (1970) administered the H.O.S. to a random sample (n = 1,405) of respondents ranging from 20 to 70 years of age. The sample contained residents of small towns and rural farms. Overall, older residents (50 years plus) scored higher on the average than did those below 50. Unfortunately, the authors did not report the variance associated with any of the means in their analyses. About one-fourth of their sample obtained "at risk" scores, i.e., raw scores over 30 points, but these persons were not broken out by age groups. Rural farm residents obtained slightly higher mean H.O.S. scores than did small-town residents, and relatively high scores were also found among nonwhites, unmarried persons, and those with lower education and income levels. In the absence of regression analyses, the relative predictive efficacy and interaction among these demographic variables remain unknown.

In order to relate demographic and socioeconomic attributes to self-reported symptoms of depression, Comstock and Helsing (1976) compared the interview data for a randomly selected sample of urban Kansas City adults (n = 1,173) with a sample of rural–urban residents (n = 2,762) of Washington County, Maryland. The primary instrument was the Center for Epidemiologic Studies Depression Scale (CES-D), a 20-item instrument assessing major symptoms of clinical depression. Approximately 650 residents were 65 years or older, with about 1,300 residents of all ages residing in small towns and rural farm areas of Washington County. Adjusting for the effects of several demographic variables (sex, marital status, education, income), elderly Washington County and Kansas City residents had a smaller percentage of high scores on the CES-D than did younger adults (3% to 10% across older samples, respectively). The authors concluded that age, per se, may actually decrease the tendency to feel depressed when the effects of associated sociodemographic factors are controlled. The authors reported that the frequency of high CES-D scores was similar across all parts of Washington County, supporting the conclusion that rural–urban differences in the prevalence of depression did not exist. Rural–urban variations in depression for older Washington County residents are not reported, though the overall percentage of older high scorers was about 3 percent across the county. This study again illustrates the importance of examining the contribution of variable domains (in this case, demographic) which may mediate or produce so-called age-group or rural–urban differences in scoring on psychiatric epidemiological measures. Comstock and Helsing (1976) have argued that studies using unadjusted rates of mental disorder are comparable only to the degree that their populations possess similar characteristics. By "equalizing" features on which communities may differ, adjustment for socioeconomic and demographic differences "yields results which should be more widely applicable," and many produce "values that are more likely to reflect causal associations" (Comstock & Helsing, 1976, p. 559).

Phillips (1966) surveyed a probability sample of 600 residents across the entire state of New Hampshire in order to identify both the true prevalence of mental disorder and the proportion of this group actually receiving treatment. Psychiatric symptomatology was assessed using the Langner Twenty-Two Item Screening Scale. Phillips reported that the true prevalence rates were associated with each of several demographic variables (education, income, marital status, and sex) and with region, but made no attempt to determine the manner in which these predictors combined to explain variation in scoring. Using a cutoff of 7+ symptoms endorsed on the Langner Psychiatric Screening Index (Langner, 1962), older residents (60 years plus) exhibited a lower percentage of caseness (6%) than did the average of all categories of younger residents (10%). Men showed slightly lower symptomatology (7.4%) than did women (9.9%). Those with higher levels of education and income displayed fewer symptoms on the Langner scale, as did those who were currently married or never married. About 12 percent of widowed residents showed mental disorder by this criterion. If the six study regions are classified by using a standard quantitative index of rurality (Windley & Scheidt, 1982), it appears that residents of the most rural regions of the state displayed higher percentages of psychopathology or caseness than did those of the more urban regions (e.g., Dartmouth–Lake Sunapee region, 15%; Seacoast region, 5%).

The actual treatment rates reported by Phillips (1966) showed considerable variation across regions, with no clear rural–urban treatment trends emerging. The lowest treatment rates occurred in one of the more rural regions (North Country, 0%), which reported the second highest true prevalence rate. This discrepancy between prevalence and treatment is attributed to the severe lack of mental health services in this area, suggesting that the elderly residents of such a rural region are receiving no formal treatment for the psychiatric complaints they exhibit. While failing to capitalize on the explanatory potential of the data, this study is not atypical of regional research which attempts to provide prevalence profiles of use to local professionals. It is unfortunate that such prevalence studies rarely emerge from even modest theoretical perspectives, the test of which might conceivably enhance the understanding of factors causally related to mental illness.

Fengler and Jensen (1981) examined the way in which several situational dimensions predicted "life-satisfaction" among a sample of randomly selected urban ($n = 385$) and nonurban ($n = 692$) elderly in Vermont. In the text the authors offered no defining criteria for distinguishing between the urban and nonurban groups. The predictor domain included a variety of perceived predictors (e.g., income, health, transportation, and housing) and a smaller number of objective predictors (e.g., living alone, population density, and the presence of someone to provide care). Selected items from Bradburn's Total Affect Balance Scale, including recent prevalence of boredom, depression, and loneliness, comprised the "life-satisfaction" measure, which might be more properly viewed as a limited temporal measure of current happiness. Overall, the predictors accounted for a greater proportion of variation of life-satisfaction scores among the urban (43%) than among the nonurban (18%) elderly. In addition, the measures of perceived status served as stronger predictors of these mood states than did the objective measures among both urban and nonurban elderly. Indeed, the authors found few objective conditions to differentiate these groups. Self-perceived income, perceived difficulties in obtaining access to suitable transportation, and objectively defined organizational participation were significantly stronger predictors for the urban than for the nonurban elderly residents. The investigators suggested that social planners would be wise to consider the impact of program interventions on the subjective appraisals of services made by elderly recipients, especially among urban elderly populations.

Despite the critical omission of criteria for defining rurality and the confusion engendered by labeling transient affect as "life-satisfaction," the Fengler and Jensen (1981) study represents a step in a needed direction. It operationalizes the advice offered by Sauer et al. (1976) that research should seek to identify those factors which have differential import for predicting satisfaction (happiness) among urban and rural elderly populations, rather than simply examining differences in level of satisfaction among these groups. Further, the research reinforces the importance of assessing both perceived and objective situational and personal variables, and of distinguishing their relative contributions to predicting aspects of mental health.

One of the most extensive studies of the well-being of older residents of small rural towns was recently conducted by Windley and Scheidt (Scheidt, 1981; Scheidt & Windley, 1982b; Windley, 1981; Windley & Scheidt, 1980, 1982). These researchers attempted to identify the degree to which several perceived physical and psychosocial community attributes affected social and psychological well-being, including mental health, of older residents across 18 small towns (2,500 and less in size) in Kansas. Towns of varying sizes within this range were selected from counties varying in their degree of rurality, the latter defined via a multidimensional quantitative index of population and occupational characteristics. Town panel members served as liaisons for the study within each community. Respondents 65 years and older ($n = 989$) were randomly selected from town population lists; those who were institutionalized or too ill to tolerate an interview were excluded. Sampling was conducted proportionally, varying by town size. Using a standard structured interview instrument, data were gathered over a one-year period, beginning in late 1978. The majority of the sample was female (64%), white (99%), Protestant (81%), and lived in single family housing (87%). Also, most were married (56%) and 37 percent were widowed. Maximum education was higher than the national average, with 30 percent high school graduates, 9 percent having some college education, and 4 percent college graduates.

The interview protocol contained several measures related to the mental health of the respondents including the Philadelphia Geriatric Center Morale Scale, Bradburn's Total Affect Balance Scale, and the Langner Twenty-Two Item Screening Index. Summated scale scores for the Philadelphia Geriatric Center Morale Scale showed 21.1 percent ($n = 209$) of the total sample displaying "low morale" (median split). Scoring of the Total Affect Balance

Scale revealed that 22.9 percent ($n = 226$) of the older residents reported being more "unhappy" than "happy." Twelve percent ($n = 120$) of the sample exhibited high Langner psychiatric symptomatology, using a defining cutoff of 7+ items endorsed. In contrast, Gaitz and Scott (1972) found that 42 percent of the older portion (65 years plus) of their urban Houston quota sample consisting of Mexican-American, blacks, and Anglos exhibited low Total Affect Balance Scores or greater unhappiness by the same criterion. High Langner symptomatology was found for 16.8 percent of the Gaitz and Scott group, a rate comparable to that found by Windley and Scheidt.

A composite mental health index was derived using the above three measures. Analyses revealed no differences in levels of mental health scoring among small-town size categories or rurality categories. These analyses indicated that a fair degree of homogeneity existed across these classification dimensions for mental health scoring in this region (Scheidt & Windley, 1982b). Using path modeling, the researchers explored possible community and personal attributes affecting the mental health of these older small-town residents. Briefly, among physical environmental dimensions impacting upon composite mental health, satisfaction with features of one's dwelling and degree of environmental constriction were most predictive of level of mental health. That is, those older persons who expressed higher satisfaction with the lighting, temperature, adequacy of space, and house and neighborhood quality exhibited more positive mental health scores. Those who reported a greater number of social and physical barriers to participation in town activities tended to display lower mental health scores, i.e., greater likelihood of "at risk" status. Two psychosocial predictors (the degree of community involvement and community satisfaction) related positively with mental health. Also, those respondents who reported feeling more isolated, seeing their communities as more youth-oriented, and perceiving town norms as fostering the disengagement of older residents from community affairs were more likely to exhibit lower mental health scores. Overall, these environmental predictors accounted for only a small portion of the variation in mental health scores (17.4%). Clearly, additional personal and environmental dimensions must be considered in modeling the ecological variables that have impact on mental health.

Scheidt and Windley (1981), using three second-order well-being factors (mental/physical health, contact with others, and activity) derived a taxonomy of diverse well-being profiles on this elderly sample. High–low splits on each of these three dimensions produced eight distinct groups. The most populated group (n = 459) consisted of those high on mental/physical health, low in contact with others, and high in activity level. The group appearing to represent those who are most "at risk" displayed a profile of low mental/physical health, low contact with others, and low activity scores (n = 83). Employing samples drawn from these two groups, as well as two others, Scheidt and Windley (1981) are conducting a short-term longitudinal study of variations in behavioral coping exhibited by elderly residents in response to problems encountered in small-town behavior settings. This research holds the promise for increasing our understanding of adaptive strategies that mediate person–environment congruence, yielding information which might generate training strategies designed to help older small-town rural residents cope more effectively with their everyday environments.

Research Implications

It is apparent that research on the status of mental health and mental illness among rural populations is woefully inadequate. The population of research studies is small, and those which exist have been conducted largely for provincial purposes. Focusing only on prevalence rates for caseness or "at risk" status, one notes significant variations across rural regions and across rural–urban populations. For reasons outlined earlier, it is almost impossible to compare these rates in a way which would afford sound generalizations about the configuration of mental disorder among the rural elderly across specific regions, much less nationally. With regard to the latter, a significant untapped resource resides within national surveys of the well-being of Americans at large, such as that of Campbell et al. (1976). The data sets for such surveys might be easily accessed to break out information addressing the mental health of older rural–urban Americans and factors related to this issue. Secondary data analysis remains largely untapped as a strategy of potential aid to mental health researchers. Further, as indicated above, research would profit from the greater use of theory and proposition testing adressing explanatory factors responsible for the state of mental health of various rural populations.

The usefulness of epidemiological field surveys (e.g., the

Health Opinion Survey or the Langner Psychiatric Screening Index) for clinical practitioners attempting to treat "at risk" older persons must be questioned. Many researchers report summary scores for measures which are clearly multidimensional, making it difficult to determine what caseness or "at risk" status really means. This problem exists over and above questionable assumptions about the validity of some of these field measures (Dohrenwend & Dohrenwend, 1965). The Langner Psychiatric Screening Index, for instance, is used often as a global summary measure of "demoralization," a construct which does not easily translate into the more traditional clinical diagnostic categories most familiar to geriatric clinicians and counselors. In this context, Dohrenwend, Shrout, Egri, and Mendelsohn (1980) have provided evidence showing that epidemiological field measures such as the Psychiatric Epidemiology Research Interview serve as adequate screening devices of psychopathology in general populations, but not of specific psychiatric diagnoses. These authors recommended a two-stage screening procedure, whereby persons exhibiting "at risk" scores on epidemiological measures (stage one) would be followed up with instruments yielding more specific diagnostic assessments (stage two).

Finally, researchers must begin to attend to the need for theoretical and operational standardization which might allow greater comparability between studies. This would apply to the testing of established models and the use of common instruments, criteria for rurality and caseness, and sampling strategies.

Mental Health Service Provision to the Rural Elderly

Although researchers investigating the mental health of rural residents face significant challenges, practitioners cannot afford to wait for research problems and controversies to be resolved (Coward, 1979). There are practical implications, however, emerging from research and the writings of applied professionals, of value to those dealing with the provision of mental health services to older rural populations.

Perhaps of most concern is the issue of actual *treatment* versus defined *need* for those elderly who reside in rural regions. Despite large variations in prevalence rates of "at risk" status among rural elderly, evidence from a variety of souces indicates that many of these persons are not receiving formal treatment for their psychological complaints. Scheidt and Windley (1982a) reported that only 1 percent of their small-town elderly sample had utilized mental health facilities during the previous year, though their data show that from 12 to 23 percent of the sample exhibited "at risk" status across three field measures of disorder. Nationally, persons over 65 years of age constitute only 4 percent of the caseload of community mental health centers (National Institute of Mental Health, 1981), a figure far below the estimates of need generated by the research reviewed above. This underutilization of community mental health services is of central concern, more so given that between 1960 and 1970 the proportion of the total institutional populations in state and county mental hospitals who were elders has decreased from 30 to 12 percent while the proportion in nursing homes and homes for the dependent aged increased from 63 to 82 percent (Redick, 1974). Thus, it would appear that elderly ex-mental patients, as well as noninstitutionalized community elderly residents, have a serious need for community treatment which is not being adequately addressed.

There are a number of service and client barriers accounting for this "treatment gap" (Coward & Smith, 1983; Flax et al., 1978). Some professionals have placed primary blame upon the failure of adequate policies for financial support. For instance, Lowy (1980) noted that less than 2 percent of medicare dollars go into mental health coverage for elderly and disabled individuals. The medicaid program emphasizes institutional care, while outpatient services receive more limited coverage. Entitlement programs often result in unnecessary institutionalization and inappropriate care for many older persons (Lowry, 1980). It remains to be seen whether the 1975 amendment to the Community Mental Health Act which provides specialized services to the elderly will aid in correcting part of this deficit in treatment (Berkman, 1977).

Others have noted the extreme national shortage of mental health professionals trained specifically to treat elderly individuals. Illustratively, a recent survey of 120 clinical psychology training programs accredited by the American Psychological Association showed only four offering formal training in the clinical psychology of aging (Cohen & Cooley, 1981). Birren and Sloane (1977) projected that by 1988 we will need an estimated 1,000 psychiatrists, 2,000 clinical psychologists, 4,000 psychiatric social workers, 8,000 nurses' aides, and 10,000 paraprofessionals to deal adequately with the mental health needs of the nation's elderly. The 1981 Conference on

Training Psychologists for Work in Aging (Older Boulder Conference) represented a major positive effort to deal with the issues
implied by the current shortage of mental health professionals (Santos & VandenBos, 1982).

There are other barriers more specifically applicable to the
provision of mental health services to the rural elderly. It is critcal
that professionals, at the outset, become familiar with rural regional or community values which have implications for the development of intervention models, modes of delivery, and, ultimately
the utilization of services by those in need. Flax et al. (1978) noted
that rural values contain themes of fatalism, subjugation to nature, an orientation to concrete places and things, and an emphasis
upon personal kinship ties. Such values may directly affect the
solutions which rural elderly and their families seek to solve their
problems (Flax et al., 1978). Moreover, some have noted that conflicts between rural values and those of the larger society may
create problems significant in the etiology of mental disorders
among rural residents (Mazer, 1976).

Ansello (1981) has suggested that rural educators and practitioners would do well to recognize that the values held by many
rural elderly may be "post figurative," emphasizing cultural stability, gradual change, and the acceptance that ways of past living
will endure into the future. Professionals who hold other values
may myopically initiate delivery programs which are destined to
fail. As Coward (1979) noted, the "spirit of independence" of many
rural elderly may make them less likely to perceive the presence of
personal and psychological problems. This value may also affect
their willingness to utilize mental health service programs, especially if such programs are perceived as state or federally sponsored entities. Mental health professionals must remain keenly
sensitive to the way in which this value gap may affect the success
of service provision to ethnic and minority groups, including
American Indians, blacks, and Chicanos (Flax et al., 1978).

It is also clear that rural mental health services must mesh
effectively with other prevailing services and informal helping networks. Windley (1983), for instance, found that while older rural
small-town Kansans used community mental health services quite
infrequently, most reported regular weekly visitation to a senior
citizen center or nutrition site. Anecdotal observations indicated
that some of the directors of these latter facilities provided much
informal counseling to elderly individuals. This highlights a clear
opportunity for ecologically sensitive intervention at such sites

through education and the placement of accepted paraprofessionals. These older Kansans visited physicians reportedly for physical complaints. It is not known to what extent these health problems disguised or resulted from psychological problems, though clinicians frequently point to these possibilities. Again, this is an instance where preventive and ameliorative treatment might be targeted outside of the formal mental health facility. It is also clear from the Kansas data that most of the small-town elderly traveled to many services in other communities (Windley, 1983), a finding which indicates that service providers should perhaps adopt regional as opposed to solely community-specific targeting of mental health programs where appropriate.

Rural service providers, especially those in transition from urban settings, must be aware of a number of more subtle personal and contextual points affecting the successful link-up between services and recipients. Bischoff (1976) advised that rural practitioners must go beyond traditional sociodemographic knowledge in becoming familiar with specific rural communities. This includes acquiring a subjective sense of a rural community and of self in relation to the community. The rural therapist must remain flexible and versatile in the face of potential professional isolation and lack of resources. Gaining acceptance may necessitate getting out of the formal facility and into the community in order to learn about local customs and norms. In many rural regions, professionals may find that they must establish their credentials as human beings before being accepted as credible service providers. Outsiders, especially service providers, are viewed suspiciously in many rural areas. Thus, in addition to prerequisite professional skills, rural mental health professionals must also develop a "streetwise" sense of the social ecology in which they will be operating.

References

Adams, D.L. Correlates of satisfaction among the elderly. *The Gerontologist,* 1971, *2,* 64–68.

Ansello, E.F. Antecedent principles in rural gerontology education. In P. Kim & C. Wilson (Eds.), *Toward mental health of the rural elderly.* Landover, Md.: University Press of America, 1981, pp. 1–14.

Berkman, B. Community mental health services for the elderly. *Community Mental Health Review,* 1977, *2,* 1–9.

Birren, J.E., & Renner, V.J. Concepts and criteria of mental health and aging. *American Journal of Orthopsychiatry*, 1981, *51*, 242–254.

Birren, J., & Sloane, R.B. *Manpower and training needs in mental health and illness of the aging.* Los Angeles: Ethel Percy Andrus Gerontology Center, 1977.

Bischoff, H.G.W. *Rural settings: A new frontier.* Paper presented at the Summer Study Program in Rural Mental Health, Madison, Wis., 1976.

Campbell, A., Converse, P.E., & Rodgers, W.L. *The quality of American life: Perceptions, evaluations, and satisfactions.* New York: Russell Sage Foundation, 1976.

Cohen, L.D., & Cooley, S. Psychology training programs for direct services to the aging. Paper presented at the Conference on Training Psychologists for Work in Aging, Boulder, Colorado, 1981.

Comstock, G.W., & Helsing, K.J. Symptoms of depression in two communities. *Psychological Medicine*, 1976, *6*, 551–563.

Coward, R.T. Planning community services for the rural elderly: Implications from research. *The Gerontologist*, 1979, *19*, 275–282.

Coward, R.T., & W.M. Smith, Jr. (Eds.). *Family services: Issues and opportunities in contemporary rural America.* Lincoln: The University of Nebraska Press, 1983.

Dohrenwend, B.P. The epidemiology of mental illness: Psychiatric epidemiology as a knowledge base for primary prevention in community psychiatry and community mental health. In G. Serban & B. Astrachan (Eds.), *New trends of psychiatry in the community.* Cambridge, Mass.: Ballinger, 1977, pp. 53–67.

Dohrenwend, B.P., & Dohrenwend, B.S. The problem of validity in field studies of psychological disorder. *Journal of Abnormal Psychology*, 1965, *70*, 52–69.

Dohrenwend, B.P., & Dohrenwend, B.S. *Social status and psychological disorder: A causal inquiry.* New York: Wiley, 1969.

Dohrenwend, B.P., Dohrewend, B.S., Gould, M.S., Link, B., Neugebauer, R., & Wunsch-Hitzig, R. *Mental illness in the United States: Epidemiological estimates.* New York: Praeger, 1980.

Dohrenwend, B.P., Shrout, P.E., Egri, G., & Mendelsohn, F. Nonspecific psychological distress and other dimensions of psychopathology: Meaures for use in the general population. *Archives of General Psychiatry*, 1980, *37*, 1229–1236.

Edgerton, J.W., Bentz, W.K., & Hollister, W.G. Demographic factors and responses to stress among rural people. *American Journal of Public Health*, 1970, *60*, 1065–1071.

Fengler, A.P., & Jensen, L. Perceived and objective conditions as predictors of the life-satisfaction of urban and nonurban elderly. *Journal of Gerontology*, 1981, *36*, 750–752.

Flax, J.W., Ivens, R.E., Wagenfeld, M.O., & Weiss, R.J. Mental health and rural America: An overview. *Community Mental Health Review,* 1978, *3* (1), 3–15.

Frank, J.D. *Persuasion and healing.* Baltimore: Johns Hopkins University Press, 1973.

Gaitz, C.M., & Scott, J. Age and the measurement of mental health. *Journal of Health and Social Behavior,* 1972, *13,* 55–67.

George, L.K. Subjective well-being: Conceptual and methodological issues. In C. Eisdorfer (Ed.), *Annual review of gerontology and geriatrics* (Vol. II). New York: Springer Publishing Co., 1981.

Gurin, G., Veroff, J., & Feld, S. *Americans view their mental health.* New York: Basic Books, 1960.

Hynson, L.M. Rural–urban differences in satisfaction among the elderly. *Rural Sociology,* 1975, *40,* 64–66.

Kaplan, B.L. Towards a working definition of mental health. *Community Mental Health Review,* 1976, *1,* 4–9.

Kay, D.W., & Bergmann, K. Epidemiology of mental disorders among the aged in the community. In J. Birren & R.B. Sloane (Eds.), *Handbook of mental health and aging.* Englewood Cliffs, N.J.: Prentice-Hall, 1980, pp. 34–56.

Langner, T.S. A twenty-two item screening score of psychiatric symptoms indicating impairment. *Journal of Health and Human Behavior,* 1962, *3,* 269–276.

Larson, R. Thirty years of research on the subjective well-being of older Americans. *Journal of Gerontology,* 1978, *33,* 109–129.

Lawton, M.P. Morale: What are we measuring? In C. Nydegger (Ed.), *Measuring morale: A guide to effective assessment.* Washington, D.C.: Gerontological Society, 1977, pp. 6–14.

Lee, G.R., & Lassey, M.L. Rural–urban differences among the elderly: Economic, social, and subjective factors. *Journal of Social Issues,* 1980, *36,* 62–74.

Link, B., & Dohrenwend, B.P. Formulation of hypotheses about the true prevalence of demoralization in the United States. In B.L. Dohrenwend et al. (Eds.), *Mental illness in the United States: Epidemiological estimates.* New York: Praeger, 1980, pp. 114–127. (a)

Link, B., & Dohrenwend, B.P. Formulation of hypotheses about the ratio of untreated to treated cases in the true prevalence studies of functional psychiatric disorders in adults in the United States. In B.P. Dohrenwend et al. (Eds.), *Mental illness in the United States: Epidemiological estimates.* New York: Praeger, 1980, pp. 133–149. (b)

Lowy, L. *Social policies and programs on aging.* Lexington, Mass.: Lexington Books, 1980.

Manis, J.G., Brawer, M.J., Hunt, C.L., & Kercher, L. Validating a mental health scale. *American Sociological Review,* 1963, *28,* 108–116.

Mazer, M. *People and predicaments.* Cambridge, Mass.: Harvard University Press, 1976.

Mueller, D.P. The current status of urban–rural differences in psychiatric disorder. *Journal of Nervous and Mental Disease*, 1981, *169*, 18–27.

National Institute of Mental Health. *Provisional data on federally-funded community mental health centers, 1978–79*. National Institute of Mental Health, Survey and Reports Branch, Division of Biometry and Epidemiology, Rockville, Md., 1981.

Neugebauer, R. Formulation of hypotheses about the true prevalence of functional and organic psychiatric disorders among the elderly in the United States. In B.P. Dohrenwend et al. (Eds.), *Mental illness in the United States: Epidemiological estimates*. New York: Praeger, 1980, pp. 95–113.

New York State Department of Mental Hygiene, Staff of the Mental Health Research Unit. A mental health survey of older people. *Psychiatric Quarterly*, 1959, *33*, 45–99.

Pasamanick, B. A survey of mental disease in an urban population: An approach to total prevalence by age. *Mental Hygiene*, 1962, *46*, 567–572.

Pfeiffer, E. Psychopathology and social pathology. In J. Birren & K.W. Schaie (Eds.), *Handbook of the psychology of aging*. New York: Van Nostrand, 1977, pp. 650–671.

Phillips, D.L. The "true" prevalence of mental illness in a New England state. *Community Mental Health Journal*, 1966, *2*, 35–40.

Redick, R. *Patterns in use of nursing homes by the aged mentally ill: Statistical Note 107*. National Institute of Mental Health, Division of Biometry, Survey and Reports Branch. Rockville, Md.: Department of Health, Education and Welfare, 1974.

Redick, R.W., & Taube, C.A. Demography and mental health care of the aged. In J. Birren & R.B. Sloane (Eds.), *Handbook of mental health and aging*. Englewood Cliffs, N.J.: Prentice-Hall, 1980, pp. 57–71.

Rosow, I. Docs: Ortho and para. *American Journal of Orthopsychiatry*, 1981, *51*, 255–259.

Santos, J., & VandenBos, G.R. (Eds.). *Psychology and the older adult: Challenges for training in the 80's*. Washington, D.C.: American Psychological Association, 1982.

Sauer, W.J., Shehan, C., & Boymel, C. Rural–urban differences in satisfaction among the elderly: A reconsideration. *Rural Sociology*, 1976, *42* (2), 269–275.

Scheidt, R.J. Psychosocial environmental predictors of the mental health of the small town rural elderly. In P. Kim & C. Wilson (Eds.), *Toward mental health of the rural elderly*. Washington, D.C.: University Press of America, 1981, pp. 53–80.

Scheidt, R.J. & Windley, P.G. *A behavior setting analysis of stress and coping in older community residents: Conceptual and methodological issues*. Paper presented at the annual meeting of the Gerontological Society of America, Toronto, November, 1981.

Scheidt, R.J., & Windley, P.G. *A behavior setting analysis of stress and coping in older community residents: Conceptual and methodological issues.* Paper presented at the Annual Meetings of the Gerontological Society of America, Toronto, 1982. (a)

Scheidt, R.J., & Windley, P.G. Well-being profiles of small-town elderly in differing rural contexts. *Community Mental Health Journal,* 1982, *18,* pp. 257–267. (b)

Schooler, K.K. A comparison of rural and non-rural elderly on selected variables. In R.C. Atchley & T.O. Byerts (Eds.), *Rural environments and aging.* Washington, D.C.: Gerontological Society, 1975, pp. 27–42.

Schwab, J., Warheit, G., & Holzer, C. Mental health: Rural-urban comparisons. *Mental Health and Society,* 1974, *1,* 265–274.

Srole, L. The city versus town and country: New evidence on an ancient bias, 1975. In L. Srole & A.K. Fischer (Eds.), *Mental health in the metropolis: The midtown Manhattan study.* New York: New York University Press, 1978, pp. 433–459.

Summers, G.F., Seiler, L.H., & Hough, R.L. Psychiatric symptoms: Cross-validation with a rural sample. *Rural Sociology,* 1971, *36,* 367–378.

Taube, C. Personal communication, March, 1982.

Wagenfeld, M.O. Psychopathology in rural areas: Issues and evidence. In P.A. Keller & J.D. Murray (Eds.), *Handbook of rural community mental health.* New York: Human Sciences Press, 1982, pp. 30–44.

Windley, P.G. The effects of ecological/architectural dimensions of small rural towns on the well-being of older people. In P. Kim & C. Wilson (Eds.), *Toward mental health of the rural elderly.* Washington, D.C.: University Press of America, 1981, pp. 81–96.

Windley, P.G. Community services in small rural towns: Patterns of use by older residents. *The Gerontologist,* 1983, *23,* 180–184.

Windley, P.G., & Scheidt, R.J. The well-being of older persons in small rural towns: A town panel approach. *Educational Gerontology,* 1980, *5,* 355–373.

Windley, P.G., & Scheidt, R.J. An ecological model of mental health among small-town rural elderly. *Journal of Gerontology,* 1982, *37,* 235–242.

6

Rural Housing: Perspectives for the Aged

Robert A. Bylund

While considerable attention has been directed toward many aspects of the housing of elders—such as micro-environments (Pastalan & Carson, 1970), intermediate housing (Bronson, 1972), retirement villages (Bultena & Wood, 1969), and nursing homes (Gubrium, 1975)—relatively little investigation has pursued the majority of elderly who live independently in their own households.[1] This lack of attention is particularly acute with regard to the *rural* elderly. Although the rural and small-town elderly comprise almost one-third of all persons over age 65, and head about one out of every five households in their communities, their housing situation has gone largely unnoticed by researchers.

It is the goal of this chapter to examine what is known about the housing of the rural elderly and to suggest areas requiring further attention. Specifically the following topics will be addressed: (1) the importance of housing to the elderly; (2) elderly–nonelderly and rural–urban differences in housing characteristics; and (3) suggestions for future research.

The Importance of Housing to the Elderly

To understand why housing is so important to older people, it is first necessary to consider what housing is and what functions it serves. At the most basic level housing can be defined as a physical structure, designed to provide shelter and accommodation for one

---

[1]About 85–90 percent of all elderly live independently in their own homes. About 5 percent are institutionalized, with the remaining 5–10 percent living with relatives other than the spouse.

or more occupants. To define housing simply in physical terms, however, would understate its importance. Carp (1966) defined housing to include the entire physical and social context. A more complete understanding of the implications of such a definition can be gained by considering the kinds of functions housing fulfills.

Smith (1970) has suggested that housing provides the individual with shelter, privacy, location, environmental amenities, and investment capacity for homeowners. In addition, Grant (1976) emphasized the importance of the location of the dwelling when access to services is considered. He argued that for housing to be "successful," it must exist within a matrix of services and opportunities—such as transportation, shopping, recreation, and medical and social services. Furthermore, he asserted that the value of the matrix may well exceed the economic value of the dwelling itself. Location within a service area becomes increasingly important for the elderly due to their often decreased physical mobility (Regnier, 1975).

Another view of the importance of housing and the functions it serves is suggested by Newmark and Thompson (1977), who portray housing as related to the "hierarchy of needs" advanced by Maslow (1970).[2] These authors maintained that housing plays a role in contributing to the fulfillment of needs at each of the levels of the hierarchy. Thus, for example, at the most basic level, physiological needs are met in part by the provision of shelter. Similarly, at the top of the hierarchy, ego needs can be served through the decor and style of the dwelling.

Housing is an integral part of everyone's life. For the elderly in particular, though, housing may assume increased importance. Montgomery (1972) stated that:

> The quality of the housing environment becomes increasingly significant in the lives of many aged families and individuals, and the quality of this limited world largely determines the extent to which they will retain their independence; the amount of privacy, auditory and visual, they will experience; how often they will visit friends; their sense of place; and their ability to exercise a measure of control over the immediate environment. Housing is a major variable physically, socially, and psychologically in the lives of older persons. (p. 38)

Emphasizing the special importance of housing to the elderly in terms of their ability to remain independent, Huttman (1977) asserted that "a major concern of . . . the elderly is housing; a ma-

---

[2]Maslow's hierarchy of needs includes physiological, security and safety, social, and self-esteem or ego needs.

jor fear is not to be able to any longer stay in one's own home or to continue an independent lifestyle. Above all it is a concern about keeping out of nursing homes" (p. vii).

The salience of the preceding statements increases when it is realized that the elderly spend an estimated 85 to 90 percent of their domestic lives within their homes (Hansen, 1971). In reality, the elderly spend more time in their homes than any other age group (Carp, 1976).

As noted earlier, despite the particular importance of housing to the elderly, there is a conspicuous lack of data on this subject. Carp (1976) noted that while most elderly individuals live in ordinary housing structures within their communities, relatively little is known about these settings, how well the structures accommodate the aged, or what the housing needs of the elderly might be. Along the same lines, Struyk (1976) noted that existing data are insufficient to answer the seemingly simple question of how well aged Americans are housed.

In spite of the paucity of data on the housing of the elderly in general, and on rural–urban differences in particular, there is a growing body of information becoming available which begins to answer many important questions and raises certain others.

Rural Housing Characteristics

An adequate understanding of the housing situation of elderly rural Americans requires an appreciation of their status on several basic housing characteristics. The first of these characteristics to be examined is housing tenure (owner-renter). Table 6.1 provides data on the housing tenure of elderly households by residence.

From these data it is apparent that the nonmetropolitan elderly are more likely to own their homes than their metropolitan counterparts. More important, perhaps, is the fact that it is the most rural sections of nonmetropolitan areas which account for the highest proportions of owned homes (see Chapter 2 for a detailed definition of metropolitan/nonmetropolitan and rural/urban). Specifically, in 1975 almost 83 percent of the housing units headed by the rural nonmetropolitan elderly were owned. This is a significantly higher proportion than in metropolitan areas, where 65 percent of the housing units were owner-occupied. The comparable figure for nonelderly households in the general population for the same year was 63 percent.

Table 6.1. Elderly Households by Metropolitan and Nonmetropolitan
Residence and Tenure

	Own		Rent	
Residence	Numbers in thousands	Percent	Numbers in thousands	Percent
Total U.S. population	10,082	70.1	4,031	29.9
Metropolitan	5,903	65.0	3,178	35.0
Nonmetropolitan	4,178	78.8	1,124	21.2
Urban	1,604	72.8	599	27.2
Rural	2,568	82.9	530	17.1

Source: Adapted from Bylund, R. A., Crawford, C. O., & LeRay, N. L. *Older American Households and Their Housing 1975: A Metro–Nonmetro Comparison.* University Park: Department of Agricultural Economics and Rural Sociology, The Pennsylvania State University, Report No. 146, 1980.

As a consequence of this greater homeownership, a higher proportion of the elderly in rural areas, compared to the metropolitan elderly, can be expected to encounter problems related to maintenance and upkeep of their dwellings as well as rising property taxes. The issue of maintenance is important because half of the housing units occupied by the elderly in rural America were built prior to 1940, compared to about 25 percent of the dwellings occupied by the nonelderly, thus increasing the likelihood of their need for repair (Bylund et al., 1980). On a more positive note, about 91 percent of rural elderly homeowners are free of mortgage payments, compared with 83 percent of elderly metropolitan homeowners, which may well contribute to their economic security (Bylund et al., 1980).

A second housing characteristic of importance is the type of dwelling occupied by the rural elderly. Table 6.2 illustrates some substantial differences between the nonmetropolitan rural and the metropolitan elderly.

The nonmetropolitan elderly in general, and the rural elderly in particular, are much more likely to live in single, detached units than are the metropolitan elderly (85.6% to 54.3%). In fact, if mobile homes are included in the tally of detached units, 93.8 percent of the rural elderly in 1975 lived in single detached units, while only 57.4 percent of their metropolitan counterparts did.

These substantial differences reinforce the point that the rural elderly are more likely to be faced with maintenance and upkeep costs than the urban elderly. Furthermore, these data suggest that

Table 6.2. Elderly Households by Metropolitan and Nonmetropolitan Residence, Tenure, and Type of Dwelling Unit

Type of dwelling	Total	%	Metropolitan Total	%	Nonmetropolitan Total	%	Urban %	Rural %
	Number (thousands)							
All households								
Mobile home	565	3.9	3.1		5.3		1.2	8.2
1 detached unit	9,207	64.0	54.3		80.7		73.8	85.6
1 attached unit	531	3.7	4.6		2.1		3.2	1.2
2–4 living units	1,879	13.0	16.0		8.0		13.8	4.0
5+ living units	2,200	15.3	22.0		3.9		8.0	1.0
Total: Percent	—	100.0	100.0		100.0		100.0	100.0
Total: Number	14,382	—	9,083		5,300		2,203	3,098
Owner								
Mobile home	519	5.1	4.6		6.0		1.5	8.8
1 detached unit	8,230	81.6	76.2		89.3		90.4	88.5
1 attached unit	343	3.4	5.2		0.8		1.3	0.6
2–4 living units	752	7.5	10.2		3.6		6.2	2.0
5+ living units	241	2.4	3.9		0.3		0.6	0.1
Total: Percent	—	100.0	100.0		100.0		100.0	100.0
Total: Number	10,085	—	5,912		4,174		1,65	2,569

133

Table 6.2. (cont.)

Type of dwelling	Total Number (thousands)	Total %	Metropolitan Total %	Nonmetropolitan Total %	Nonmetropolitan Urban %	Nonmetropolitan Rural %
Renter						
Mobile home	45	1.1	0.4	2.8	0.5	5.4
1 detached unit	981	22.8	13.5	49.1	29.1	71.6
1 attached unit	187	4.4	3.6	6.6	8.5	4.5
2–4 living units	1,123	26.1	26.7	24.4	34.2	13.4
5+ living units	1,962	45.6	55.8	17.1	27.7	5.1
Total: Percent	—	100.0	100.0	100.0	100.0	100.0
Total: Number	4,298	—	3,172	1,127	598	529

Source: Adapted from Bylund, R. A., Crawford, C. O., & LeRay, N. L. Older American Households and Their Housing 1975: A Metro–Nonmetro Comparison. University Park: Department of Agricultural Economics and Rural Sociology, The Pennsylvania State University, Report No. 146, 1980.

effective community housing programs must begin to reflect these substantial differences between rural and urban communities. Thus, the housing services most likely to be required in rural areas are those such as handyman services, weatherization, and low-cost home improvement loans, whereas in urban areas there is more need for services such as rent subsidies and renter organizations to push for needed repairs, rent control, protection against condominium conversion, and other issues relevant to renters.

A final interpretation consistent with the above data is that the lack of desirable alternatives in rural communities contributes to the large proportion of rural elderly who live in detached dwellings. Indeed, the higher proportion of rural elderly living in mobile homes (8% or about twice the proportion in metropolitan areas) can be construed as indicating that when options are available they are exercised. That is, since zoning laws tend to be less restrictive in rural areas, mobile homes become a more viable option than they are in more urbanized areas.

The Quality of Rural Housing

Before an informed assessment of housing quality can be attempted, it is necessary to consider what is meant by the concept. The term implies the presence or absence of certain characteristics by which a dwelling can be evaluated or judged as to its adequacy. The determination of exactly which characteristics are to be included in assessing housing quality is, however, problematic because there are no absolute standards by which essential attributes can be delineated. For example, should equal emphasis be placed on the physical features of a dwelling and the location of the dwelling in terms of proximity to services? What attributes are most essential in assisting the elderly to live independently in their homes? Does proximity to services lose some of its importance when adequate transportation is available? How important is proximity to family and friends? It becomes apparent that a broad conceptualization of housing quality presents numerous difficulties in specifying the essential components of housing and their interrelationships.

An additional problem is deciding from whose point of view quality should be evaluated. Hamovitch and Peterson (1969) found that interviewers' ratings of dwellings did not always coincide with occupants' evaluations. What may be physical shabbiness in the view of the outsider may be quite otherwise to the occupant. Whose view is appropriate? Whose view is most accurate? Although arguments have been made for both, there is a strong tendency in the literature to accept the outside observers' objective evaluations of attributes of the dwelling.[3]

Even when the parameters of housing quality are limited to objective housing characteristics (e.g., plumbing, heating, sewer) reported by the respondent, it does not resolve all of the problems. For example, a reasonably common procedure for measuring housing quality involves the utilization of single-item indicators. The most frequently used are the presence of indoor plumbing, crowding (number of persons per room), and age of structure (Beyer, 1965; Bird, Beverly, & Simmons, 1968; Kampe, 1975; Mikesell, 1977). While such items do allow for a direct interpretation and do provide important information about the dwelling, they tend to provide a very narrow view of housing quality. One consequence of this is a likely underestimate of the number of substandard units, because dwellings with other deficiencies are missed (Sumka, 1977). Goedert and Goodman (1977) argued that "no single housing feature is a reliable indicator of the presence or absence of a wide range of housing quality indicators" (p. 26).

The discussion that follows concentrates on studies that have used multiple indicators of quality. Research on the quality of housing for individuals of all ages indicates that rural and nonmetropolitan housing is generally of lower quality than urban and metropolitan housing (Bird & Kampe, 1977; Steward & Meyers, 1972; Weicher, 1980). The data also indicate that substantial improvements have taken place over the past few decades in both metropolitan and nonmetropolitan areas. It is important to note, however, that while the overall quality of housing has been improving, the elderly have occupied a growing proportion of substandard homes. According to Bird and Kampe (1977),[4] the numbers of substandard housing units occupied by the nonmetropolitan elderly decreased from 1,653,000 units in 1950 to 673,000 units in 1975. However, this reflects a general improvement in rural housing which is proceeding more rapidly among younger than older persons. In 1950, 18.2 percent of all substandard housing units

[3]While Dillman, Tremblay, and Dillman (1979) have noted the importance of housing norms in evaluating housing quality, the implications in relation to "objective" measures and housing policy are not clear.
[4]Substandard housing was defined as units which were (1) delapidated or (2) lacked one or more of the following facilities: hot running water, flush toilet for private use, bathtub or shower for private use.

were occupied by the elderly; this figure had increased to 35.0 percent by 1975 (Bird & Kampe, 1977), even though only 23 percent of all nonmetropolitan households were headed by elderly persons. This increase is due in part to the growing number of older persons who live alone, in both rural and urban areas (Bird & Kampe, 1977; Kobrin, 1976), but it nonetheless indicates that the rural elderly are disproportionately afflicted by low-quality housing.

Three relatively recent studies, all using national data sets, indicate that the housing quality of the rural elderly is not as high as that found in metropolitan areas (Atchley & Miller, 1975; Bylund, 1979; Struyk, 1976). The fact that each of these studies used multiple "objective"[5] indicators (but different procedures) provides a certain degreee of convergent validity to the findings.

Furthermore, Bylund (1979) found that, in addition to dichotomous rural and metropolitan differences in housing quality, size of place of residence on a six-point continuum was directly related to housing quality. This relationship is shown in Table 6.3. On both the Facility Index (e.g., heating, plumbing, and kitchen facilities) and the Condition Index (e.g., peeling paint, cracked plaster, and leaks) the proportion of households with zero deficiencies is substantially greater in larger areas. On the Facility Index the percent of dwellings with no deficiencies was 68.1 percent in rural areas, compared with 87.6 percent in metropolitan areas. Comparable figures for the Condition Index indicate an even greater disparity (28.6% to 65.7%). Indeed, even within rural areas substantial farm–nonfarm differences are apparent, a finding also reported by Struyk (1976).

Accounting for Rural–Urban Differences in Housing Quality

There is ample evidence that the housing quality of the rural and nonmetropolitan elderly is significantly lower than that of their metropolitan counterparts; however, it is less clear what accounts for these differences. Certainly part of the relationship between

---

[5]The multiple indicators included housing quality items such as plumbing, heating, kitchen facilities, cracks in walls, leaks in roof, etc. Bylund (1979) constructed indicators using standard scaling techniques. Struyk (1976) utilized "key indicators" based on a scheme relating deficiencies to household incomes. Atchley and Miller (1978) used a summation process in which the deficiencies were added together for each household.

Table 6.3. Percent Distribution of Elderly Households in the United States by Facility and Condition Index and Size of Place of Residence

Quality index	Residence					
Facility	<2,500 Farm	<2,500 Nonfarm	2,500– 4,999	5,000– 19,999	20,000– 50,000	>50,000 SMSA
0	68.1	72.6	83.4	85.2	88.7	87.6
1	13.8	14.0	11.4	8.6	7.4	8.4
2	18.1	13.4	5.2	6.1	4.0	4.0
Total %	100.0	100.0	100.0	100.0	100.0	100.0
n^a	904	2,194	573	1,045	583	9,069
Condition						
0	28.6	46.1	53.1	49.5	58.3	65.7
1	41.1	33.1	33.8	38.3	29.8	25.0
2	18.9	11.9	9.8	7.3	8.9	5.6
3	11.4	8.9	3.3	4.9	3.0	3.6
Total %	100.0	100.0	100.0	100.0	100.0	100.0
n^a	904	2,194	573	1,045	583	9,069

[a]Numbers in thousands.

Source: Adapted from Bylund, R. A., Crawford, C. O., & LeRay, N. L. *Older American Households and Their Housing 1975: A Metro–Nonmetro Comparison.* University Park: Department of Agricultural Economics and Rural Sociology, The Pennsylvania State University, Report No. 146, 1980.

place of residence and housing quality can be accounted for by income and education differentials. Elderly individuals living in rural and nonmetropolitan areas typically have lower income and lower educational levels than their urban metropolitan counterparts (Atchley & Miller, 1975; Kampe, 1975; Lee & Lassey, 1980). Yet even when these variables are controlled, the residence differences in housing quality remain largely intact (Bylund, 1981). There are a number of other factors which could still produce these differences. For example, the comparative lack of housing programs for the elderly in rural areas (Lawton, Hoover, & Kostelc, 1978; Taietz & Milton, 1979; White House Conference on Aging, 1973) may be reflected in the quality of housing. In addition, several researchers have charged that the administrative structure of many of the available housing programs (e.g., requirements or bureaucratic red tape) often precludes their use by both rural and urban older Americans (McFarland & Thompson, 1975; Montgomery, Stubbs, & Day, 1980).

The low visibility of existing substandard units in rural environments can further compound the problem. McFarland and Thompson (1975) stated that substandard rural housing is often "literally out of sight to everyone except those who suffer from it. In the city, suburb, in town, civic and charitable organizations, churches, minority groups, and community and neighborhood groups, press for solutions to housing problems and contribute to their solutions with time, ideas, and money. No such organized concern has been mobilized in rural areas" (pp. 145–146).

Another possible factor influencing the quality of housing in rural areas is the attitudes held by many elderly toward seeking or accepting governmental assistance. Montgomery et al. (1980) reported in their study of rural households that even elderly persons living in substandard dwellings neither sought nor wished to secure any governmental assistance to improve their homes. Several studies (Glenn & Hill, 1977; Willits, Beales, & Crider, 1974) have found rural residents to be more traditional or conservative than urban dwellers in terms of their willingness to accept governmental assistance. If the rural elderly are more reluctant to seek or receive assistance than their more urbanized counterparts, it should ultimately be reflected in a higher incidence of low-quality housing in rural areas (Osgood, 1977).

The implications of health for the housing quality of the rural elderly must also be considered. Larson and Youmans (1978) proposed that some elderly may not be able to perform improvement tasks in their homes due to health problems, or afford to have others do them due to income constraints. Among the elderly, health status is positively related to size of place of residence (McCoy & Brown, 1978). Thus poor health may combine with limited financial resources to prevent many older persons from maintaining the quality of their homes.

In summary, research has shown rural residents to be markedly disadvantaged, in comparison to their urban counterparts, in terms of income, education, health, and service availability, and to be less interested in or willing to accept governmental assistance in maintaining or improving their homes. These factors, singly and in combination, account for a major portion of the substantial rural deficit in the quality of housing for the elderly.

Neighborhood Characteristics and Housing Quality

To this point, the evaluation of housing quality has centered around characteristics of the dwelling itself. However, some research has expanded the definition of housing quality to include neighborhood characteristics such as crime, noise, and litter (Struyk, 1976). When this broader definition is used, there is evidence that the rural elderly are somewhat better off than the urban. Struyk (1976) commented that:

> It is only in the area of neighborhood conditions—street noise, crime, trash and litter, etc.—that the rural elderly are better off on the average than their urban counterparts. These "neighborhood factors" are particularly problematic because of the speed at which neighborhood downgrading can occur. One effect can be to leave elderly homeowners effectively trapped in their dwellings as falling property values destroy a major portion of their equity. This contrasts sharply with the relatively stable market conditions encountered by the rural elderly. (p. 12)

However, with respect to other neighborhood characteristics such as access to medical facilities and care, transportation and shopping availability, the housing of the rural elderly is likely to once again be judged deficient.

Subjective Evaluations

In spite of the fact that there is a significant number of rural elderly living in housing that is judged to be deficient, those living in such situations are for the most part uncomplaining. The majority report that they are satisfied with their current living arrangements and very few express any desire to move, even though their dwellings may have been judged to have several serious deficiencies (Montgomery et al., 1980). Furthermore, the evidence indicates that few anticipate making home improvements even when deficiencies are present (Lawton, 1978).

The explanation of this seeming lack of housing aspiration is not obvious or simple. Montgomery et al. (1980) suggested that either cohort or aging effects may account for this phenomenon. They noted that early in this century, when today's elderly were growing up, the federal government was involved in very few efforts to assist the poor and was not expected to do so. Thus, those growing up at this time were socialized to "take care of themselves" and to "stay in their own place," the result being a continuing reluctance to accept governmental assistance. In contrast, they also suggested that aspirations may decrease with age. They concluded that the difficulty in separating the two effects (with their data) precluded a definitive answer, and therefore, both explanations remain as possibilities.

It also seems likely that income is a significant factor, although it still is not clear at what point income becomes sufficient to ensure adequate housing. The U.S. Department of Housing and Urban Development has estimated that 42 percent of the elderly would have to spend an excessive amount of their income to obtain unflawed housing in the housing market (U.S. Department of Housing and Urban Development, 1979). In addition, it is not clear what priority housing has to the elderly themselves. That is, in view of the limited resources of many elderly, perhaps housing cannot take priority over other needs and requirements.[6]

A final consideration in understanding the paradox between objective measures of the quality of housing of the elderly and their own judgment may involve the definitions of housing quality mentioned previously. That is, rather than focusing on indicators

[6]The percentage of elderly below the poverty level ranges from 9.0 percent for elderly families to 31 percent for unrelated individuals (U.S. Bureau of the Census, 1977).

such as plumbing, heating, or leaking roofs, the elderly may emphasize the more positive aspects of the rural living environment. For example, the rural elderly may give a greater weight to the fact that rural communities have less violent crime (and therefore they feel "safer") than they do to the fact that there are cracks in their walls. This possibility suggests a need to reevaluate the appropriateness of most current definitions of housing quality and to begin to examine the policy implications of alternative definitions.

It seems reasonable to conclude that by most "objective" standards of quality, the rural elderly are at a disadvantage when compared to their counterparts in metropolitan areas and to the non-elderly population. There are still, however, a number of important questions regarding subjective perceptions and definitions of housing quality which remain unanswered. Further research is needed if these issues are to be adequately explained.

Housing Services and Programs

The desire of the elderly to retain their independence and remain in their own homes is well documented. Their ability to do so, however, is influenced by a number of variables such as health, income, and the ability to maintain their dwelling. When independent living is threatened, community housing services can be a major factor in avoiding institutionalization. While the distinction between housing services and other social services is not necessarily clear-cut, this discussion will be limited to those services directly related to housing. It is useful for discussion purposes to categorize housing services into two types: physical services and income-supporting services.

Physical Services

These include building and construction programs for new housing units or the rehabilitation of existing units. The U.S. Department of Housing and Urban Development's (HUD) major housing programs for the elderly (Public Housing, Section 8, Section 202, and Section 236) have several major deficiencies for rural residents. Relatively little of the money from these programs ever finds its way to rural areas (Parente, 1973). Furthermore, all of the programs cited apply only to renters, not to homeowners, and thus the majority of the rural elderly are ineligible. Those HUD programs that are for homeowners (such as Section 115 and Section 312) are comparatively small programs, and program eligibility requirements render them largely unavailable or irrelevant to the rural elderly. Awards for Section 115 Rehabilitation Grants, for example, have been based on categorical entitlement criteria (i.e., urban renewal and code enforcement areas) which are not applicable in rural areas (Lawton, 1978).

A review of the major Farmers Home Administration (FmHA) housing programs (Section 502 and Section 504) that are pertinent to the rural elderly also reveals some major flaws. For example, in 1976, 8 percent of the funds from FmHA (representing some 9,000 units) were used to upgrade or create new housing for the rural elderly (Special Committee on Aging, 1977). The inadequacy of this investment is apparent when the fact that elderly comprise some 20 percent of all households in rural areas is coupled with the estimates of low housing quality discussed earlier. In addition, there is reason to doubt whether those elderly most in need will go through the necessary bureaucratic procedures and commit themselves to long-term monthly repayments.

There is also a variety of support services funded through federal, state, and local sources which are potentially important for the retention of independent living. Included among these are small repair, maintenance, handyman, and weatherization programs. These services may well keep small problems from becoming major ones. The availability of these programs, however, is far from universal, and evidence indicates that they are scattered, with rural communities providing fewer than urban areas (Lawton, 1978).

To summarize, a number of factors have been noted which contribute to the substantial gap between existing federal housing programs and the needs of older people in rural areas. First, many rural areas are not eligible for certain federal programs. Second, the programs for which they are eligible are often aimed at loans for the construction of multi-unit rental structures, although the majority of rural residents are homeowners. Third, the nature of many federal programs, in terms of eligibility requirements, loan approval procedures, and repayment stipulations, appears to largely bypass those most in need. Fourth, the homeowner programs available are clearly underfunded. Finally, the attitudes of the rural elderly themselves toward governmental housing assistance may also contribute to the lack of congruence between programs and needs (Atchley & Miller, 1975; Montgomery et al., 1980). Montgomery et al. (1980) summed up the situation as follows: "By and large, federal housing programs as now conceived and administered appear irrelevant to the rural elderly . . ." (p. 451).

The implications of the preceding discussion are several. It appears that increased resources must be directed toward rural elderly homeowners, who have thus far largely been bypassed. Increased efforts must be made to improve service delivery mechanisms and to improve the availability of and access to services. Furthermore, research must further illuminate the subjective meaning of housing quality to the rural elderly themselves. Without a better appreciation of the subjective meaning, it will not be possible for service providers to adequately formulate functional assistance programs (through formal or informal channels) for the rural elderly.

Income-supporting Services

This is the second category of housing services. The primary programs in this category are housing allowances, reverse annuity mortgages, and tax relief. The housing allowance programs apply primarily to renters in multi-unit structures in the form of rent subsidies. This is of little use to most rural elderly since few of them live in such structures.

Both of the remaining services are geared toward homeowners. Tax relief, in the form of tax breaks for elderly homeowners, is available in many (but by no means all) states and localities. The impact this has on housing is probably quite small, however, as homeowners are not likely to apply tax savings directly to their housing. Reverse annuity mortgages allow homeowners to use directly the equity they have in their homes. The availability of such programs is dependent, however, on local lending institutions and they are not presently available in many rural areas. In addition, many elderly feel that their homes are a resource which should be left for their children and, thus, may be hesitant to participate in such a program. Finally, while the money gained may well help those involved (a relatively small number) to retain their independence, the direct effect on housing quality is unknown. That is, the question remains as to whether income from reverse annuity mortgages would be utilized to upgrade housing.

In conclusion, income-support services are most likely to affect housing quality for renters. For homeowners the effect is more indirect since these programs act to increase disposable income, which may or may not be used to offset housing costs.

Housing Options

It is useful to approach the topic of housing options by considering how housing decisons are made. Lawton (1981) asserted that the major factors affecting the housing decisions are support requirements, enablement, and preference. Support requirements refers to the degree of assistance the individual needs to carry out the activities of daily living. Enablement refers to the combination of personal and physical factors which "enable" the individual to live in a particular housing environment desired by the individual. The housing options within a community should provide some variation in these factors.

In terms of required support, major housing options range from totally independent living to institutionalization. They include independent residences, planned community housing, boarding homes, domiciliary care, personal care, and nursing homes. It should be noted that there is a great deal of overlap between these categories in terms of the range of support provided. Thus, for any given individual, one of several options might provide the support needed. This is an important consideration when the availability of these options is considered. While figures on the distribution of these housing options are not generally available, it is likely that they follow the pattern of other social services: the full range of options is likely to be less available in rural areas. Given the overlap among these options, however, it is likely that most individuals could find a place which will meet their support requirements among the types described above (Lawton, 1981). Thus, while there may still be a need for improvement in quality of care and for an increased number of options, the range of care available is probably adequate.

The more limiting factors in housing options tend to be in the areas of enablement and preference. That is, are the rural elderly able to find and maintain the kind of housing they prefer? It is clear that the majority of rural elderly wish to and do live in their own homes. Given this priority, increased attention to services which would allow them to remain there seems to be in order.

Other, less traditional housing options for the independent elderly include shared housing, granny flats, cooperatives, and mobile homes. It is safe to say that of these options, mobile homes are the most frequently found option in rural areas, where zoning laws and regulations tend to be less restrictive. Little is known at this point about those elderly living in these dwellings, but there is evidence that the number of elderly living in mobile homes is increasing substantially (Raush & Hoover, 1980). Questions such as who they are, why they chose this option, and how satisfied they are thus deserve increased attention. The remaining options mentioned tend to exist only on an experimental basis in urban centers and are not likely to have sponsors or initiators in most rural areas.

It would seem that the independent rural elderly who do not wish to maintain their own homes have relatively few options. Indeed, it is possible that part of the reason for such high ownership rates in rural areas is that few other options are open to the elderly. Apartments are generally not readily available, and many rural areas are poorly equipped organizationally to secure government loans for such projects. Further resources should go toward maintaining those who wish to remain in their homes (a majority), increasing the rental unit availability (for a substantial minority), and making other, less utilized options available to create a real measure of choice.

Research Needs

There remain many issues on which further research on housing for the rural elderly could produce fruitful results. An area of primary concern, which has not received adequate attention, is how the rural elderly themselves view their housing. That is, how do elders' perceptions of their housing correspond to the more "objective" indicators of quality usually used? How should the perceptions of the elderly affect policy decisions? If their evaluations are that their housing is adequate, should intervention take place if the dwelling is deficient in terms of socially accepted definitions of adequacy? Indeed, is effective intervention possible without an admission or perception of need?

In the area of housing services it is clear that an important research issue revolves around underutilized and often ineffective governmental programs. This will require a closer examination of both the attitudes of the rural elderly and the delivery mechanisms of present housing services. It may well be that alternative delivery modes such as using established rural organizations would be more effective.

Finally, further work is needed to explore the demand for and the receptiveness to the provision of additional housing options.

While the majority wish to remain in their homes, some may do so because they perceive few other desirable, available, or affordable options. Many important issues pertaining to the housing situation of elderly rural Americans remain unresolved. If effective and informed housing policies for the elderly in rural areas are to be developed, it is essential to obtain information concerning these issues. Without greater information, it will be difficult to meet the goal stated in the Housing Act of 1947—and reaffirmed many times since—of providing a "decent home and suitable environment" for every American.

References

Atchley, R. C., & Miller, S. J. Housing and the rural aged. In R. C. Atchley & T. O. Byerts (Eds.), *Rural environments in aging.* Washington, D.C.: Gerontological Society, 1978, pp. 95–143.

Beyer, G. H. *Housing and society.* New York: Macmillan, 1965.

Bird, R., Beverly, L., & Simmons, A. *Status of rural housing in the U.S.* Washington, D.C.: U.S. Department of Agriculture, Economic Research Service, Report No. 144, 1968.

Bird, R., & Kampe, R. *25 years of housing progress in rural America.* Washington, D.C.: U.S. Department of Agriculture, Economic Research Service, Report No. 373, 1977.

Bronson, E. P. An experiment in intermediate housing facilities for the elderly. *The Gerontologist,* 1972, *12,* 22–26.

Bultena, G. L., & Wood, V. The American retirement community: Bane or blessing. *Journal of Gerontology,* 1969, *22,* 209–217.

Bylund, R. A. *Housing quality of the rural elderly.* Unpublished Ph.D. dissertation. The Pennsylvania State University, 1979.

Bylund, R. A. *Housing quality of the elderly: The importance of size of place of residence.* Paper presented at the Annual Meetings of the Rural Sociological Society, Guelph, Ontario, Canada, 1981.

Bylund, R. A., Crawford, C. O., & LeRay, N. L. *Older American households and their housing 1975: A metro–nonmetro comparison.* University Park: Deparment of Agricultural Economics and Rural Sociology, The Pennsylvania State University, Report No. 146, 1980.

Carp, F. M. (Ed.). *Patterns of living and housing of middle-aged and older adults.* Washington, D.C.: U.S. Government Printing Office, 1966.

Carp, F. M. Housing and living environments of older people. In R. H. Binstock & E. Shanas (Eds.), *Handbook of aging and the social sciences.* New York: Van Nostrand Reinhold, 1976, pp. 244–271.

Dillman, D. A., Tremblay, K. R., & Dillman, J. Influence of housing norms and personal characteristics on stated housing preferences. *Housing and Society,* 1979, *6,* 2–19.

Glenn, N. D., & Hill, L., Jr. Rural–urban differences in attitudes and behavior in the United States. *The Annals of the American Academy of Political and Social Science,* 1977, *429,* 36–50.

Goedert, J. E., & Goodman, J. L., Jr. *Indicators of the quality of U.S. housing.* Washington, D.C.: The Urban Institute, 1977.

Grant, D. P. Creating living environments for older adults within existing contexts. In W. Donahue (Eds.), *Proceedings of the international symposium for housing and environmental design for older adults.* Washington, D.C.: International Center for Social Gerontology, 1976, pp. 37–45.

Gubrium, J. F. *Living and dying at Murray Manor.* New York: St. Martin's Press, 1975.

Hamovitch, M. B., & Peterson, J. E. Housing needs and satisfactions of the elderly. *The Gerontologist,* 1969, *9,* 30–32.

Hansen, G. D. Meeting housing challenges: Involvement—The elderly. In American Association of Housing Educators, *Proceedings of the fifth annual meeting.* Lincoln, Neb.: 1971.

Huttman, E. *Housing and social services for the elderly.* New York: Praeger, 1977.

Kampe, R. E. *Household income—How it related to substandard housing in rural and Farmers' Home Administration areas by state and race, 1970.* Washington, D.C.: U.S. Department of Agriculture, Economic Research Service, Report No. 287, 1975.

Kobrin, F. E. The primary individual and the family: Changes in living arrangements in the United States since 1940. *Journal of Marriage and the Family,* 1976, *38,* 233–239.

Larson, D. K., & Youmans, E. G. *Problems of rural elderly households in Powell County, Kentucky.* Washington, D.C.: U.S. Department of Agriculture, Economic Research Service, Report No. 655, 1978.

Lawton, M. P. The housing problems of community-resident elderly. In R. P. Boynton (Ed.), *Occasional papers in housing and community affairs* (Vol. 1). Washington, D.C.: U.S. Department of Housing and Urban Affairs, 1978, pp. 39–74.

Lawton, M. P. Alternative housing. *Journal of Gerontological Social Work,* 1981, *3,* 61–81.

Lawton, M. P., Hoover, S., & Kostelc, J. *Community housing choices for older Americans: An early summary of program and policy suggestions.* Philadelphia: Philadelphia Geriatric Center, 1978.

Lee, G. R., & Lassey, M. L. Rural–urban differences among the elderly: Economic, social, and subjective factors. *Journal of Social Issues,* 1980, *36,* 62–74.

Maslow, A. H. *Motivation and personality* (2nd ed.). New York: Harper and Row, 1970.

McCoy, J. L. & Brown, D. L. Health status among low-income elderly persons: Rural–urban differences. *Social Security Bulletin,* 1978, *41,* 6.

McFarland, C., & Thompson, M. M. *Current and future housing needs of elderly Pennsylvanians.* Washington, D.C.: International Center for Social Gerontology, 1975.

Mikesell, J. J. *Population change and metro–nonmetro housing quality.* Washington, D.C.: U.S. Department of Agriculture, Economic Research Service, Report No. 388, 1977.

Montgomery, J. E. The housing patterns of older families. *The Family Coordinator,* 1972, *21,* 37–46.

Montgomery, J. E., Stubbs, A. C., & Day, S. The housing environment of the rural elderly. *The Gerontologist,* 1980, *20,* 444–451.

Newmark, N. L., & Thompson, P. J. *Self, space and shelter: An introduction to housing.* San Francisco: Canfield Press, 1977.

Osgood, M. H. Rural and urban attitudes towards welfare. *Social Work,* 1977, *22,* 41–47.

Parente, J. R. The provision of housing for the rural elderly under major federal housing programs. In *Report of the U.S. Senate Subcommittee on Rural Development.* Washington: U.S. Government Printing Office, 1973, pp. 8–10.

Pastalan, L. A., & Carson, D. H. (Eds.). *Spatial behavior of older people.* Ann Arbor: University of Michigan Press, 1970.

Raush, K., & Hoover, S. *Mobile home elderly: Structural characteristics of their dwellings.* Philadelphia: Philadelphia Geriatric Center, 1980.

Regnier, V. Neighborhood planning for the elderly. In D. S. Woodruff & J. E. Birren (Eds.), *Aging: Scientific perspectives and social issues.* New York: Van Nostrand, 1975, pp. 295–312.

Smith, W. F. *Housing: The social and economic elements.* Berkeley: University of California Press, 1970.

Special Committee on Aging. *Development in aging, 1976. Part I.* Washington, D.C.: U.S. Government Printing Office, 1977.

Steward, D. D., & Myers, P. R. *Housing 1970: Differences between SMSA's and non-SMSA'S by region with state data.* Washington, D.C.: U.S. Department of Agriculture, Economic Research Service, Report No., 230, 1972.

Struyk, R. *The housing situation of elderly Americans.* Washington, D.C.: The Urban Institute, 1976.

Sumka, H. J. Measuring the quality of housing: An econometric analysis of tax appraisal records. *Land Economics,* 1977, *53,* 298–309.

Taietz, P., & Milton, S. Rural–urban differences in the structure of services for the elderly in upstate New York counties. *Journal of Gerontology,* 1979, *34,* 429–437.

U.S. Bureau of the Census. Characteristics of the population below the poverty level: 1975. *Current population reports,* Series P-60, Number 106. Washington, D.C.: U.S. Government Printing Office, 1977.

U.S. Department of Housing and Urban Development. *How well are we housed? The elderly.* Washington, D.C.: U.S. Department of Housing and Urban Development, Office of Policy Department and Research, 1979.

Weicher, John C. *Housing: Federal policies and programs.* Washington, D.C.: American Enterprise Institute for Rural Policy Research, 1980.

White House Conference on Aging, 1971. *Toward a national policy on aging: Final report II.* Washington, D.C.: U.S. Government Printing Office, 1973.

Willits, F. K., Bealer, R. C., & Crider, D. M. The ecology of social traditionalism in a rural winterland. *Rural Sociology,* 1974, *39,* 334–347.

7

Family and Kin Relations of the Rural Elderly

Gary R. Lee and Margaret L. Cassidy

Reviewers of similar topics have frequently noted the dearth of empirical studies regarding the family relatons of the rural elderly (Powers, Keith, & Goudy, 1979, 1981; Lee & Cassidy, 1981). We are, in fact, in imminent danger of having more reviews of studies than we have studies on this topic. Nonetheless, the opportunity to review our knowledge in this area may serve several useful purposes. One is to contribute further to the synthesis and organization of existing knowledge, scarce though it may be. Another is to emphasize that there is little conformity between prevalent stereotypes regarding the families of older rural residents and empirical knowledge. Finally, we will identify areas in which more and better research is needed to provide information and illuminate explanatory theory. We will attempt to accomplish these objectives by formulating empirical generalizations where sufficient information is available, and hypotheses where available information is insufficient to permit empirically documented conclusions.

In addition to the shortage of studies and data, we must also attend to a problem created by the prevalent methods of organizing and presenting data in previous studies and available statistical sources. Specifically, many sources distinguish between farm and nonfarm residents as if the distinction reflected or represented rural–urban differences. It does not. Only a small fraction of rural populations reside on farms. The farm–nonfarm distinction treats over 95 percent of the American population (the "nonfarm" segment) as residentially homogeneous. While the farm population may be distinctive in many ways, it does not follow that the environments of all nonfarm residents are alike. Unfortunately, many potential sources of information fail to distinguish between residents of small towns and those of large cities. This constraint seriously hinders our efforts to apprehend the effects of different residential environments upon family relations. It does, however, contribute to our understanding of how farm families differ from other families. The review that follows will demonstrate that we know more about the effects of farm residence upon family patterns than we do about the implications of any other residential context.

For older people, family relations fall into two categories: (1) *marriage,* including phenomena such as divorce, widowhood, and lifelong singlehood, as well as the dynamics of the husband–wife relationship; and (2) *kinship,* under which we have classified relationships with grown children, as well as those with more "distant" kin. Our primary objective is to determine whether the marital and kinship relations of the rural elderly differ from those of their urban counterparts. Where differences do exist, we will attempt to explain them and investigate their implications for both rural sociology and social gerontology.

Marriage

Marital Status

One of the basic demographic differences between rural and urban families is that divorce rates are lower among rural residents (Brown, 1977, 1981; U.S. Bureau of the Census, 1978, 1980; Woodrow, Hastings, & Tu, 1978). Brown (1981) has documented that differences in the divorce rate between rural and urban areas narrowed somewhat between 1950 and 1970, but that differences still remain. Since divorce is more likely to occur in the earlier than the later years of marriage, rural–urban differences in divorce may be particularly pronounced among the current generation of older persons.

There are several possible explanations for this difference. Perhaps the most obvious is that marriages among rural residents are more stable because they are happier. If true, this would conform to popular stereotypes about the idyllic lives of rural families. Previous research, however (Campbell, Converse, & Rodgers, 1976; Mitchell, 1976; Schumm & Bollman, 1981; Targ, 1981), has found that marital satisfaction and/or adjustment does not vary by residential location. Our own data, obtained from a sample of residents of Washington State aged 55 and over, show that this pattern also holds among the elderly (see Table 7.1). It is interesting to note that, in these data, farm men are lower on marital satisfaction than any other category of males, while farm women are higher than any other category of females. These differences, however, do not approach statistical significance and should be regarded as random fluctuations. It appears safe to conclude that residential differences in divorce rates cannot be explained by residential differences in marital satisfaction, for the elderly or for other age categories.

Another possibility is that the normative structure in rural areas is less favorable (or more unfavorable) toward divorce. "Traditional" family values, including the value of marital stability, may be held more strongly by rural residents. We have some evidence that this is indeed the case (Bescher-Donnelly & Smith, 1981; Glenn & Hill, 1977; Larson, 1978; Schumm & Bollman, 1981). Furthermore, it appears that these "traditional" values are espoused. more strongly by older than younger rural persons (Glenn, 1974; Lind, 1976; Schumm & Bollman, 1981). Thus, at any given level of marital conflict or discord, the rural elderly may be less likely to perceive divorce as a viable solution than are other segments of the population.

Additional factors may be operative for those rural families who are engaged in farming. Rosenblatt and Anderson (1981) have argued that the necessity of working together, and the mutual involvement in an economic as well as a domestic enterprise, may create tensions and exacerbate interpersonal conflicts among farm family members. These people appear to adjust their behavior patterns and activity schedule to maximize privacy, however, thus minimizing opportunities for tension and conflict. Powers et al.

Table 7.1. Marital Satisfaction by Residence and Sex

	Males		Females	
Residence	$\overline{X}$	n	$\overline{X}$	n
Farm	21.00	130	20.55	109
Rural nonfarm	21.65	238	20.21	225
Small town	21.39	128	20.38	120
Small city	21.77	243	20.31	198
Large city	21.01	260	20.45	228
Total	21.39	999	20.36	880

Source: A survey of Washington State residents aged 55 and over, conducted by Gary R. Lee and Steven R. Burkett, 1980. Scores were obtained from a six-item marital satisfaction scale on which possible scores ranged from 6 (low) to 30 (high).

(1981) reported that, in a sample of rural and small-town older men, farmers spend less time interacting with their families (including spouses) than did members of any other occupational category. Thus, while farm life may create somewhat unique opportunities for marital discord, farm couples have apparently developed strategies to deal with the problem.

The great economic interdependence of farm couples may also militate against divorce for purely pragmatic reasons. According to the U.S. Bureau of the Census (1980), 3.4 percent of all nonfarm residents in the United States aged 65 and over are divorced; this figure is identical for males and females. Among the elderly farm population, however, only 1.0 percent of the males and 0.9 percent of the females are divorced. It is likely that those farm residents who do divorce either remarry quite rapidly (Woodrow et al., 1978) or move off the farm. Marriage may be a singular advantage for farm residents because farming is still a family enterprise, depending in large measure upon a complementary division of labor between spouses. While the economic interdependence of farm couples probably depresses the divorce rate, those who do experience divorce face severe economic exigencies. If a farm family is broken by divorce, property settlements almost inevitably force at least one spouse to leave; the remaining spouse may have great difficulty in maintaining the operation without remarrying.

The same logic may explain the fact that widows are underrepresented in the farm population. Census data (1980) reveal that, for the nonfarm population aged 65 and over, 14.3 percent of the males and 52.6 percent of the females are widowed. Among elderly farm residents, however, only 11.6 percent of the men and 32.8 percent of the women are widowed. This pattern cannot be explained in terms of differences in the probability of widowhood due to differential life expectancies. Instead, it appears that farm residents whose marriages are terminated, whether by widowhood or divorce, are quite likely to either remarry or leave the farm.

The few existing studies of rural–urban differences in the experience of widowhood (Berardo, 1967; Youmans, 1963) have not found major differences according to residence. Berardo (1967) reported, however, that widowhood seemed to have a greater adverse effect upon the financial status of women in rural than urban areas. Rural widowers, in contrast, were economically better off than were their urban counterparts. There is considerable evidence to the effect that low levels of emotional adjustment among widowed persons are attributable in large part to the decrease in financial resources which often accompanies widowhood (Balkwell, 1981; Chatfield, 1977; Morgan, 1976). We would thus expect rural women to be particularly disadvantaged by widowhood, in comparison to both urban women and rural men.

Studies of widowhood among rural residents suggest, however, that widowhood may be a more difficult experience for men than for women. A study by Pihlblad and associates (Pihlblad & Adams, 1972; Pihlblad, Adams, & Rosencranz, 1972) found that participation in friendship relations and voluntary associations were both substantially reduced by widowhood among small-town men; no comparable differences were observed between married and widowed women. Both types of social participation were positively related to life satisfaction, suggesting that the emotional well-being of rural widowed men is particularly adversely affected by the paucity of their social contacts. This conforms with Berardo's (1967) finding that widowers who lived in small towns were more socially isolated than were either farm or urban widowers.

Powers and Bultena (1976), on a statewide sample of elderly Iowans, observed that men reported having more friends than did women, but women had more intimate friends. Widowhood was associated with an increase in intimate friendship for men, but not for women. Kivett (1979), on the other hand, found that neither sex nor marital status was related to friendship interaction among rural North Carolina residents, but that women and widowed persons were more likely to report feelings of loneliness.

Our own data (see Table 7.2) show that loneliness is increased by widowhood for women and urban men, but not for rural or small-town men. Among widowed men, rural residents are the least lonely and urban residents the most; among women, small-town widows are more lonely than are either rural or urban widows. But the most striking feature of these data is the generally small impact of widowhood upon loneliness, regardless of sex or residence. Why should this be the case?

We believe that part of the answer is contained in the third and fourth columns of Table 7.2, which show the relationship between marital status and friendship interaction by residence. In each residential category, and for both sexes, widowed persons interact more frequently with friends than do married people. It appears that the function of companionship may be taken over, in part, by friendship relations when widowhood occurs. Rural people do not differ substantially from urban in this regard.

Table 7.2. Friendship Interaction and Loneliness by Residence and Sex

	Males			
	Loneliness		Friendship interaction	
Residence	Married	Widowed	Married	Widowed
Rural	21.05	20.73	4.65	4.85
Small town	21.22	21.14	4.64	5.69
Urban	20.81	22.30	4.88	5.78
Total	21.00	21.60	4.74	5.52
n	(585)	(48)	(585)	(48)

	Females			
	Loneliness		Friendship interaction	
Residence	Married	Widowed	Married	Widowed
Rural	20.84	21.26	4.85	5.32
Small town	21.53	22.07	4.72	5.38
Urban	20.70	21.20	4.96	5.38
Total	21.01	21.53	4.86	5.37
n	(425)	(266)	(425)	(266)

Source: A survey of Washington State residents aged 55 and over, conducted by Gary R. Lee and Steven R. Burkett, 1980. Scores were obtained from a 10-item loneliness scale and 2 items measuring frequency of visiting friends in one's own home and friends' homes.

Table 7.2 does contain one interesting anomaly, however. Among widowed men, rural residents obtained the lowest scores on both the loneliness and the friendship interaction measures, while urban men scored highest on both measures. This suggests that friendship relations do not necessarily reduce loneliness, although these two variables are in fact negatively correlated.

These results, along with those of other studies noted above, show generally small differences in the effects of widowhood according to residence. It does not appear reasonable to conclude that widowhood is, in general, a more isolating or demoralizing experience for rural than urban residents. Further research on more broadly based samples is clearly needed, however, since studies done in different areas of the country have produced differing results.

The Marital Relationship

We have already noted that research has found no major differences in marital satisfaction or adjustment according to residential location, and that this generalization appears to apply to the elderly as well as to other age categories. This does not mean, however, that there are no residential differences in the nature of marriage, although most reviewers have concluded that these differences are relatively small (Schumm & Bollman, 1981; Targ, 1981).

One of the most consistent and recurrent themes in the sparse research literature on rural marriage is the apparently greater conservatism or traditionalism of rural couples (Bescher-Donnelly & Smith, 1981; Glenn, 1974; Powers, 1971; Powers et al., 1979). Many studies have found rural people to be more conservative in terms of attitudes and values, including those pertaining to family matters (Bayer, 1975; Fischer, 1975; Glenn & Hill, 1977; Lowe & Peek, 1974). It is also the case that older people tend to be more conservative than do younger people (Cutler & Kaufman, 1975; Foner, 1974; Glenn, 1974). This is not because people's attitudes become more conservative with age, but rather because of cohort differences. Nonetheless, this suggests that older rural couples may be particularly traditional on marriage-related dimensions.

Glenn and Hill (1977) have reported that the endorsement of marriage and parenthood without employment as a preferred lifestyle is more common among rural than urban women. According to Powers et al. (1979), traditional sex-typed divisions of domestic labor are highly characteristic of older rural couples. It is tempting to attach a simple "traditionalism" explanation to these rural–urban differences. Structural features of rural family life, however, may be in a large part responsible for the greater traditionalism of rural couples in terms of both attitudes and behaviors.

Blood and Wolfe (1960), in their now-classic study of marital relations in the Detroit vicinity, found that farm wives were more likely than were urban wives to assume unilateral responsibility for traditionally "feminine" tasks such as cooking and housekeeping. They also found, however, that farm wives were more likely to perform normatively "masculine" tasks such as household repairs and yard work, either entirely or in part, than were urban wives. This suggests a structural, rather than a cultural, explanation. Blood and Wolfe (1960) concluded that rural–urban differences in the division of household labor between spouses

> ... can hardly be attributed to rural conservatism. . . . In many ways, [men's] farm work is like women's work—it's never done. . . . If this interpretation is correct, the farmer's perennial involvement in his work makes him relatively unavailable for household tasks, whereas the city husband's separation from his place of work makes him highly available for part-time "employment" at home. (pp. 58–59)

This interpretation is consistent with the study by Powers et al. (1981), in which farm men were found to spend less time interacting with other household members, including spouses, than were rural men of other occupational categories. This clearly contradicts some popular stereotypes about the family centered lives of farm families (see Coward & Smith, 1982 for a discussion of such myths), but also illustrates the real problems which may arise from too much togetherness (see also Rosenblatt & Anderson, 1981). The difference at issue here, however, is actually an occupational rather than a residential difference, since it distinguishes between farm and nonfarm families and thus does not entirely explain why rural couples in general seem to evidence more marital-role segregation than do urban couples.

Another stereotype about the marital relations of elderly rural couples involves decision-making authority in marriage: older rural couples are often thought to be more "traditional" in the sense that husbands predominate in directing family activities. A number of studies have indeed shown that rural residents are more likely than are urban to endorse relatively partriarchal norms (Bescher-Donnelly & Smith, 1981; Bayer, 1975; Fischer, 1975; Roberts & Kowalski, 1978). Blood and Wolfe (1960), however, found no residential differences in marital decision-making patterns. If there are behavioral differences in the authority structures of rural and urban marriages, these differences appear to be quite small.

The findings with respect to age are less equivocal, but contrary to the stereotype. Blood and Wolfe (1960), Centers, Raven, and Rodrigues (1971), and others have found that the husband's power tends to decrease with both age and length of marriage. Sawer (1973), in a study of farm families, hypothesized that the wife's role in decision making would decrease with age because older couples "may be influenced by perceptions of traditional sex roles" (p. 421). She found, however, a small positive relationship between age and the involvement of wives in decision making.

Patterns such as these cannot be explained in terms of traditionalism among elderly or rural couples. The data reported by

Sawer (1973) support Blood and Wolfe's (1960) resource theory of marital power rather than a normative or cultural explanation. Sawer found the strongest antecedents of wives' decision-making influence to be the extent of information-seeking activity and degree of involvement in farm-related tasks. Thus, competence seems to be a major antecedent of marital authority among rural couples, outweighing the effects of cultural or normative factors. The rural elderly are probably no different from other Americans in terms of either typical distributions of marital power or the factors which determine these distributions.

Kinship Relations

One of the most pervasive beliefs in the American cultural system is that kinship relations and extended family ties are stronger among rural than urban populations (Lee, 1980). This belief is, to a considerable degree, shared by sociologists. At this point in the course of research on kinship, we cannot conclude that it is demonstrably wrong. As we have noted elsewhere (Lee & Cassidy, 1981), however, the results of research on residential differences in kinship networks have been surprisingly equivocal.

Virtually all studies of kinship relations implicate the elderly in some way, since kinship contact frequently involves interaction between the generations. Of the studies which have examined rural–urban differences in kinship interaction, the slight majority have found kinship interaction to be more frequent among rural residents or persons from rural backgrounds (Berardo, 1966; Heller, Quesada, Harvey, & Warner, 1981a, 1981b; Hendrix, 1976; Klatzky, 1972; Mirande, 1970; Shanas, Townsend, Wedderburn, Friis, Milhoj, & Stehouwer, 1968; Straus, 1969; Winch & Greer, 1968). Several other studies, however, have found either no significant difference (Key, 1961) or that urban residents interact more frequently with kin than do rural (Bultena, 1969; Youmans, 1963). The latter two studies, not incidentally, employed elderly persons as respondents, as did Shanas et al. (1968).

Two of the studies noted above specifically examined differences between agricultural workers and others (Klatzky, 1972; Shanas et al., 1968). Both found interaction between the generations to be somewhat more frequent among agricultural workers than among either white-collar or blue-collar urban workers. Klatzky (1972) noted, however, that this difference is almost entirely attributable to differential distance from kin: the adult male farmers in her sample tended to live closer to their parents than did other types of workers. The fact that her study dealt exclusively with interaction between fathers and sons may be partially responsible for this, since we know that farm families tend to live nearer to the husband's parents than the wife's (Wilkening, Guerrero, & Ginsberg, 1972). These generalizations, however, may not apply to rural nonfarm families, which include the overwhelming majority of the rural population.

The implications of the occupation of farming for kinship relations may stem from the fact that farming is a family business which relies upon land, a tangible resource which is often acquired through the process of inheritance. This means that instrumental ties in the male line are often of particular importance. Their importance emanates from farming as an occupation, not from the fact that farmers are rural residents. Thus, differences between farmers and industrial workers will not necessarily be replicated in comparisons of rural nonfarm and urban residents. Klatzky (1972), for example, found no residential differences in kinship interaction in comparisons which did not include farmers. Berardo (1966) found that residents of a small city who had grown up on farms interacted with kin more than did those who had not, suggesting that norms develop among farm families which promote kinship interaction even after leaving the farm. Klatzky (1972) and others, however, have not found this pattern.

Hendrix (1976) studied people who lived in a small Ozark community, comparing people who had moved away with those who had remained in the home town. He found that kinship interaction was most frequent among home-town residents, followed by those who had moved to a town of less than 50,000. Those who had moved to larger cities were least likely to interact with kin. This was true even when availability of kin was controlled by examining these relationships only among respondents who had two or more related households living in their communities. Thus, Hendrix concluded that migration decreased the opportunity to interact with kin (see also Winch & Greer, 1968), and residence in an urban area decreased the motivation to interact with kin.

There are, however, two points that need to be considered before the latter conclusion can be accepted. First, all respondents in this study were migrants from or residents of one small community; these people may well be quite different from lifelong urban residents. Second, having kin residing in one's own community may well mean very different things, in terms of the actual accessibility of these kin, in large rather than small cities. We know that geographic distance is the single most important antecedent of kinship interaction (see Lee, 1980, for a summary). Therefore, the accessibility of kin is not, in fact, held perfectly constant in Hendrix's (1976) study.

Recent research by Heller et al. (1981a, 1981b) demonstrated the importance of both geographic distance and geographic region of the country for kinship interaction. In an earlier study, Heller and Quesada (1977) compared rural Virginia residents with rural Nevada residents and found a much stronger orientation toward extended kin in the Virginia sample. Specifically, they found the Virginians expressed stronger feelings of closeness to extended kin; were more likely to marry within the extended-kin group; visited more frequently with kin than with friends; and turned to relatives for help. They attributed these differences in part to the much greater geographic proximity of Virginians to other members of their kin networks; Nevadans had many fewer kin residing within any proximate distance. Distance is not only a causal variable in this set of relations, however. Virginians were markedly less mobile than were Nevadans. Heller and Quesada (1977) argued that "a lack of geographic mobility may partly constitute a desire to maintain one's immersion within the extended-kin group" (p. 229). These results imply that rural residents are not homogeneous with respect to kinship and that the strong extended-kin bonds we typically associate with rural families may be unique to eastern or southeastern rural families.

Subsequently, Heller et al. (1981a, 1981b) compared their rural Virginia and Nevada respondents with a sample of residents from Akron, Ohio, intended to represent urban families. They found the Akron sample to be very similar to rural Nevadans on each of the dimensions noted above; the urbanites and the Nevadans thus differ from the Virginians in many of the same ways, even though they differ from each other on the rural–urban dimension as well as in terms of geographic region of the country.

Studies of the kinship relations of elderly persons which have included rural–urban comparisons (Bultena, 1969; Youmans, 1963) have found the urban elderly to interact with kin (particularly adult children) somewhat more frequently than do the rural. The reasons for this finding differ between the two studies, however. Bultena (1969), studying a Wisconsin sample, found higher interaction with children among the urban elderly because of more proximate residence. Many of the children of rural elderly had moved away (often, presumably, to urban areas); the children of the urban elderly were more likely to live in the same community or vicinity as their parents.

Youmans (1963), however, found higher interaction rates among urban elderly in spite of lesser proximity to their children. In his sample of Kentucky residents, more older rural than urban persons had children living nearby, but the urban elderly visited with their chlidren more frequently. Part of the explanation for this pattern may reside in the generally low level of financial resources possessed by the rural elderly in Youmans' sample. Rural respondents were much less likely than were urban to initiate visits with their children; they were instead more dependent upon the children's motivations. This suggests that the ability of the rural elderly to traverse even relatively short distances may have been hampered by their lack of resources. The rural–urban difference which Youmans reports may thus be, in part, a class or income difference. This is particularly interesting because Youmans' data come from the same general region of the country where, according to Heller and his associates (Heller & Quesada, 1977; Heller et al., 1981a, 1981b), rural kinship ties are the strongest.

Our data, obtained from the state of Washington, may shed a little light on this subject. For the analyses shown in Table 7.3, the sample consisted of over 1,400 men and 1,700 women (the exact cell sizes vary becaues of item-specific nonresponse and because persons who have no children and/or no grandchildren are excluded from the appropriate tabulations). These data indicate that farm residents of both sexes are more likely than are residents of any other type of area to visit with children (who do not live with them) more than once a week, and to visit with grandchildren more than once a month. This appears to stem in part from the greater proximity of elderly farm residents to their children; they are significantly more likely than are members of any other residence category to have at least one child living within a mile of their homes.

This difference evaporates, however, when the definition of proximity is expanded to a 10-mile range. Here, residents of large cities (in this case, Seattle) are more likely to live within 10 miles of at least one child. This suggests that a fairly high proportion of the children of the urban elderly remain within the general metropolitan area, although not often in the same neighborhood as their parents. When the children of the farm elderly move away they

Table 7.3. Kinship Interaction by Residence and Sex

Males	Farm	Rural nonfarm	Town	Small city	Large city	Total
Visit with children more often than once per week	30.6	13.9	23.0	15.5	18.6	19.6
Visit with grandchildren more often than once per month	48.6	35.9	41.7	39.9	45.2	41.8
Almost always spend holidays with children	35.5	32.4	34.9	33.6	43.5	36.5
Have at least one child within 1 mile	23.0	12.2	17.2	12.2	14.7	15.3
Have at least one child within 10 miles	46.0	35.1	48.2	52.0	58.0	49.0
Females						
Visit with children more often than once per week	29.1	17.5	28.5	26.6	19.9	24.1
Visit with grandchildren more often than once per month	53.2	44.9	48.6	49.3	46.8	48.0
Almost always spend holidays with children	49.6	48.1	47.2	51.6	53.5	50.0
Have at least one child within 1 mile	35.8	15.4	22.3	16.4	17.3	19.8
Have at least one child within 10 miles	47.7	43.8	54.0	53.2	60.2	53.3

Source: A survey of Washington State residents aged 55 and over, conducted by Gary R. Lee and Steven R. Burkett, 1980.

appear to move farther away, perhaps to urban areas. This severely restricts opportunities for interaction. It is also interesting to note that the rural nonfarm elderly are the least likely to have proximate children of any residential category under either definition of proximity. This is probably due to limited occupational opportunities for young nonfarming adults in areas of low population densities.

Data from Table 7.3 also suggest that interaction between elderly farm residents and their children is perhaps somewhat more instrumental, and correspondingly less expressive, than is such interaction for urban residents. The rural and small-town elderly of both sexes are slightly less likely than are their urban counterparts to report that they almost always spend holidays with children. The difference here is certainly small, but the fact that it is opposite in direction to differences in routine interaction frequency may be significant. Similarly, farm residents were more likely than were other respondents to report that the child with whom they interacted most frequently was a son rather than a daughter. Nearly 56 percent of farm males, as opposed to less than 45 percent of all other males, see sons more often than daughters. This suggests, in combination with the information on holiday interaction, that a higher proportion of the intergenerational interaction engaged in by elderly farm residents is instrumental in nature, perhaps involving farming operations or related aspects of joint economic endeavors.

These data add further credibility to Klatzky's (1972) argument that higher frequencies of interaction between aging parents and their adult children among farm families are attributable to economic factors rather than to stronger traditions of "familism" among rural populations. She concluded that differences between farmers and nonfarmers in interaction frequency

> derive from the fact that farmers remain closer in physical distance to their parents, a situation which may mean that they cultivate land owned by or obtained from their parents, or more generally, that farming is one of the few remaining occupations where residing near the family of orientation promotes one's occupational interests. (p. 39)

Our data confirm Klatzky's on this point, even though ours come from the aging parents and hers were obtained from the grown children. Furthermore, our data show that the greater interaction frequencies sometimes found among rural kin networks are attributable to higher rates of interaction among farmers, not rural people generally. Rates of interaction between aging parents and their lineal descendents are, in most cases, as high among residents of large cities as among rural nonfarm or small-town residents.

Summary

Many scholars have noted the prevalence of stereotypes about rural American families which portray "country living and family life as simple, pure, and wholesome; slower paced; free from pressures and tensions; and surrounded by pastoral beauty and serenity" (Coward & Smith, 1982, p. 77). This is obviously much different than our stereotypes of urban and suburban families which are widely known to be afflicted by all manner of problems.

While common stereotypes of rural and urban families are dramatically different, their realities are very similar. Rural married couples divorce less often than do urban, but not because their marriages are any more gratifying. Farm families evidence a somewhat more sex-segregated divison of labor between spouses, and older persons who live on farms experience slightly more contact with their adult children than do others; but these differences are small and, in all probability, have minimal effects upon the daily lives of the rural elderly. With respect to the family patterns of the elderly, residential location has very little explanatory utility.

It is usually the case that findings of no difference attract little interest and are quickly forgotten, by both the scientific community and those responsible for the formulation and implementation of public policies and programs. In this case, we feel that such an outcome would be extremely unfortunate. Stereotypes about the rural elderly and their family lives are so prevalent that they may be frequently employed as rationales for concentrating upon the more visible and commonly recognized problems of the urban elderly. If the rural elderly really were uniquely advantaged by embeddedness in strong, supportive kin networks, in contrast to the "isolated nuclear families" of the urban elderly (see Lee, 1980), their needs for public services might indeed be less. The fact is that they are not. Other chapters in this volume document the relative deprivation of the rural elderly in terms of economic resources (Chapter 3), housing (Chapter 6), availability of services (Chapter 9), and other critical determinants of the quality of life. We do not claim to have found any comparable "deficiencies" in the quality of family life among the rural elderly. But we do contend that the available evidence should serve, at least, to demolish the myth that rural families possess any unique strengths which ameliorate the effects of other privations upon their elderly members. We therefore cannot assume that the needs of the rural elderly for supportive public services are any less than are those of other groups because the "classical family of Western nostalgia" (Goode, 1963, p. 6) is alive and well and living in the country. It is not.

References

Balkwell, C. Transition to widowhood: A review of the literature. *Family Relations*, 1981, *30*, 117–127.

Bayer, A. E. Sexist students in American colleges: A descriptive note. *Journal of Marriage and the Family*, 1975, *37*, 391–397.

Berardo, F. M. Kinship interaction and migrant adaptation in an aerospace-related community. *Journal of Marriage and the Family*, 1966, *28*, 757–768.

Berardo, F. M. *Social adapation to widowhood among a rural–urban aged population*. Pullman: Agricultural Experiment Station Bulletin No. 689, Washington State University, 1967.

Bescher-Donnelly, L., & Smith, L. W. The changing roles and status of rural women. In R. T. Coward & W. M. Smith, Jr. (Eds.), *The family in rural society*. Boulder, Colo.: Westview Press, 1981, pp. 167–185.

Blood, R. O., Jr., & Wolfe, D. M. *Husbands and wives: The dynamics of married living*. New York: The Free Press, 1960.

Brown, D. L. Recent changes in the demographic structure of the rural family. In R. T. Coward (Ed.), *Rural families across the life span: Implications for community programming*. West Lafayette: Indiana Cooperative Extension Service, 1977, pp. 18–41.

Brown, D. L.. A quarter century of trends and changes in the demographic structure of American families. In R. T. Coward & W. M. Smith, Jr. (Eds.), *The family in rural society*. Boulder, Colo.: Westview Press, 1981, pp. 9–25.

Bultena, G. L. Rural–urban differences in the familial interaction of the aged. *Rural Sociology*, 1969, *34*, 5–15.

Campbell, A., Converse, P. E., & Rodgers, W. L. *The Quality of American life: Perceptions, evaluations, and satisfactions*. New York: Russell Sage, 1976.

Centers, R., Raven, B. H., & Rodrigues, A. Conjugal power structure: A re-examination. *American Sociological Review*, 1971, *36*, 264–278.

Chatfield, W. G. Economic and sociological factors influencing life satisfaction of the aged. *Journal of Gerontology*, 1977, *32*, 593–599.

Coward, R. T., & Smith, W. M., Jr. Families in rural society. In D. A. Dillman & D. J. Hobbs (Eds.), *Rural society in the U.S.: Issues for the 1980s*. Boulder, Colo.: Westview Press, 1982, pp. 77–84.

Cutler, S. J., & Kaufman, R. L. Cohort changes in political attitudes: Tolerance of ideological nonconformity. *Public Opinion Quarterly*, 1975, *39*, 69–81.

Fischer, C. S. The effect of urban life on traditional values. *Social Forces*, 1975, *53*, 420–432.

Foner, A. Age stratification and age conflict in political life. *American Sociological Review*, 1974, *39*, 187–196.

Glenn, N. D. Recent trends in intercategory differences in attitudes. *Social Forces*, 1974, *52*, 395–401.

Glenn, N. D., & Hill, L., Jr. Rural–urban differences in attitudes and behavior in the United States. *Annals of the Academy of Political and Social Science*, 1977, *429*, 36–50.

Goode, W. J. *World revolution and family patterns*. New York: The Free Press, 1963.

Heller, P. L., & Quesada, G. M. Rural familism: An interregional analysis. *Rural Sociology*, 1977, *42*, 220–240.

Heller, P. L., Quesada, G. M., Harvey, D. L., & Warner, L. G. Rural familism: Interregional analysis. In R. T. Coward & W. M. Smith, Jr. (Eds.), *The family in rural society*. Boulder, Colo.: Westview Press, 1981, pp. 73–85. (a)

Heller, P. L., Quesada, G. M., Harvey, D. L., & Warner, L. G. Familism in rural and urban America: Critique and reconceptualizaton of a construct. *Rural Sociology*, 1981, *46*, 446–464. (b)

Hendrix, L. Kinship, social networks, and integration among Ozark residents and out-migrants. *Journal of Marriage and the Family*, 1976, *38*, 97–104.

Key, W. H. Rural–urban differences and the family. *Sociological Quarterly*, 1961, *2*, 49–56.

Kivett, V. *The rural by-passed elderly: Perspectives on status and needs*. Greensboro: North Carolina Agricultural Research Service Bulletin No. 260, University of North Carolina at Greensboro, 1979.

Klatzky, S. R. *Patterns of contact with relatives*. Washington, D.C.: American Sociological Association, 1972.

Larson, O. F. Values and beliefs of rural people. In T. R. Ford (Ed.), *Rural U.S.A.: Persistence and change*. Ames: Iowa State University Press, 1978, pp. 91–112.

Lee, G. R. Kinship in the seventies: A decade review of research and theory. *Journal of Marriage and the Family*, 1980, *42*, 923–934.

Lee, G. R., & Cassidy, M. L. Kinship systems and extended family ties. In R. T. Coward & W. M. Smith, Jr. (Eds.), *The family in rural society*. Boulder, Colo.: Westview Press, 1981, pp. 57–71.

Lind, R. W. Sex knowledge, birth control, and marital attitudes of a rural population. *Journal of Home Economics Research*, 1976, *5*, 47–53.

Lowe, G. D., & Peek, C. W. Location and lifestyle: The comparative explantory ability of urbanism and rurality. *Rural Sociology*, 1974, *39*, 392–420.

Mirande, A. M. Extended kinship ties, friendship relations, and community size: An exploratory analysis. *Rural Sociology*, 1970, *35*, 261–266.

Mitchell, R. M. *Paths to happiness: Residence locality and interpersonal relations*. Unpublished Ph.D. dissertation, University of Notre Dame, South Bend, Ind. University Microfilms No. 76–27, 1976.

Morgan, L. A. A re-examination of widowhood and morale. *Journal of Gerontology*, 1976, *31*, 687–695.

Pihlblad, C. T., & Adams, D. Widowhood, social participation, and life satisfaction. *International Journal of Aging and Human Development*, 1972, *3*, 323–330.

Pihlblad, C. T., Adams, D., & Rosencranz, H. Social-economic adjustment to widowhood. *Omega*, 1972, *3*, 295–305.

Powers, E. A. The effect of wife's employment on household tasks among post-parental couples: A research note. *International Journal of Aging and Human Development*, 1971, *2*, 284–287.

Powers, E. A., & Bultena, G. L. Sex differences in intimate friendships of old age. *Journal of Marriage and the Family*, 1976, *38*, 739–747.

Powers, E. A., Keith, P. M., & Goudy, W. J. Family relationships and friendships among the rural aged. In T. O. Byerts, S. C. Howell, & L. A. Pastalan (Eds.), *Environmental context of aging: Life styles and living arrangements*. New York: Garland STPM Press, 1979, pp. 80–101.

Powers, E. A., Keith, P. M., & Goudy, W. J. Family networks of the rural aged. In R. T. Coward & W. M. Smith, Jr. (Eds.), *The family in rural society*. Boulder, Colo.: Westview Press, 1981, pp. 199–217.

Roberts, A. E., & Kowalski, G. S. *Farm residence or background and women's sex role attitudes*. Paper presented at the Annual Meetings of the Rural Sociological Society, San Francisco, Calif., 1978.

Rosenblatt, P. C., & Anderson, R. M. Interaction in farm families: Tension and stress. In R. T. Coward & W. M. Smith, Jr. (Eds.), *The family in rural society*. Boulder, Colo.: Westview Press, 1981, pp. 147–166.

Sawer, B. J. Predictors of the farm wife's involvement in general management and adoption decisions. *Rural Sociology*, 1973, *73*, 412–426.

Schumm, W. R., & Bollman, S. R. Interpersonal processes in rural families. In R. T. Coward & W. M. Smith, Jr. (Eds.), *The family in rural society*. Boulder, Colo.: Westview Press, 1981, pp. 129–145.

Shanas, E., Townsend, P., Wedderburn, D., Friis, H., Milhoj, P., & Stehouwer, J. *Old people in three industrial societies*. New York: Atherton Press, 1968.

Straus, M. A. Social class and farm-city differences in interaction with kin in relation to societal modernization. *Rural Sociology*, 1969, *34*, 476–495.

Targ, D. B. Middle age in rural America: Adapting to change. In R. T. Coward & W. M. Smith, Jr. (Eds.), *The family in rural society*. Boulder, Colo.: Westview Press, 1981, pp. 187–198.

U.S. Bureau of the Census. Special studies: Social and economic characteristics of the metropolitan and nonmetropolitan population, 1977 and 1970. *Current population reports*. Series P-23, No. 75. Washington, D.C.: U.S. Government Printing Office, 1978.

U.S. Bureau of the Census. Population characteristics: Marital status and living arrangements, March 1979. *Current population reports,* Series P-20, No. 349. Washington, D.C.: U.S. Government Printing Office, 1980.

Wilkening, E. A., Guerrero, S., & Ginsberg, S. Distance and intergenerational ties of farm families. *Sociological Quarterly,* 1972, *13,* 382–396.

Winch, R. F., & Greer, S. A. Urbanism, ethnicity, and extended familism. *Journal of Marriage and the Family,* 1968, *30,* 40–45.

Woodrow, K., Hastings, D. W., & Tu, E. J. Rural–urban patterns of marriage, divorce, and mortality: Tennessee, 1970. *Rural Sociology,* 1978, *43,* 70–86.

Youmans, E. G. *Aging patterns in a rural and an urban area of Kentucky.* Lexington, Ky.: Agricultural Experiment Station Bulletin No. 681, University of Kentucky, 1963.

8

Aging in Rural Society: Non-Kin Community Relations and Participation

Vira R. Kivett

The importance of non-kin relationships to the general well-being of older adults is receiving increased recognition. Non-kin relationships and community participation provide for continuity in role performance over the adult years as well as for the replacement of roles lost through retirement, widowhood, and other late-life events. Non-kin relationships, while expanding the life space of older adults, are also important for their reference group function. In turn, older adults, through community participation, make valuable contributions to society through leadership, volunteerism, and other supportive behaviors. Although considerable research in community participation and informal relationships in later life has accumulated, results are frequently equivocal and difficult to generalize (Coward, 1979; Larson, 1978; Lee & Lassey, 1980).

Non-kin community relationships can be divided into two types: (1) associations through *formal organizations* such as voluntary participation in clubs, civic and social groups, or the church; and (2) immersion in *informal networks* that occur through interactions with neighbors and friends. The primary purpose of this chapter is to examine the participation of older rural adults in the broader community and the implications of this participation for general well-being. The chapter examines the extent of participation of older rural adults in formal organizations and their patterns of interaction with non-kin, the factors influencing participatory behaviors, and the significance of social interaction for psychological well-being. Where possible, rural and urban contrasts are addressed throughout. The chapter concludes with an identification of research priorities in the area of non-kin community relations and participation, especially as they relate to older rural populations.

Participation in Formal Organizations

Research shows that membership in voluntary associations extends well into the later years, although considerable variation in participation is found according to the type and location of the organization. Babchuk, Peters, Hoyt, and Kaiser (1979), in an investigation of a large nonmetropolitan sample of persons 65 years or older, found that 80 percent belonged to at least one organization while 50 percent belonged to more than one. Similarly, Cutler (1977) observed high levels of participation among the urban elderly. On the other hand, McKain (1967) reported that older rural adults only infrequently belonged to clubs and organizations, and Cutler (1976) found membership (excluding church groups) among a General Social Survey sample ranged from a low of 3 percent (in national groups) to a high of 18 percent (in fraternal groups). In terms of participatory involvement, a Harris Poll in 1975 showed only 17 percent of the public 65 and over reported themselves as giving a "lot of time" to participating in fraternal or community organizations or clubs (Harris and Associates, 1975).

The extent of continuity in participation in organizational activity over the adult years is also unclear. Rosow (1967) found that, with age, adults hold fewer offices in organizations and become less active. Cutler (1977), however, observed few changes in the participatory activity of older urban adults over a two- to four-year period. A greater drop in participation with advancing age has usually been observed for men than for women (Berghorn, Schafer, & Steere, 1978; Riley & Foner, 1968). Sex differences have also been observed in membership choices (Babchuk et al., 1979; Berghorn et al., 1978). Women have been found more likely than men to belong to church-related and to social expressive voluntary groups.

Several factors may account for changes in participation in the later years. Bild and Havighurst (1976) have explained declines in the level of social participation to be precipitated by changes associated with aging: the death of a spouse and friends, decreased mobility, poor health and finances, and other problems which reduce life space such as lack of transportation. Also, few organizations have catered to the needs and interests of men or women after the fifth decade. A particular deficiency in this regard is the void of associations or organizations focused on the needs and interests of older men. This probably accounts in part for the sex differences in participation described above.

The loss of membership roles in later life deprives older adults of important central group supports as well as responsibility, power, privilege, resources, and prestige. Rosow (1967) has argued that the weakening of group ties forces the older individual to be more dependent upon the immediate environment for social life and support, for friendships, and for associations. This may be especially critical for older adults with few or no family members, those living in rural or other isolated areas, and persons with limited informal social networks.

Of particular interest in studies of social interaction is the variation in participation found *within* groups of older adults. Berghorn et al. (1978), for example, found large within-group differences in the amount of formal social activity in an elderly urban sample. This variability appeared to be due in part to the composition of the neighborhood. This finding supported other data that indicated higher levels of social interaction among the elderly in neighborhoods with high concentrations of older persons (Rosow, 1967). Berghorn and associates (1978) interpreted this to suggest that age-homogeneous environments are less stressful to the elderly and consequently facilitate more social interaction. Similarly, the researchers concluded that people in neighborhoods with a high density of the elderly have higher levels of social aptitude and behaviorally express it with higher levels of activity.

Other factors also have been found to have impact on the participation patterns of older adults. These include socioeconomic status, health, activity, and race (Bauder & Doerflinger, 1967; Clemente, Rexroad, & Hirsch, 1975; Riley & Foner, 1968). Membership in organizations is more frequent among adults from higher socioeconomic backgrounds and those who are healthy, active, and well integrated into other social roles. Clemente et al. (1975) contrasted large comparable samples of older metropolitan blacks and whites. Their data supported previous reports in the literature of higher participation and attendance rates among older blacks than older whites. Clemente and his associates attributed these higher rates to the "compensatory theory" or to the observation that blacks compensate for discrimination in the larger society by more frequently joining and participating in organizations.

Rural–Urban Comparisons in Group Participation

Although there is a paucity of research contrasting the participation levels of the rural and urban elderly, limited evidence suggests that rural adults are less likely to participate in organizations than urban adults. Schooler (1975) found that older rural persons were less likely to belong to organizations and to attend meetings than corresponding urban adults. Lozier and Althouse (1975) suggested that the rural elderly were less likely than the urban elderly to remain highly involved in social and community activities.

The work of several investigators indicates reasons for rural–urban differences in participation where they might exist. Lee and Lassey (1980) suggested that older rural adults might be less likely than the urban elderly to be participants in organizations because of "objective" factors such as lower incomes, poorer health, less transportation, and other limited resources. Similarly, observations by Harbart and Wilkinson (1979) of the extreme differences in general status and quality of life between rural and urban populations indicated the potential for less organization participation among rural than urban elderly. Adams (1975) pointed to differences in the socialization patterns between urban and rural adults which have implications for group participation. Besides having been socialized to a different society, older rural individuals have been socialized to a different speed of expected social change. As a result, new social opportunities such as those associated with recently developed senior citizens programs might be expected to gain slower acceptance in rural than in urban areas.

Age density has also been used to explain rural–urban differences in organization participation. The findings are mixed, however, with regard to the direction of the effect. Berghorn et al. (1978) found that urban areas with low densities of older people tended to stimulate greater participation in organized activity in efforts to offset isolation. In sharp contrast, other evidence has suggested that where there are high densities of older adults, such as is sometimes observed in rural areas, more group participation will occur, especially in activities that are age-graded (Rosow, 1967).

There is also evidence that suggests differences by residence in the type of organizations in which older adults participate. As might be expected, participation in professional and civic organizations is more frequent among the urban elderly, while older rural residents are more likely to be involved in associations such as the programs of the Extension Service of the U.S. Department of Agriculture and certain other farm organizations (Sanders, 1977). There is also some indication that the church is a more prominent force in the lives of the rural than the urban elderly, especially among minority groups (Clemente et al., 1975).

The Rural Elderly and Formal Organizations

Research findings through the 1960s showed few older persons living in rural areas taking part in formal organizations. Youmans (1963) found that less than 20 percent of older rural Kentuckians participated regularly in any group activity, excluding church. Stubbs (1968) showed that rural husbands and wives in the age groups of 45 to 64 had limited participation in engrossing leisure-time activities that included group activity.

More recent data suggest that these patterns have changed little since the preceding decades. In terms of actual participation, Kivett and Scott (1979), in a study of rural southern white and black elderly, found that approximately 67 percent of adults 65 years or older got together with other people for organized activity (e.g., civic, social, and church groups) two or more times a month, while 16 percent said they seldom or never participated in group activities. The high percentage of participants, however, appeared to be due in large part to participation in church-related activities. Other data showed that approximately 80 percent of the older adults listed church activities as a favorite pastime, whereas only 20 percent mentioned participation in clubs and civic organizations.

Several organizations or programs appear to dominate voluntary association opportunities for older adults in rural farm communities. Sanders (1977) referred to three of these as the agricultural cooperative, special-interest farm organizations (such as the Grange and Farm Bureau), and the national political parties. In many cases, Grange halls have served as major social centers in predominantly agricultural areas.

A recent survey of the membership of the National Extension Homemakers Association, a support and volunteer group within the Extension Services of many states (70% of whom reside in rural areas or places of less than 10,000), indicated that 39 percent of the sample was 60 years or older (U.S. Department of Agriculture, 1981). Blalock (1979) has reported still further evidence of the outreach of the programs of the Extension Service. In North Carolina the annual report of the Extension Service noted that 3,898 senior volunteers (a significant percentage of the overall membership) had served on Extension boards, councils, and committees, as club officers, and in other leadership roles during the preceding year (School of Agriculture and Life Sciences, 1981). During this same period, peer counseling groups established by the Extension Service, churches, and/or mental health organizations involved approximately 5,400 widows, widowers, and peer leaders. [It should be noted that although Extension's roots, and strengths, lie in rural America, some research (Coward, 1978) has indicated that Extension involves only a small percentage of the total rural population. This trend is perhaps heightened by the inmigration of urbanites, unfamiliar with Extension as a resource, that has occurred in the 1970s and 1980s.]

The rural church has been singled out as providing one of the few frequent opportunities for older adults to assume meaningful status roles outside the family or occupation (Loomis & Beegle, 1975). This observation applies in particular to certain socioeconomic and minority groups. Religion appears to have a compensatory function which has been found to increase with social isolation. Smith (1967) emphasized the centrality of the church in the social life of rural blacks and, in particular, elderly blacks. In many cases the church has served an unduplicated role in social welfare and social reform for the poor and other powerless subgroups. In view of its strategic position in the community, the church has been criticized for failing to take more initiative in meeting the full range of needs of both the rural and the urban elderly (White House Conference on Aging, 1981a).

Rural areas are only now beginning to receive closer to their fair share of monies from the Older Americans Act, a radical departure from earlier policy (Coward, 1979; National Strategy Conference on Improving Service Delivery to the Rural Elderly, 1979; Green Thumb, 1981). This increased flow of federal resources is seen in the growing numbers of rural elderly participating in senior center programs. A recent report revealed that of the 26 percent of Americans 55 years or older who say that they attend senior centers, 48 percent are from rural areas (National Council on the Aging, 1979). This percentage is higher than the proportion of older persons living in rural areas and reflects, at least, no rural deficit in senior center participation. Other studies, however, suggest considerable regional departure from national figures and attest to the infrequency with which many older rural adults still participate in senior citizens programs. Scott (1981), for example, found that among a representative group of 200 older Americans and Mexican-Americans in Texas, 14 percent used senior centers, 7 percent visited congregate meal programs, less than 1 percent participated in the R.S.V.P. (a volunteer program), and none were affiliated with the Foster Grandparents program. Scott observed that only 13 percent of the elderly participated in other organizations specifically designed for older adults such as the National Retired Teachers Association (NRTA) and the American Association for Retired Persons (AARP). In many cases, low participation rates reflect lack of opportunity rather than lack of interest. Given adequate outreach strategies, the recent emphasis on rural funding for a number of programs under the Older Americans Act could result in the involvement of larger numbers of rural adults in programs such as those provided through the national network of area agencies on aging.

The contributions that older rural adults can make through volunteerism and civic participation have been largely overlooked. Although some hold leadership positions in community organizations, little effort has been made to increase these opportunities. Recommendations resulting from the 1981 White House Conference on Aging stress the importance of utilizing the talents of the rural elderly in local communities through employment, volunteer activities, and advisory planning boards and committees (Green Thumb, 1981; White House Conference on Aging, 1981b). The structure for delegate selection for the 1981 Mini-Conferences on Aging for the White House Conference, as well as for the 1981 White Conference on Aging itself, serve as excellent models for the incorporation of older adults into policymaking structures. Criteria for state delegations for the Mini-Conferences on Rural Aging, for example, required that 90 percent of the representatives be 55 years or older (Green Thumb, 1981).

Factors Influencing the Rural Elderly's Participation

Observing the complexity of factors which affect participation in rural areas, McKain (1967) cautioned against the dangers of overgeneralizing. His broad review of the literature of the 1960s pointed out a number of factors that influence rural adults' participatory behaviors, including the extent of farming operations, extent of public assistance, place of birth, health, education, and length of time in the community. Social activity was found to be greater among adults with large farm operations, the native born, persons who had good health and higher education, and those who were not receiving public assistance. Older adults living in nonfarm rural areas were more likely than other rural adults to participate in clubs and organizations. More recent data for comparison are lacking.

Living in a rural area may have both positive and negative effects on participation in voluntary associations in still other ways. The high proportion of older people in many rural areas may be viewed as a positive force in group participation. High age density, for example, may lead to less age grading and isolation than in a more age-heterogeneous population. In contrast, older rural adults may be eliminated from participation in voluntary associations through low population density, geographic isolation, and a lack of transportation. This observation appears to be especially true for older rural widows, many of whom have never learned to drive (Kivett, 1979). Older rural groups particularly vulnerable to the effects of inadequate transportation are adults whose children have moved from the general area and the nondriving childless elderly (Kivett & Learner, 1980). The high cost of car maintenance and operation makes social participation in formal organizations prohibitive for numerous rural elderly, many of whom live at or below the poverty level. A general lack of public transportation in outlying areas as well as fear of criminal assault, poor vision for night driving, poor health, and the limited availability of voluntary associations further reduce opportunities for group participation among the rural elderly.

Attitudes toward leisure can also exert considerable influence on the participation rates of older rural adults. Two widely held values in American society strongly condition the attitudes of older adults toward the acceptance of leisure pursuits. They have been described as the value attached to work as opposed to leisure and the value placed on youth rather than age. These attitudes are especially pronounced in rural areas (McKain, 1967; Youmans, 1973). The work ethic and adherence to traditional achievement values may still account for a part of the variation in the participatory behavior of the rural elderly. The societal emphasis on youth has also shaped the nature of free-time activities. As a result, many voluntary associations within the community place emphasis on activities based on youthful capabilities, interests, and leadership. The result is to discourage the participation of older persons whose interests and energies may be quite different from those of younger adults.

The growing numbers of older people moving to rural areas may have important implications for the future demand and structure of rural voluntary associations. It might be expected that elderly migrants to rural areas will participate in community organizations in significant numbers. This is likely because older inmigrants to rural areas generally have higher levels of income and education than the resident elderly, are more independent, and often move to areas in which they have many family and friendship ties (Glasgow, 1980). Because the majority of metropolitan inmigrants are married, organizations and other leisure pursuits designed for both males and females may become more popular. Because this increasingly important group tends to relocate in the most rural areas of nonmetropolitan regions, transportation will become an increasingly important determinant of sustained participation among the very old.

In summary, participation in clubs, organizations, and related groups appears to extend well into old age. Membership rates among both urban and rural groups vary considerably within each group. Common factors influencing participation choices include geographic location, sex, socioeconomic status, and race. The mobility of the older individual, depending on health and transportation, also is a prominent factor in sustained activity in organizations. There is some indication of membership differences between rural and urban elderly. Less participation among the rural than the urban elderly appears to be due in part to fewer opportunities or options for membership, less likelihood of established patterns of group membership, fewer economic and social resources, and more geographic isolation. The high density of older adults frequently found in rural areas may, however, be a positive force for social participation unequaled in many urban areas. There is some indication that recent federal programs for older Americans are affording new membership opportunities for larger numbers of older rural adults. A continuing influx of the metropolitan elderly to rural areas will no doubt bring important changes to the future membership profile of older rural Americans.

Patterns of Interaction in Informal Networks

Friends and neighbors play important roles in the helping networks of older adults. Part of the value of informal networks is the role modeling they provide for widowhood, retirement, grandparenthood, and other critical life events. Peer groups also may serve as important refuges and support structures to cushion the shock of status loss. Payne (1977) has indicated the importance of friends as reference groups to provide feedback for age-appropriate behaviors. Kivett and Scott (1979) found that 84 percent of rural elders reported having a confidant, i.e., a major referent.

Interactions with friends and neighbors greatly expand the social network of older adults. Shanas, Townsend, Wedderburn, Friis, Milhoj, and Stehouwer (1968) found that older people with nonlocal children were extremely involved in compensatory neighboring. As former group ties weaken, older adults become increasingly dependent upon their immediate environments for social life and support, for friendships and associations (Rosow, 1967). Although friends and neighbors often overlap, differences may be observed in the roles of the two groups. Litwak and Szelenyi (1969) argued that whereas neighbors may be valued more for their close proximity, especially in terms of emergency assistance and regular checkups, friends provide an important reference group and social outlet. Both, however, are in contrast to the unique position of the family in its long-term commitment to the needs of older adults.

Numerous studies have been conducted on friend and neighbor networks in later life (Litwak & Szelenyi, 1969; Powers, Keith, & Goudy, 1975; Rose, 1967; Rosenburg, 1976; Rosow, 1967; Shanas et al., 1968). Most evidence suggests that the number of friends and informal relationships declines as age increases, and that these relationships in general become less intense. The extent of satisfaction received from friends, however, does not appear to decrease with age. In contrast, some data show that interaction with nonrelatives may be among the most rewarding relationships in later life (Powers et al., 1975).

Rural–Urban Comparisons in Informal Networks

There is some evidence to suggest differences in the levels of informal interaction of rural and urban adults. Schooler (1975) found that the rural elderly were more likely to have contact with friends and neighbors than the urban elderly. Older rural adults were also more likely to perceive themselves as situated conveniently to friends and relatives and to report having a confidant. Similarly, McKain (1967) reported that rural Kentuckians engaged in more informal visiting than the urban elderly, were more likely to know people within the community, and identified a larger number of persons as close friends. McKain observed that withdrawal from work roles in rural areas involved less change in interaction patterns than in urban areas. That is, with severence from the work role, older urban men were less likely to have continuing contact with friends than rural men.

The fact that income is lower and transportation less available among older rural adults has important implications for rural–urban differences in informal interactions. Not only is an adequate income associated with maintaining many social relations, but transportation must also be available for continued interaction. The extent to which rural and urban areas differ in age density, social class, and ethnicity are also important to informal networks. In areas where there are high concentrations of older adults (such as frequently observed in rural areas), more interaction will occur. This interaction will increase among members of similar ethnic and socioeconomic groups. Research on both the rural and urban elderly demonstrates that the number of friends and frequency of contact will increase with social class and will be higher in ethnically homogeneous areas (Graham, 1979; Reisman, 1979; Rosow, 1967).

Significant changes during the 1970s such as faster growth among rural and small-town areas than urban areas, greater population increases in open-country rural counties than in adjacent urban areas, and nonmetropolitan industrial growth (Dillman & Hobbs, 1982) have had important implications for both rural and urban older adults and their social networks. As pointed out earlier, the age structures of communities may be altered in ways that either limit or increase social opportunities for peer relationships. The inmigration of elders of varying socioeconomic status, ethnicity, and orientation to leisure holds the potential to effect negatively the established friendship patterns and participation in community associations. On the other hand, concentrations of older individuals of similar age and status may increase social activity. Elderly outmigration may have considerable negative impact on the remaining older residents through disrupted or terminated friendships. The current migration stream of older adults to rural areas may be sufficiently large to stimulate the attention of policymakers to the special needs of older rural adults (Glasgow, 1980). Included here are improved transportation and increased opportunities to enlarge informal social networks.

The Rural Elderly and Informal Networks

Informal social participation assumes added significance among older adults in rural areas because of the sometimes limited avenues of social expression that are available to them (McKain, 1967). Continuing contact with friends and neighbors in rural areas is also of considerable instrumental value. Friends and neighbors may be a major source of transportation or a resource in a medical or other emergency. Futhermore, visiting with friends and neighbors may enable older rural adults to share pleasant moments and to keep alive their current interests; it also has the important function of reinforcing older adults' roles in the community (McKain, 1967).

The majority of the rural elderly have been found to have moderate to high friend-neighbor contact, possibly because of high age densities. Schooler (1975) observed that among a national sample of older rural adults, 47 percent showed "high neighbor contact." Britton and Britton (1972), in a study of older northern rural adults, found that the majority of the sample reported having 10 or more friends. Kivett and Scott (1979) reported that 71 percent of a representative sample of southern rural adults 65 years or older had either occasional or frequent visits with friends and neighbors, approximately 29 percent seldom or never visited; and over 40 percent talked on the phone at least once daily to friends or family. Scott (1981) also found relatively high levels of contact among older rural adults. She reported that 56 percent of older Texans frequently visited with friends and neighbors, 26 percent visited occasionally, 15 percent seldom visited, and only 3 percent never visited. These data were compatible with the earlier report by McKain (1967), which noted that approximately 60 percent of a sample of older rural Kentuckians had either frequent or occasional visiting with friends and neighbors.

Relationships have been observed between participation in groups and frequency of interaction in informal networks. Kivett and Scott (1979) found that the extent to which older rural people are engaged in formal organizations such as clubs and churches is positively related to the frequency of their informal social involvement. Similarly, McKain (1967) observed an association between declines in interests in formal associations in the community and opportunities for informal social participation.

Factors Influencing the Informal Relationships of Older Rural Adults

A number of factors may affect the extent to which the rural elderly interact with friends and neighbors. The most obvious of these are the density of older people in the area and the extent of spatial isolation. Dispersed populations and low population density can affect opportunities for social interaction in some geographical areas. Where the outmigration of the young from rural areas has left high ratios of older adults, the availability of peers for interaction is high. If, however, neighbors and friends are not in close proximity, there is low population density, health is poor, and transportation is limited or unavailable, isolation may become a severe problem.

The friendship networks of the rural elderly are based strongly on their length of residence in the area, the stability of the neighborhood and its social homogeneity, and the extent to which family and friends have remained in the area or are still living (Powers et al., 1975). Relatively high degrees of homogeneity and low residential mobility in rural areas foster long-term, reciprocal relationships. Although few studies have been conducted on the importance of social class to the informal relationships of older rural adults, urban findings may be of some applicability. Urban studies have indicated, for example, that among the working class the role of neighbor becomes more salient after retirement. Patterns of friendship in the neighborhood also become closely linked to class-related factors in the community such as income, occupational background, and race (Rosenburg, 1976). With the increasing infirmity and loss of resources of older rural adults, the neighborhood becomes even more important to informal networks.

In many cases, the friendships of older adults in rural areas are found to be aged-graded; i.e., similar age groups interact (Powers et al., 1975; Rosow, 1967). Age grading in friendship and neighboring appear to be related to age density rather than to a conflict between generations. The importance of age density to friendship is greater among women because of the proportionally larger numbers of females who are relatively immobile due to older ages and limited physical and economic resources.

In summary, limited information on the informal network of older rural adults shows relatively high levels of friend-neighbor contact. This level of interaction, however, is lower than in earlier adulthood. Informal interaction appears to be more frequent than participation in organized groups. Much information on the factors influencing the rural elderly's interaction with friends and neighbors must be generalized from urban studies. This information suggests that where there is a high density of older adults (a characteristic generally associated with rural areas), more informal interaction will occur among age peers. The low residential mobility and relative homogeneity of most rural areas probably contribute to a stronger informal network among the rural than the urban elderly. On the other hand, restricted resources such as low incomes, poor health, and inadequate transportation may be potentially greater inhibitors to social interaction of rural than urban adults.

The continuing migration of the metropolitan elderly to rural areas will have important implications for the informal networks of both rural and urban elderly, especially as it affects age and sex distributions, population density, and social and ethnic homogeneity. The overall effect of these shifts may be to cause increasing similarity in the social networks of older rural and urban adults.

The Importance of Social Interaction to Psychological Well-Being

Both disengagement theory and activity theory have stimulated considerable research on the relationship between the degree of social involvement and psychological well-being. These studies have used a wide variety of measures of activity and well-being as well as populations. Although findings vary (Lee & Lassey, 1980), there probably is more evidence to support than to refute the existence of a positive association between psychological well-being and level of activity. Larson (1978), in a comprehensive review of the literature on subjective well-being, found the range of correlations to be from low to moderate ($r = .10$ to .30). Larson's review showed that while the positive relationship is clear for general indices of social activity, the results for more specific measures are less consistent. The review also indicated that some relationships between activity and well-being are not as salient for persons with higher status and good health.

Findings on the relationship of social interaction to well-being vary according to the type of social activity. There appears to be more evidence of a relationship between subjective well-being and *informal* social activity than formal activity. Several studies have shown a significant positive association between the life satisfaction of the elderly and the frequency of their nonfamilial social participation such as visiting in the homes of friends and neighbors (Edwards & Klemmack, 1973; Lemon, Bengtson, & Peterson, 1972; Pihlblad & Adams, 1972; Smith & Lipman, 1972). Lemon et al. (1972), from observations of a representative group of retirement-home dwellers, reported that only interaction with friends (from among several types of activities) was significantly related to life satisfaction.

It has been suggested that *perceived* adequacy of interaction may be an important mediator between level of social activity and emotional well-being. From a study of older rural adults, Heltsley and Powers (1975) concluded that regardless of the amount of interaction of the elderly with their children and others, satisfaction with the interaction may not be achieved. This they attributed to the tendency of the elderly to perceive current interactions relative to (1) the level of interaction achieved in earlier life, (2) the amount of time currently available for interaction, and (3) the decreasing number of opportunities for interaction.

Most studies have reported little or no difference in the well-being of urban and rural adults (Bull & Aucoin, 1975; Cavan, Burgess, Havighurst, & Goldhamer, 1949; Harris and Associates, 1975; Sauer, Shehan, & Boymel, 1976). Two studies, however, report higher well-being among the rural elderly (Donnenwerth, Guy, & Norvell, 1978; Hynson & Lawrence, 1975), whereas Schooler (1975) found the rural elderly to have lower morale and to feel more alienated than older urban adults. Important rural–urban differences have been noted in the relationship of social activity to subjective well-being. The life satisfaction of rural and small-town groups has been found to increase with group participation, especially church activity and club participation (Edwards & Klemmack, 1973; Palmore & Luikart, 1972; Pihlblad & Adams, 1972; Pihlblad & McNamara, 1965). In general, no relationship is found between group participation and subjective well-being among the urban elderly (Bull & Aucoin, 1975; Cutler, 1973; Lemon et al., 1972).

The Rural Elderly and Correlates of Social Activity

Work by Kivett (1979) and Kivett and Scott (1979) has reported two additional dimensions of well-being, loneliness and morale, to be related to formal social activity among the rural elderly. Older adults who had low levels of participation in organized social activities were high risks for loneliness. With respect to morale, the frequency of organized social activity was fourth in importance in a set of predictors following health, perceived adequacy of income, and adequacy of hearing. Morale increased with the number of times per month that older rural adults participated in group activities. Other information from the same data set, however, indicated no relationship between life satisfaction and activity in organizations. The greater specificity of the variables of loneliness and morale, as contrasted with the more abstract concept of life satisfaction, may account for this discrepancy, although this interpretation is contrary to that by Larson (1978). In another investigation with rural widows, Kivett (1978) reported that the level of loneliness decreased significantly with more frequent interaction.

The magnitude of the relationship between social interaction and subjective well-being varies greatly according to the specificity of the dimension of well-being that is measured and the group that is observed. Interactions with friends and neighbors appear to be more important in determining the subjective well-being of the elderly than participation in organized groups. There are few data available, however, on urban–rural differences in importance of the type of social activity. Available information suggests that participation in formal organizations may be more salient to the wellbeing of the rural than of the urban elderly. Explanations for these rural–urban differences are unclear. It is plausible that because of fewer resources and opportunities for leisure-time pursuits, participation in groups may take on more meaning among the rural elderly. It may also be that when the rural elderly choose to join groups, those groups become more meaningful.

Current Research Priorities in Non-Kin Community Relations

Perhaps in no other area of rural gerontology is the need for research as great as in the area of non-kin relationships. A review of existing research suggests the following five major needs: (1) basic information on informal and formal participation; (2) information on the factors associated with various types of social activity; (3) data on the quality of relationships and activities; (4) data on the relationship of social activity to subjective well-being; and (5) new and improved methodology,

Basic information on informal and formal participation among older rural adults is scant. Delineations between types of activities are unclear, and categories of activities are overlapping and poorly defined. There is a need for better conceptualization of organization types, i.e., reducing or factoring voluntary associations according to generic type. Problems in comparing studies are created by the diverse ways in which rates of participation are measured and activity indices constructed. These measurement weaknesses account, in part, for many of the discrepancies that are found between studies.

Scant information is available on the relative importance of different types of social activity in later adulthood. More information is needed on the friend and neighbor networks of both older rural and urban adults, the conditions under which such networks operate, and the interpersonal dynamics that sustain such relationships.

A second general research priority is the need for information on the factors associated with various social activities of the elderly, e.g., the extent to which sex and race are related to social interaction, the importance of age to social activity, and the extent to which social activity varies with geographical area. Information is lacking on the relationship between the extent to which there are class differences in interaction with friends and neighbors in rural areas. Many questions remain unanswered with regard to the effect of age-graded organizations on the level of participation of the rural elderly. Data are also lacking on the effects of age density on the formal and informal social activity of both rural and urban adults. A question seldom formally addressed through research is, to what extent does adherence to the Western work ethic still exist among the rural elderly and what is its impact on the quality of time freed through retirement?

Most of the research on social participation has dealt exclusively with the *frequency* of participation; therefore, a third research priority is the need for data on the *quality* of social interaction. Before this can take place, however, better quantitative methods must be developed. Few studies have addressed the distinctions between activities that are meaningful to the rural elderly and those that merely fill time. Questions dealing with the quality of social activity also need to speak to the importance of reciprocity in friendships and neighboring.

The fourth area in which more research is needed involves the relationship between subjective well-being and social activity. What types of activity contribute to the psychological well-being of older rural adults? In particular, why are certain types of participation more strongly related to the psychological well-being of the rural than the urban elderly?

Finally, a number of research needs in the area of social activity relate to methodological issues, including the need for longitudinal research to show trends in social activity over the life cycle. There is also a continuing need for more multivariate studies in the area of social activity and well-being. In particular, more information is needed on the direct as well as the indirect effects of numerous demographic and social factors on social activity.

In conclusion, information on the non-kin relations of older rural adults is limited and characterized by contradictory findings. A portion of this difficulty stems from the poor conceptualization and measurement of activity variables in previous research. A significant void in the literature is the relative lack of research comparing the social activity of the rural elderly to that of urban populations. Such comparisons would point to the unique situations and problems of the rural elderly and might suggest directions that could be followed in strengthening their social networks. Increased knowledge in the area of non-kin networks of the rural elderly will help assure that support groups are strengthened and opportunities for social involvement expanded.

References

Adams, D.L. Who are the rural aged? In R.C. Atchley, T.O. Byerts, & M. Arch (Eds.), *Rural environments and aging*. Washington, D.C.: The Gerontological Society, 1975, pp. 11–25.

Babchuk, N., Peters, G.R., Hoyt, D.R., & Kaiser, M. The voluntary associations of the aged. *Journal of Gerontology*, 1979, *34*, 579–587.

Bauder, W., & Doerflinger, J. Work roles among the rural aged. In E.G. Youmans (Ed.), *Older rural Americans*. Lexington, Ky: University of Kentucky Press, 1967, pp. 22–43.

Berghorn, F.J., Schafer, D.E., & Steere, G.H. *The urban elderly: A study of life satisfaction*. Montclair, N.J.: Allanheld and Osmun, 1978.

Bild, B.R., & Havighurst, R.J. Senior citizens in great cities. *The Gerontologist*, 1976, *16*, 63–69.

Blalock, T.C. Statement before U.S. House of Representatives Subcommittee on Human Resources During Oversight Hearings on Older Americans' Program. Raleigh, N.C.: McKimmon Center, North Carolina State University, 1979.

Britton, J.H., & Britton, J.O. *Personality changes in aging*. New York: Springer Publishing Company, 1972.

Bull, C.N., & Aucoin, J.B. Voluntary association participation and life satisfaction: A replication note. *Journal of Gerontology*, 1975, *30*, 73–76.

Cavan, R., Burgess, S., Havighurst, R.J., & Goldhamer, H. *Personal adjustment in old age*. Chicago: Science Research Associates, 1949.

Clemente, F., Rexroad, P.A., & Hirsch, C. The participation of the black aged in voluntary associations. *Journal of Gerontology*, 1975, *30*, 469–472.

Coward, R.T. Greater awareness: Extension's key to program success. *Journal of Extension*, 1978, *16*, 11–17.

Coward, R.T. Planning community services for the rural elderly: Implications from research. *The Gerontologist*, 1979, *19*, 275–282.

Cutler, S.J. Voluntary associations participation and life satisfaction: A cautionary research note. *Journal of Gerontology*, 1973, *28*, 96–100.

Cutler, S.J. Membership in different types of voluntary associations and psychological well-being. *The Gerontologist*, 1976, *16*, 335–339.

Cutler, S.J. Aging and voluntary association participation. *Journal of Gerontology*, 1977, *32*, 470–479.

Dillman, D.A., & Hobbs, D.J. (Eds.) *Rural society in the U.S.: Issues for the 1980s*. Boulder, Colo.: Westview Press, 1982.

Donnenwerth, G.V., Guy, R.F., & Norvell, M.J. Life satisfaction among older persons: Rural–urban and racial comparisons. *Social Science Quarterly*, 1978, *59*, 578–583.

Edwards, J.N., & Klemmack, D.L. Correlates of life satisfaction: A re-examination. *Journal of Gerontology*, 1973, *28*, 497–502.

Glasgow, N. The older metropolitan migrant as a factor in rural population growth. In A.J. Sofranko & J.D. Williams (Eds.), *Rebirth of rural America*. Ames, Iowa: North Central Regional Center for Rural Development, 1980, pp. 153–170.

Graham, A.A. *A sociology of friendship and kinship*. London, England: George Allen and Unwin Ltd., 1979.

Green Thumb, Inc. *Rural America: Coming of age*. Rural Mini-Conference Report, White House Conference on Aging. Washington, D.C.: Green Thumb, Inc., 1981.

Harbart, A.S., & Wilkinson, C.W. Growing old in rural America. *Aging*, 1979, Nos. 291–292 (Jan.–Feb.), 36–40.

Harris, L., and Associates. *The myth and reality of aging in America*. Washington, D.C.: The National Council on Aging, 1975.

Heltsley, M.E., & Powers, R.C. Social interaction and perceived adequacy of interaction of the rural aged. *The Gerontologist*, 1975, *15*, 533–536.

Hynson, L. M., Jr. Rural–urban differences in satisfaction among the elderly. *Rural Sociology*, 1975, *40*, 64–66.

Kivett, V.R. Loneliness and the rural widow. *Family Coordinator*, 1978, *27*, 389–394.

Kivett, V.R. Discriminators of loneliness among the rural elderly: Implications for intervention. *The Gerontologist*, 1979, *19*, 108–115.

Kivett, V.R., & Learner, R.M. Perspectives on the childless rural elderly: A comparative analysis. *The Gerontologist*, 1980, *20*, 708–716.

Kivett, V.R., & Scott, J.P. *The rural by-passed elderly: Perspectives on status and needs*. Raleigh: North Carolina Agricultural Research Service, Technical Bulletin No. 270, 1979.

Larson, R. Thirty years of research on the subjective well-being of older Americans. *Journal of Gerontology*, 1978, *33*, 109–125.

Lee, G.R., & Lassey, M.L. Rural–urban differences among the elderly:

Economic, social and subjective factors. *Journal of Social Issues*, 1980, *36*, 62–74.

Lemon, B.W., Bengtson, V.L., & Peterson, J.A. An exploration of the activity theory of aging: Activity types and life satisfaction among in-movers to a retirement community. *Journal of Gerontology*, 1972, *27*, 511–523.

Litwak, E., & Szelenyi, I. Primary group structures and their functions: Kin, neighbors, and friends. *American Sociological Review*, 1969, *34*, 465–481.

Loomis, C.P., & Beegle, J.A. *A strategy for rural change*. New York: Schenkman, 1975.

Lozier, J., & Althouse, R. Retirement to the porch in rural Appalachia. *International Journal of Aging and Human Development*, 1975, *6*, 7–15.

McKain, W.C. Community roles and activities of older rural persons. In E.G. Youmans (Ed.), *Older rural Americans*. Lexington: University of Kentucky Press, 1967, pp. 75–96.

National Council on the Aging. *NCOA public policy agenda, 1979–1980*. Washington, D.C.: National Council on the Aging, 1979.

National Strategy Conference on Improving Service Delivery to the Rural Elderly. *Improving services for the elderly*. Washington, D.C.: Farmers Home Administration, U.S. Department of Agriculture, 1979.

Palmore, E., & Luikart, C. Health and social factors related to life satisfaction. *Journal of Health and Social Behavior*, 1972, *13*, 68–80.

Payne, B. The older volunteer: Social role continuity and development. *The Gerontologist*, 1977, *17*, 355–361.

Pihlblad, C.T., & Adams, D.L. Widowhood, social participation and life satisfaction. *Aging and Human Development*, 1972, *3*, 323–330.

Pihlblad, C.T., & McNamara, R.L. Social adjustment of elderly people in three small towns. In A.M. Rose & W.A. Peterson (Eds.), *Older people and their social world*. Philadelphia: F.A. Davis, 1965, pp. 49–73.

Powers, E.A., Keith, P.M., & Goudy, W. Family relationships. In R.C. Atchley, T.O. Byerts, & M. Arch (Eds.), *Rural environments and aging*. Washington, D.C.: The Gerontological Society, 1975, pp. 67–90.

Reisman, J.M. *Anatomy of friendship*. New York: Irvington, 1979.

Riley, M.W., & Foner, A. *Aging and society. Volume one: An inventory of research findings*. New York: Russell Sage, 1968.

Rose, A.M. Perspectives of the rural aged. In E.G. Youmans (Ed.), *Older rural Americans*. Lexington: University of Kentucky Press, 1967, pp. 6–21.

Rosenburg, G.S. Age, poverty, and isolation from friends in the urban working class. In B.D. Bell (Ed.), *Contemporary social gerontology*. Springfield, Ill.: Charles C Thomas, 1976, pp. 247–255.

Rosow, I. *Social integration of the aged*. New York: The Free Press, 1967.

Sanders, I.T. *Rural society.* Englewood Cliffs, N.J.: Prentice-Hall, 1977.

Sauer, W.J., Shehan, C., & Boymel, C. Rural–urban differences in satisfaction among the elderly: A reconsideration. *Rural Sociology,* 1976, *41,* 269–275.

School of Agriculture and Life Sciences. *Annual Report.* Raleigh: North Carolina State University, 1981.

Schooler, K. A comparison of rural and non-rural elderly on selected variables. In R.C. Atchley, T.O. Byerts, & M. Arch (Eds.), *Rural environments and aging.* Washington, D.C.: Gerontological Society, 1975, pp. 27–42.

Scott, J.P. *Older rural adults: Perspectives on status and needs: A progress report.* Lubbock: Department of Home and Family Life, Texas Tech University, 1981.

Shanas, E., Townsend, P., Wedderburn, D., Friis, H., Milhoj, P., & Stehouwer, J. *Old people in three industrial societies.* New York: Atherton Press, 1968.

Smith, S.H. The older rural Negro. In E.G. Youmans (Ed.), *Older rural Americans.* Lexington: University of Kentucky Press, 1967, pp. 262–280.

Smith, K.J., & Lipman, A. Constraint and life satisfaction. *Journal of Gerontology,* 1972, *27,* 77–82.

Stubbs, A.C. *Use of leisure time: In middle years and anticipated use in older age.* College Station: Texas Agricultural Experiment Station, 1968.

U.S. Department of Agriculture. *National extension homemakers.* Washington, D.C.: 1981 (August).

White House Conference on Aging. *Executive summary of Technical Committee on Creating an Age Integrated Society: Implications for spiritual well-being.* Washington, D.C., 1981.(a)

White House Conference on Aging. Committees' Recommendations from the White House Conference on Aging. Washington, D.C., 1981.(b)

Youmans, E.G. Perspectives on the older American in a rural setting. In J.G. Cull & R.E. Hardy (Eds.), *The neglected older American.* Springfield, Ill.: Charles C Thomas, 1973, pp. 65–85.

Youmans, E.G. *Aging patterns in a rural and an urban area of Kentucky.* Lexington: Kentucky Agricultural Experiment Station, Bulletin No. 681, 1963.

Part III

Social Interventions and the Elderly in Rural Society

The chapters in this section assess the state of service delivery and the development of public policy for the rural elderly population. Each chapter points to the continuing need to consider the rural elderly population as more than an aggregate of individuals with somewhat distinctive collective characteristics. Researchers and practitioners need to take into account the special environmental and ecological conditions of rural areas and the ways in which these factors impede or, on rare occasions, facilitate social interventions to improve the quality of life of the rural elderly.

Coward and Rathbone-McCuan, in Chapter 9, assess the current state of knowledge regarding the development and delivery of human services to older rural residents. This assessment is multidimensional, convering issues relating to availability, accessibility, quality, utilization, and cost of service provision. These issues are, of course, interrelated. The authors demonstrate that existing data are insufficient to document the full extent of the rural deficit on each dimension. They also state that much of our "knowledge" in this area is actually based on presumption rather than data. For example, the widely held belief that the rural elderly are more resistant than others to accepting services provided by governmental units has not been sufficiently documented. Elderly people in general highly value their personal independence and auton- omy, and it has not been adequately established that this value is any less widespread or less firmly entrenched among the urban than the rural elderly. In the absence of such evidence, we should not make the mistake of attributing lower service utilization rates among the rural elderly to distinct cultural patterns or valuative predispositions antitheti- cal to such utilization. Instead, we need to direct attention at the interaction between individual characteristics, structural conditions, and environmental constraints.

Coward and Rathbone-McCuan also suggest a framework for developing and assessing services for the rural elderly premised on the assumption that, in many dimensions at least, the structure of service systems *should be different* in rural than urban areas. They argue that rural service delivery systems are often simply scaled-down versions of urban systems. But because of the distinctive features of the rural social and physical environments as well as the rural elderly population, very different strategies for solving problems and delivering services may be necessary in rural than in urban areas.

Watkins and Watkins continue this theme of distinctiveness in their discussion of the development of policy for the elderly in Chapter 10. They examine three central issues regarding social policy development: (1) whether policies should emphasize the provision and maintenance of adequate incomes or the creation and delivery of necessary services; (2) whether programs should be directed toward people with particular needs regardless of age or toward designated segments of the population, such as the elderly, which are likely to have many diverse needs; and (3) whether the fulfillment of needs is best accomplished through a competitive free-market system or through governmental programs. There are no easy solutions to any of these dilemmas; the issues are complex, and choices ultimately reflect gradations and combinations of options rather than dichotomous alternatives. The central message of the chapter, however, is that different policies may well be appropriate under different sets of contingencies, and rural residence poses a different set of contingencies than does urban residence. Policy options which may be perfectly viable in urban settings may be unworkable in rural areas, and vice versa.

Watkins and Watkins demonstrate clearly that the policy alternatives they examine, and the choices among them, are interdependent. They also illustrate that each option has advantages and disadvantages and that the mixture of benefits and costs pertaining to each option varies, slightly or radically, according to the residential environment in which the policy would be implemented. This suggests that policy formulation must be carried on in full recognition of the necessity for flexibility and a high level of abstraction. That is, policies which affect the elderly must be designed to encompass a diversity of needs and a diversity of methods through which these needs may be most effectively met. No single policy or programmatic strategy will succeed in meeting the needs of our heterogeneous elderly population unless this heterogeneity, in terms of both the characteristics of individuals and the characteristics of their environments, is an integral component of the social intervention.

9

Delivering Health and Human Services to the Elderly in Rural Society

Raymond T. Coward and Eloise Rathbone-McCuan

Amid debates about the magnitude and nature of differences in the needs of rural and urban elders, there appears to be consensus that the development and delivery of social services in small towns and rural communities has unique features that distinguish it from similar processes in large, urban centers (Bachrach, 1981; Cedar & Salasin, 1979; Coward & Smith, 1983; Farley, Griffiths, Skidmore, & Thackeray, 1982; Ginsberg, 1976; Johnson, 1980; Keller & Murray, 1982; Kim & Wilson, 1981; Wagenfeld, 1981). Although the exact nature of these uniquenesses have not always been well articulated (Albers & Thompson, 1980), both clinical and empirical evidence suggests that there are distinctive features about rural environments that influence the delivery of social services (Coward, DeWeaver, Schmidt, & Jackson, 1983).

In some aspects of life, data imply that the needs of the rural elderly may be greater than those of their urban counterparts—for example, see Chapter 3 for a description of the financial situations of the rural elderly or Chapter 6 for a discussion of their housing. In contrast, there are other aspects of life where the rural elderly are judged to be advantaged—specifically, repeated observations have documented that rural residents experience better environmental quality in regard to air, noise levels, and scenic beauty; that they are more satisfied with their communities; and that they perceive their neighborhoods as safer (Tremblay, Walker, & Dillman, 1983). In still other aspects of life, the needs of elders are exacerbated by their rural residence—for example, emergency care needs are compounded by the lesser training of the personnel that staff emergency vehicles in rural areas and the longer distances necessary to reach proper medical care (U.S. House of Representatives, 1979); and the reduced number of alternative housing arrangements for elders in rural areas may contribute to premature institutionalization (Greene, 1982). When rural elders do experience crises in their lives, there is sufficient evidence to predict that formal helping services will be less available and narrower in range (Nelson, 1980; New York State Senate Research Service, 1980; Taietz & Milton, 1979).

For decades it has been a fundamental principle of effective social service practice that programs should be congruent with the social environment and culture of the communities they purport to serve (Frank, 1973; Morris, 1982). Consequently, to design programs for the elderly that are consistent with the realities of their rural lifestyle, practitioners must be able to clarify those distinctive features of rural environments that impinge upon service development and delivery (Coward, 1979; Coward et al., 1983; Coward & Kerchkhoff, 1978). In recent years several authors have tried to illuminate and organize these characteristics. In preparing this chapter, our efforts have benefited from the earlier contributions of Bachrach (1981), Coward et al. (1983), Ecosometrics (1981), Flax, Wagenfeld, Ivens, and Weiss (1979), Jackson (1983), and Martinez-Brawley and Munson (1981).

We begin this chapter by reviewing rural–urban comparisons of community services for elders, directing particular attention to the issues of availability, accessibility, quality, utilization, and cost. We then examine a previously advanced organizational framework to determine its utility for considering the development of services for the rural elderly. We also analyze the degree of congruence between the educational preparation of providers and the realities and demands of rural service delivery. Finally, we identify critical topics that require further research and investigation.

Rural–Urban Comparisons of Current Services

Comparisons of this sort are not made easy by a wealth of appropriate data. Indeed, as is so often the situation when studying rural phenomena, generalizations are complicated by the lack of direct rural–urban comparative data in most studies, by serious methodological complications involving both definition and measurement, and by the diversity that exists between rural communities. Nevertheless, there are some studies which can be reviewed to shed light on the availability, accessibility, quality, utilization, and cost of health and human services for the rural elderly.

Availability

Investigations by Taietz and Milton (1979) and Nelson (1980) provide the best comparative perspectives on the availability of services to the elderly. The first study compared rural and urban counties in upstate New York. The data are particularly useful because they include a time element: inventories were completed on services in the *same* counties in 1967 and 1976. On the average, in both years the urban counties had significantly more services available for their elders than did the rural counties. Although the number of services in both rural and urban counties had increased dramatically by 1976, rural counties still lagged behind their urban counterparts in the average number of services available (see Table 9.1).

The authors had comparative data across time and residence on 25 specific services. Analysis of these data indicated that in 19 of the services the largest percentage increases between the two data points had occurred in the rural counties (see Table 9.2 for a list of the specific services compared by residence and time). For the most part, however, the enormous percentage increases registered by the rural counties were a function of the very small availability of services found in 1967 in those settings. In 1976, significant rural–urban discrepancies remained for certain services. For example, five of the services were more than twice as likely to be found in urban as compared to rural counties (special adult education courses, senior centers, preretirement courses, foster homes service for the

Table 9.1. Rural–Urban Comparisons of the Availability of Selected Services, 1967 and 1976

	Number of counties	Average number of services available	SD	t-value	P
1967					
Urban	16	7.9	4.9	4.34	0.0001
Rural	37	3.2	2.8		
1976					
Urban	16	27.9	4.3	3.54	0.0001
Rural	36	21.8	6.3		

Source: Taietz, P., and Milton, S. Rural–urban differences in the structure of services for the elderly in upstate New York counties. *Journal of Gerontology,* 1979,*34* (3), 429–437.

Table 9.2. Percentage Comparisons of the Availability of Services in Rural and Urban Counties in 1967 and 1976

Service	1967 Urban (n=16)	1967 Rural (n=37)	1976 Urban (n=16)	1976 Rural (n=36)	Percentage Increase Urban	Percentage Increase Rural
Visiting nurse	63	8	100	97	59	1113
Information and referral	44	17	100	97	127	471
Homemaker services	69	56	100	92	45	64
Reduced taxes	63	36	94	95	49	164
Home health aides	50	14	100	92	100	551
Meals-on-Wheels	19	3	94	86	395	2,767
Discount on general purchases	6	3	88	86	1,367	2,767
Escort service	6	8	100	78	1,567	875
Discount on medicines	25	0	94	75	276	0
Special library program	63	39	94	75	49	92
Home repair service	6	6	88	75	1,367	1,150
Discount on public events	63	11	88	69	40	527
Public housing for elderly	56	17	94	58	68	241
Shopping assistance	6	8	81	64	1,250	700
Friendly Visitor Service	50	28	88	53	76	89
Special adult education courses	50	17	100	47	100	176
Job training and placement	44	3	75	44	70	1,367
Sheltered workshop	19	3	75	44	295	1,367
Senior center	56	17	94	31	68	82
Discount on transportation	0	3	75	39	0	1,200
Special media features	19	11	69	33	263	200
Special outlets for sale of products	19	6	31	44	63	633
Vacation planning service	38	6	50	28	32	367
Preretirement courses	13	3	56	22	331	633
Foster home service for elderly	0	6	38	17	0	185

Source: Taietz, P., and Miller, S. Rural–urban differences in the structure of services for the elderly in upstate New York counties. *Journal of Gerontology,* 1979, 34 (3), 429–437.

elderly, and media features), whereas rural counties were only very slightly advantaged in regard to two services (reduced taxes and special outlets for sale of products). It is important to recognize that for six of the most prevalent elderly services, rural–urban differences by 1976 had been reduced to less than 10 percent (visiting nurse; information and referral; homemaker services, home services, and home health aides; Meals-on-Wheels; and discounts on general purchases). In a subsequent study, Taietz (1982) has replicated these results with data collected in California.

Nelson (1980) reported the results of a survey of a stratified national sample of Area Agencies on Aging (AAAs) classified as rural or urban as a function of the composition of their planning and service areas. His analysis indicated that urban agencies tended to have a larger number of services available—out of a possible 14 discrete services, the average number of services offered in rural areas was 4.7 as opposed to 6.1 for urban areas (see Table 9.3 for a list of the services and rural–urban comparisons). Furthermore, 40 percent of the rural agencies, as opposed to 14

Table 9.3. Rural–Urban Comparisons of Percentage of Area Agencies on Aging that Reported the Availability of Selected Services: Budget Year 1976–1977

Service	Percentage of rural area agencies (n=60)	Percentage of urban area agencies (n=77)
Day care	3	24
Counseling	16	21
Foster care	2	8
Health related	23	46
Homemaker/chore	50	72
Housing	36	42
Information and referral	85	94
Legal	31	51
Meals	34	51
Protective services	8	14
Recreational	40	52
Transportation	93	100
Residential care	4	5
Employment/education	28	28
Other[a]	14	13

[a] Unable to discriminate specific service types.
Source: Nelson, G. Social services to the urban and rural aged: The experience of Area Agencies on Aging. *The Gerontologist,* 1980, *20* (2), 200–207.

percent of the urban agencies, offered only between 1 and 3 services, whereas 39 percent of the urban and 23 percent of the rural
agencies had between 8 and 12 services available (see Table 9.4 for
more details).

The availability of services is influenced by a number of factors, not the least of which are the distribution of funds and professionals. Figure 9.1 presents an analysis prepared by the New York
State Senate Research Service (1980) that visually illustrates the
rural–urban discrepancies in the per capita expenditures, for the
elderly, of major federal grant programs. These inequities, as well
as those reported by others (Kivett & Learner, 1981; Parkinson,
1981), are inextricably linked to the availability of services. Similarly, the maldistribution of health and human service professionals in the United States has many direct and indirect effects on
service availability. The rural shortages involve many professions
that are essential to the development of a comprehensive system of
gerontological services. These include physicians, dentists, and
nurses (Ahearn, 1979); social workers (Munson, 1980); mental
health workers (Wagenfeld & Wagenfeld, 1981); psychiatrists
(National Institute of Mental Health, 1973); and psychologists
(Keller, Zimbleman, Murray, & Feil, 1980).

Accessibility

Although distance is a major determinant of accessibility, it is not
the only factor that must be entered into a formula predicting
access. Many service characteristics must be considered when judg-
ing the overall accessibility of a program to rural residents, e.g.,
knowledge of services, client eligibility, fiscal constraints, psychological constraints, and administrative practices (Ecosometrics,

Table 9.4. Rural–Urban Comparisons of Range of Services Available: Budget
Year 1976–1977

Number of services available	Percentage of rural area agencies ($n=60$)	Percentage of urban area agencies ($n=77$)
1–3	70	14
4–7	27	47
8–12	23	39

Source: Nelson, G. Social services to the urban and rural aged: The experience of Area
Agencies on Aging. *The Gerontologist,* 1980, *20* (2), 200–207.

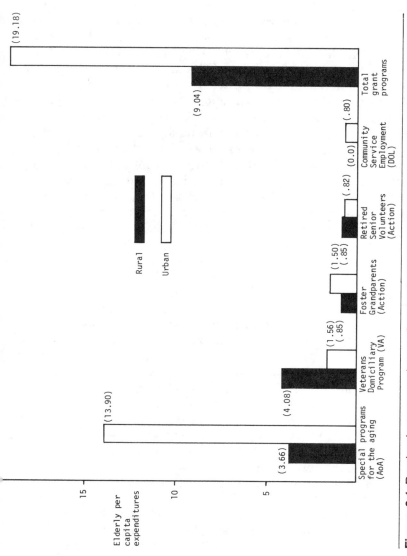

Figure 9.1 Rural–urban comparisons of major federal grant programs for the elderly: Outlays per elderly capita in FY 1976.

(*Source:* New York State Senate Research Service. *Old Age and Ruralism: A Case of Double Jeopardy—A Report on the Rural Elderly.* Albany, N.Y.: Senate Standing Committee on Aging, May 1980.)

1981). Nevertheless, Parkinson (1981) has noted that distance "represents the most formidable barrier to the development of programs for rural areas" and argued that it "complicates the delivery of every service, and often removes the rural elderly from life's basic necessities" (p. 227). In many rural areas, the effects of distance are compounded by harsh weather, poor road conditions, and the rising cost of fuel. Schooler (1975) reported that 82 percent of the rural elderly, as contrasted with 10 percent of the urban elderly, in a national sample perceived that they lived far from a core set of services. Ambrosius (1981) commented that in "a bureaucracy fueled by 'the numbers game' rural areas continue to be unduly penalized because of distance, terrain, and climatic factors" (p. 292).

The circumstances of rural elders without private transportation are made worse by the absence of public transportation in many small towns. Parkinson (1981) has stated that about 60 percent of rural areas with a population less than 2,500 have no taxi service. As a consequence, many rural social service programs must administer costly transportation services that consume human and fiscal resources.

Service Utilization

The rural elderly are often characterized as being resistant to formal services. They are portrayed as independent, self-reliant, and unwilling to participate in programs of social welfare. Traditional wisdom of this type, however, must be tempered by reality. First, we must remember that formal services are deemed the last resort by most elders—black or white, rich or poor, urban or rural. The majority of elders would prefer not to be dependent on others. When they are unable to maintain independence, most would first choose to receive assistance from their personal social network of family and friends (Cantor, 1977). Such attitudes are not unique or peculiar to the rural elderly.

Are these attitudes of self-reliance more prevalent or stronger among the rural elderly? Empirical data on this are equivocal and suffer from severe methodological problems including the lack of comparative rural and urban samples and inadequate controls for need (e.g., health status or mobility) or personal characteristics (e.g., income or family status). Futhermore, the acceptability of a service by rural elders is influenced by both the type of service that is being offered and the person or group that is sponsoring and delivering the service (Coward, 1980).

It would be a mistake to suggest that differences in receptivity are the only source of variation in service utilization patterns. To the extent that such attitudinal differences exist, they interact with contextual variables like availability and accessibility. Service providers must be aware of these potential psychological constraints; however, attempts to increase service utilization by those in need will require programs to simultaneously confront a number of other factors.

For example, another factor that contributes to utilization is knowledge of services. As most often conceptualized, the knowledge-of-services variable includes more than just the mere awareness that a service exists. Rather, it refers to accurate information on program characteristics such as location, purpose, hours of operation, eligibility, and fees. Fowler (1970) proposed that this variable was the most significant factor in predicting the underutilization of services.

Recognizing the importance of knowledge about services, the Older Americans Act, since 1973, has required that AAAs provide for information and referral services (I&R) to enhance the matching of client needs with available services. Even with the wide variability of services and strategies that exist within the I&R category, there appear to be some rural–urban differences. For example, Ecosometrics (1981) concluded that "while I&R services are generally available, rural communities are relatively underserved" (p. 205). They found that smaller towns tended to have fewer specialized referral systems and were less likely to have staff assigned exclusively to this task. Nelson (1980) presented evidence from his national survey of AAAs that was consistent with this interpretation—in 1976, 94 percent of the urban agencies, compared to 85 percent of the rural, funded I&R services, although this was the second smallest rural–urban difference in the availability of services that was reported by the author (see Table 9.3 for details). In addition to a somewhat lesser availability, rural environments contain unique obstacles to the delivery of I&R services: poorer telephone communication systems, larger service areas sometimes requiring toll calls for access, and higher percentages of households without phones. Collectively, these unique problems of delivering I&R services combined with a somewhat smaller availability may hamper the widespread knowledge among rural residents of the services that are available and, thus, negatively affect the patterns of utilization.

Quality of Services

To our knowledge, comparative information relevant to this issue is almost nonexistent. The attention to the special life circumstances of *rural* elders is relatively recent (see Chapter 1). To this point, most investigations of services for rural elders have focused on their distribution, accessibility, and utilization. Detailed assessments of the *quality* of rural programming are lacking and represent a significant gap in the available knowledge.

Some indirect indicators of quality, however, can be examined. For example, there are some who insist that a quality social service system for elders requires that a continuum of care be available. From this perspective, rural environments appear to be at a distinct disadvantage with regard to quality. Nelson (1980) reported that more than one-third of the rural AAAs in his sample (34%) lacked any of the services directed primarily to the frail or otherwise at-risk aged (e.g., day care, homemaker/chore services, protective services, health screening, or foster care). Similarly, Greene (1982) has argued that the lack of alternative-care settings in rural areas has forced elders living in those communities into nursing homes at earlier ages and with less disability. Although these studies do not offer direct comparisons of the quality of services delivered in rural versus urban environments, they indicate that as a consequence of the narrower range of services and alternatives that are available, rural environments find it difficult to create a quality community system of services that is defined as the availability of a full range of care settings.

The importance of information and referral services to enhancing the knowledge of services among elders was described in a previous section. Some uniquely rural features, however, threaten the quality and effectiveness of such services as they are traditionally structured: the often poorly functioning phone system of rural areas (New York State Senate Research Service, 1980); the higher percentages of rural elderly households without telephones—12.7 percent compared to 6.9 percent (Bylund, LeRay, & Crawford, 1980); and the large geographical size of rural service areas which often necessitates a toll call (New York State Senate Research Service, 1980).

Although comparative studies of the quality of specific services are infrequent, there are reasons to be concerned. For example, if the per capita amount of program dollars spent in rural areas is less, if the number of health and human service professionals is fewer in rural areas, if the recruitment and retention of professionals is more difficult in rural areas, if program models are urban biased and thus inappropriate in important ways for rural areas, if certain critical services are nonexistent or difficult to access, and if distance and transportation are barriers to service delivery, then the quality of services offered to the rural elderly may need to be scrutinized closely. These are, needless to say, a lot of "ifs"—but when taken collectively, they are sufficient to warrant concern about the overall quality of rural programming.

Costs

It has been argued that the lack of economies of scale in rural areas causes higher costs for services (Kranzel, 1980). This principle states that lower per unit costs can be achieved when program expenditures can be spread across the maximum number of clients who can be served efficiently and effectively. In rural areas, this maximum efficiency is seldom achieved because of the smaller population base. Thus, a home chore service that might function most efficiently and effectively with 20 clients may not be able to identify that many elders who need the service in a small town. Nevertheless, certain fixed expenditures must be recouped. Third-party reimbursement rates are often not adjusted to match these service-delivery cost differentials. The result is a higher cost per unit of service that is transferred to the client or absorbed by the agency as a deficit.

There are few studies that have made direct comparisons between rural and urban costs of services for the elderly, and the results of those analyses that are available are equivocal. Ecosometrics (1981) reviewed six unpublished analyses of costs and reported that three studies indicated higher costs in rural areas for certain services (homemaker and home health, nutrition, recreational, education, employment, and chore), whereas three other studies, sometimes focused on similar services (nutrition) but other times not (transportation), indicated lower costs in rural areas. In still further contrast, Hu (1981) compared the marginal costs of delivering nine different services in urban and rural areas of Pennsylvania and concluded that there were no significant differences (he compared the following services: counseling, home delivered meals, homemaker and health aides, legal aid, diagnostic services, transportation, life skills education, group dining, and social recreation). He maintained that possible differences in total costs "will be in the amount of utilization of social services between the urban elderly and the rural elderly" (p. 13).

These inconsistent findings are difficult to integrate. Indeed, after a comprehensive review of the literature, Ecosometrics (1981) concluded that it was impossible to reach definitive conclusions about the magnitude of rural as compared to urban costs. They determined that accurate comparisons were hampered by the following shortcomings in the literature: (1) the service costs used in analyses were not from the same years; (2) the reports contained varying definitions for the services provided; (3) the measures of units of service were inconsistent; (4) the reports were often unclear as to what expenditures were included in the service unit; and (5) it was impossible to control for local service quality specifications. Nevertheless, Ecosometrics (1981) concluded that:

> it appears that the cost to produce a basic unit of service (e.g., an hour of nursing staff time) is greater in urban areas than in rural areas. However, the cost of a unit of service actually utilized or consumed by the elderly (e.g., one elderly person utilizing nursing services) is greater in rural areas. Those services which have units of service which are production measures (e.g., Homemaker-staff hours) appear to have higher unit costs in urban areas. Those services for which we have units of service which are consumption measures (e.g., Social Services—persons served) have unit costs which are higher in rural areas or which are approximately equal. (p. 253)

The confusion caused by our inability to answer this seemingly simple, straightforward question—is there a difference in cost in delivering services to rural and urban environments?—is symptomatic of the disarray that exists in our knowledge of services for the rural elderly. The answer to this question has serious policy implications (funding formulas based on head counts, for example, ignore such residential variations in cost if they exist); yet a well designed, comprehensive program of research would have to be implemented in order to alleviate the methodological problems cited above.

A Framework for Developing Services for Rural Elders

Many authors have advanced the notion that delivering services in small-town, rural America differs significantly from practices in urban environments (Bachrach, 1981; Cedar & Salasin, 1979; Coward & Smith, 1983; Ginsberg, 1976; Johnson, 1980; Keller & Murray, 1982; Kim & Wilson, 1981; Wagenfeld, 1981). These con-

clusions are based primarily on personal experiences, on-site observations, and logical deductions rather than on the comparison of
systematically collected data. Indeed, in a study where data were
collected in a comparative, orderly design, Fitzpatrick, Edwards,
and Olszewski (1981) uncovered some substantial *similarities* between rural and urban practice. From interviews of providers in
county departments of social services across the state of New York
(n = 137), the authors reported few differences between rural and
urban workers in the frequency with which they performed job tasks
in three categories (i.e., case management, special client and inter-
viewing tasks, and generic work tasks); their perceptions of the
importance of these tasks; or their perceptions of the degree to
which training on the task would enhance their job performance.
Yet despite these findings, the authors would not dismiss fully the
hypothesis of rural–urban practice differences; rather they commented that "variation may occur in the *means* by which these tasks
are performed" (p. 43). Similarly, amid emerging data identifying
similarities between rural and urban practice, Ginsberg (1981) has
argued that rural providers *should* be behaving differently. He has
accused common funding sources of obscuring the differences that
should exist. He cautioned that "rural communities, which have
fewer resources, fewer agencies, and significant numbers of unmet
needs, require something more than the direct, specific services required of rural workers" (p. 15).

There is another way of approaching this issue. Rather than
attempting to document whether or not current rural and urban
providers function differently, Coward et al. (1983) have identified
"marked differences in the physical and social environment between rural and urban communities" that should lead to service
providers adopting "different practices and strategies for intervention" (p. 1). Although the framework was presented in the context
of mental health practice, its relevance to geriatric services is
easily apprehended.

Coward et al. (1983) identified three major categories under
which the distinctive features of rural environments could be organized (see Figure 9.2 for the original framework): (1) distinctive
features of rural client populations; (2) distinctive features of rural
social and physical environments; and (3) distinctive features of
the provision of rural services. While all categorization schemes
suffer from some degree of arbitrariness, a strength of this frame of
reference is its simple, straightforward organization, the implications of which may be easily translated into practice terms.

Figure 9.2 Distinctive features of rural environments: A frame of reference for mental health practice.

(*Source:* Coward, R.T., DeWeaver, K.L., Schmidt, F.E., and Jackson, R.W. Mental health practice in rural environments: A frame of reference. *International Journal of Mental Health,* 1983, *12* (1–2), 3–24.)

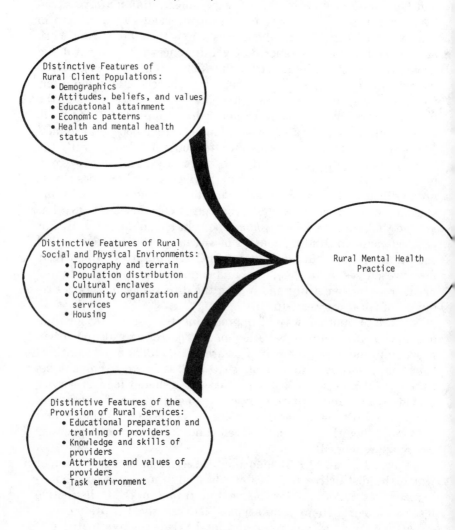

Throughout this collection readers have uncovered examples of differences in the first category of the framework—the *rural elderly client population*. In particular, the opening chapters of the book have reviewed differences in basic demographics, lifestyles, income, attitudes, and health and, thus, represent sufficient evidence that rural elders differ significantly from their urban counterparts. Yet these differences are infrequently used as a base for designing uniquely rural delivery systems. Rather, more often than not rural program designs are little more than scaled-down versions of big-city programs.

With regard to gerontological services, the remaining two categories in the framework—rural social and physical environments and the provision of rural services—share much in common with the literature reviewed in the original Coward et al. (1983) article, although some uniquenesses do exist. For example, within the social and physical environment, the rural–urban housing differences discussed in the original article may be exacerbated for the elderly (see Chapter 6 of this collection) because features of the physical dwelling are so intimately entwined with the ability of older people to maintain their independent living status. Similarly, within the category of rural service provision, the discussion of task environment (the intraorganizational and interorganizational context in which services are developed and delivered) may be particularly relevant to gerontologists. Sauer (1983) has speculated, for example, that whereas urban AAAs most often contract with other agencies for the delivery of services (providing an overall coordinating or watchdog function), rural agencies, because of the frequent absence of other agencies with which to contract, are more apt to end up actually delivering services.

The identification of those distinctive features of aging in rural environments that influence the delivery of social services, using either the organizational framework advanced by Coward et al. (1983) or another appropriate schema, would permit future research, theory building, training, and practice for rural gerontologists to proceed from a common referent. These distinctive features, when fully understood and appreciated by both policymakers and providers, would necessitate the creation of program development and delivery strategies that differ from traditional urban practices. The substantially disadvantaged state of rural services described earlier in this chapter in terms of availability, accessibility, utilization, and quality has resulted, in part, from

the abject failure of the American health and human service bureaucracy to comprehend the distinct and unique features of rural
systems.

The Training of Rural Gerontologists

For many programs, training for nonmetropolitan social service
practice includes little beyond a practicum in a rural environment.
Certainly such on-site experiences are invaluable in exposing students to the unique features of rural practice. Although practicums
are a necessary component of training, however, they are not a
sufficient technique, in and of themselves, for properly preparing
rural service providers. Preservice programs must modify class-
room experiences as well as field experiences to prepare gerontologists for rural practice. To accomplish this, however, will require
that the knowledge and skill base that underlies this specialization
be identified.

Kim (1980) has described an educational model for a specialization in rural gerontology that included "independent courses (both
basic and specialized) on rural social gerontology as well as specific
disciplinary courses in health, government and politics, mental
health, law, family relationships, and other subjects, as these might
relate to the special rural context" (p. 393). In a similar manner, the
Task Panel on Rural Mental Health (1978) has argued that an effective training program would include a supervised field experience in
a rural setting, coursework in the sociology of rural life, competence
in teamwork and collaboration with other human service programs,
program evaluation and other techniques of research, and proficiency in program administration. Bachrach (1981) proposed a five-
part taxonomy describing the factors that affect the delivery of human services to rural people: (2) nonsocial factors, (1) demographic
and ecological factors, (3) socioeconomic factors, (4) interpersonal
factors, and (5) ideological factors. In her judgment it is these ingre-
dients that would form the core of the knowledge base that would
adequately prepare rural practitioners. Martinez-Brawley (1980)
has emphasized the importance of knowledge from allied disciplines
for the preservice training of rural practitioners. Specifically, she
mentioned rural economics, rural politics and community organization, regional planning, and rural employment patterns. Munson
(1980) has echoed this need and mentioned the rural literature in
related disciplines such as history, political science, geography, eco-

nomics, and especially sociology. Currently there are at least three conceptual frameworks in the literature that could serve as the underpinnings of a training program for rural gerontologists— Bachrach (1981), Coward et al. (1983), and Martinez-Brawley and Munson (1981).

In addition to those authors who have attempted to define the knowledge base that should form the foundation for rural service delivery, others have endeavored to identify those skills associated with successful rural practice (Ginsberg, 1982; Johnson, 1977; Nooe, 1980; Southern Regional Education Board, 1976; Walsh, 1981; Wodarski, Giordano, & Bagarozzi, 1981). In this regard, a wide range of skills has been suggested: the ability to work with, and relate to, other disciplines and agencies; special skills in analyzing the rural community with respect to needs; knowledge of community power structures; the competence both to provide direct services and to perform administrative tasks; clinical styles that reflect authenticity and attention to the subtleties of hierarchy in the treatment relationships; and the capacity to implement a range of practice intervention modalities. Unfortunately, there is a severe absence of empirical verification for any of these assertions. The rigorous, comparative research which would define the "skills, attitudes and knowledge that facilitate the success of human service practitioners in rural areas" (Coward & Smith, 1982, p. 83) is lacking. Indeed, it is probably not a unique set of skills that are necessary for rural practice. Rather, the relative importance of different skills probably varies according to whether services are being provided in a rural or an urban location (Coward et al., 1983).

The absence of uniquely rural social service delivery models is another factor that has been accused of hampering the training of rural providers (Cedar & Salasin, 1979; Jackson, 1983). Most traditional and contemporary service delivery strategies have emerged from urban professionals analyzing urban problems and promoting solutions congruent with urban realities. As a consequence, rural practitioners have often been frustrated in their attempts to adapt or modify these service models to the distinctive circumstances of rural communities. "Aspects of program development that [were] of little concern when developing models for urban areas suddenly [become] major obstacles to rural implementation" (Coward, 1979, p. 276). In recent years, however, as increasing attention has been focused on the special problems of rural environments, some distinctly rural human service delivery models have emerged and have been discussed in the literature (Coward, 1983)—e.g., circuit riders, satellite programs, and resident generalists. As more service delivery models emerge that are designed exclusively for rural environments and that reflect the distinctive features of rural practice, training programs will no longer be limited by the urban bias of current strategies.

Finally, rural preservice programs have been hampered by an inability to define the proper mixture between training generalists and specialists. Bachrach (1981) and Ginsberg (1982) have argued that the effective rural practitioner must be able to cope with a wide range of problems, service needs, and circumstances. From this perspective, rural service providers are seen as fulfilling "many demands for a wide range of both of direct and indirect services to individuals and the community" (Hargrove, 1982, p. 173). These transcend several territorial lines—e.g., working at both the micro and the macro levels of service; providing help that exceeds the narrow mandates of legislation; and crossing restrictive, traditional professional boundaries. In contrast, another group of educators has blamed the generalist approach for a number of shortcomings of the current rural social service system (Jackson, 1983; Nooe, 1980). They stress that rural residents would be better served by a system that encouraged specialization. Recently a compromise approach has been described by Irey (1980), who proposed a generalist who had specialized skills. Nevertheless, this remains a critical dilemma for programs of rural gerontology. Sufficient in-depth, specialized training must be acquired so that the provider can work effectively; yet it is rather easy to predict that the work of community-based rural gerontologists will range at least over the issues of housing, health care, social adjustment, transportation, nutrition, taxes, income, and insurance.

Despite the considerable ambiguity and uncertainty about the specifics of a training program, it is probably safe to argue that health and human service professionals interested in working with rural elders must become aware of the rapidly expanding informational base in two areas: (1) the special life circumstances elders in rural society, and (2) the distinctive features of developing and delivering health and human services in rural environments. It appears to us that collectively, these two fields of enquiry create a sufficient knowledge base upon which a specialization in rural gerontology can be constructed.

Future Research

Rural human services delivery may have reached a productive and creative peak during the decade of the 1970s when rural priorities were a popular and prevalent national theme. It was an era when significant research funding was designated for rural projects (see Chapter 1 for more details). However, this favored status was short-lived. Specific rural gerontology research has suffered, along with other special populations, from reduced funding. Many well conceptualized research projects were left vulnerable by the shift away from rural priorities that occurred when the new federal administration took office. These shifts in priority have also had an impact on those national organizations that were dedicated to rural issues (Sleeper, 1981). Currently, those groups are less active in stimulating the interests of social scientists in rural questions, devote less attention to integrating and coordinating overlapping research projects, and spend fewer resources communicating the results of rural-oriented research to policymakers as part of their social advocacy and policy formulation functions.

For researchers interested in rural gerontological services, the challenge of the immediate future is to ensure that the present lack of funding and general deemphasis of rural problems becomes a "productive" lull. It may be, for example, an ideal time for researchers to reexamine existing data sets that have not previously been fully analyzed or presented in published form. More importantly, it may be a period when researchers elect to reevaluate the existing theoretical frameworks that form the foundations of rural studies, review the relevance of past research efforts and concentrations, or explore alternative designs and data collection strategies. A period of reflection, reevaluation, and intellectual innovation would have a positive impact on the future of research in this area of study.

Numerous critical research questions remain inadequately addressed or ignored. Some of the issues which most directly impinge on the delivery of services to the rural elderly include (1) determining the differential costs of rural service provision, (2) identifying the unique features of rural service provision, (3) examining the appropriateness of service utilization concepts for rural patterns, (4) exploring the quality of services delivered to rural elders, and (5) verifying strategies for the continued expansion and improvement of services. In the text below, each of these issues is briefly reviewed.

Research into the differential costs of rural and urban service provision is difficult to complete because of the ever-present problems of data availability and relevance. In the past, rural service delivery agencies have often lacked the resources (specifically knowledge and staff) to collect extensive and carefully monitored service cost information and, thus, researchers have expressed reservations about the use of such data (Hu, 1981). Future cost analysis research, however, may be forced to rely more extensively on existing data bases which have been generated for management and administrative reasons because there will be precious few financial resources to produce additional information. Monies to collect data exclusively for research purposes will be exceedingly rare.

Furthermore, rural service delivery agencies are gradually becoming more sophisticated and precise in their collection and processing of service cost information. These improvements are the result of both third-party reimbursement requirements and governmental accountability demands. These increased demands for accurate cost data as part of agency accountability will probably continue and may accelerate. Greater cooperation between researchers and agency administrators to make continuous improvements in the quality of the data base related to service costs is a desirable future step for research in this area.

With regard to the second issue of identifying the unique features of rural service provision, our gaps in information about the *quality* of rural services have promoted a lack of focus on specific service provider tasks. The trend in research has been to collect very general information about service delivery roles without detailed knowledge about the specific array of tasks and functions that rural practitioners perform. For example, the significance of case management services for the elderly is relevant in both rural and urban agencies. Typically, however, the prescribed model for case management is an urban-generated approach. It reflects the inter- and intrasystem demands of urban communities, which differ from rural situations. To reach a better understanding of the similarities and differences in rural and urban practice, studies must employ specific task and competency inventories in both urban and rural settings.

As a third high-priority focus for future research, we strongly encourage a reexamination of service usage data in order to clarify the appropriateness of traditional concepts and measures of utilization. It is essential that we illuminate the extent to which service utilization patterns are influenced by transactions between the individual and the environment. Examining the interactive context of rural service utilization will require a careful weighting of those factors associated with the individual (e.g., perceptions, preferences, or abilities) and those related to the environment (e.g., community norms, resource availability, or physical barriers). The current trend to examine service utilization as the result of either individual *or* environment seems counterproductive. The newly developed single-subject design approaches may be readily adaptable to the study of the role of extrapersonal factors in service utilization. These designs have the benefit of requiring small sample sizes; yet they yield a significant amount of data about the response of clients to services.

The fourth priority, research on the quality of services provided to the rural elderly, is fraught with some of the same problems that persist in urban population studies. The rural data base is particularly deficient in research involving experimental and control group designs and the systematic follow-up of service outcomes. The economic resources needed to implement such evaluation designs are most often awarded to urban-based service demonstration projects. Comparable data are not available on rural populations. Perhaps more disturbing, for the most part the urban-biased information base and the absence of rural perspectives goes unchallenged, ignored, or, even worse, unrecognized.

Finally, rural gerontologists are in a unique position to exert influence on the future development of rural health and human services through their research. To maximize the effect of their input, however, will require a strong commitment among researchers to design and conduct investigations that are relevant to the needs of the elderly in the communities where the studies are based. Researchers can assume a positive role in the planning and development process by making their data available to service agencies and by assuming responsibility for communicating the relevance of their data to service planners. Data collected on rural projects often have diverse and direct significance for the goal formulation of the program design. The applicability of the data to the planning process may require additional analysis or reexamination in order to sharpen their utility as planning information.

Human service researchers committed to rural studies face a very difficult future. In the short run, rural researchers may be able to compensate for some of the lost momentum caused by shifting federal priorities by increasing their collaborative efforts with rural service providers. The time may be singularly appropriate to combine the limited resources that are available both to provide services and to account for their impact. Within many communities, service delivery agencies are being forced to consider a variety of coalitions to ensure survival. In some instances researchers who have established their credibility with the service community are being invited to participate in these efforts. Within these collaborative efforts, territoriality over data is reduced. Despite the existence of these optimistic adaptations, however, cooperation remains a neglected survival strategy and resource competition continues to prevail in many settings. As a consequence, many service systems remaining unevaluated and significant numbers of researchers are without the data to ensure the continued growth of the discipline.

One concluding point seems relevant. The impetus to support special programs for the rural aged may be slipping and losing ground. The responsibilities for sustaining and/or rebuilding the interest rests, in part, with rural researchers and service providers. Ruralists need to persist within the structures of national research and professional organizations to maintain a focused perspective on the distinctive service needs of the rural aged and the necessity for research to enlighten the development and delivery of service.

References

Ahearn, M.C. *Health care in rural America.* Washington, D.C.: U.S. Department of Agriculture, Economics, Statistics and Cooperatives Service, Information Bulletin No. 428, 1979.

Albers, D.C., & Thompson, J.V. *Social work education and rural practice: What's in a name? Plenty!* Paper presented at the Canadian Rural Social Work Forum, St. Joseph, New Brunswick, 1980.

Ambrosius, G.R. To dream the impossible dream: Delivering coordinated services to the rural elderly. In P.K.H. Kim & C.P. Wilson (Eds.), *Toward the mental health of the rural elderly.* Washington, D.C.: University Press of America, 1981, pp. 289–316.

Bachrach, L.L. *Human services in rural areas: An analytical review.* Rockville, Md.: Project SHARE, A National Clearinghouse for Improving the Management of Human Services, 1981.

Bylund, R.A., LeRay, N.L., & Crawford, C.O. *Older American households and their housing, 1975: A metro–nonmetro comparison.* University Park: The Pennsylvania State University, Agricultural Experiment Station, January 1980.

Cantor, M.H. *Neighbors and friends: An overlooked resource in the infor-*

mal support system. Paper presented at the 30th Annual Meeting of the Gerontological Society of America, San Francisco, Calif., 1977.

Cedar, T., & Salasin, J. *Research directions for rural mental health.* McLean Va.: The MITRE Corporation, 1979.

Coward, R.T. Planning community services for the rural elderly: Implications from research. *The Gerontologist,* 1979, *19* (3), 275–282.

Coward, R.T. Research-based programs for the rural elderly. In W.R. Lassey, M.L. Lassey, G.R. Lee, & N. Lee (Eds.), *Research and public service with the rural elderly.* Corvallis, Ore.: Western Rural Development Center, 1980, pp. 39–56.

Coward, R.T. Serving families in contemporary rural America: Definitions, importance and future. In R.T. Coward & W.M. Smith, Jr. (Eds.), *Family services: Issues and opportunities in contemporary rural America.* Lincoln: The University of Nebraska Press, 1983, pp. 3–25.

Coward, R.T., DeWeaver, K.L., Schmidt, F.E., & Jackson, R.W. Mental health practice in rural environments: A frame of reference. *The International Journal of Mental Health,* 1983, *12,* 1–2, 3–24.

Coward, R.T., & Kerckhoff, R.K. *The rural elderly: Program planning guidelines.* Ames, Iowa: North Central Regional Center for Rural Development, 1978.

Coward, R.T., & Smith, W.M., Jr. Families in rural society. In D.A. Dillman & D.J. Hobbs (Eds.), *Rural society in the U.S.: Issues for the 1980s.* Boulder, Colo.: Westview Press, 1982, pp. 77–84.

Coward, R.T., & Smith, W.M., Jr. (Eds.), *Family services: Issues and opportunities in contemporary rural America.* Lincoln: The University of Nebraska Press, 1983.

Ecosometrics, Inc. *Review of reported differences between the rural and urban elderly: Status, needs, services, and service costs.* Washington, D.C.: Administration on Aging (Contract No. 105-80-065), July 1981.

Farley, O.W., Griffiths, K.A., Skidmore, R.A., & Thackeray, M.G. *Rural social work practice.* New York: The Free Press, 1982.

Fitzpatrick, J.L., Edwards, R.L., & Olszewski, C. Job priorities of rural services workers: Implications for training and practice. *Arete,* 1981, *6* (4), 35–44.

Flax, J.W., Wagenfeld, M.O., Ivens, R.E., & Weiss, R.J. *Mental health in rural America: An overview and annotated bibliography.* Washington, D.C.: National Institute of Mental Health (DHEW Publication No. (ADM) 78-753), U.S. Government Printing Office, 1979.

Fowler, F.J. *Knowledge, need and use of services among the aged.* Paper presented at the 19th Annual Southern Conference on Gerontology, University of Florida, February 1970.

Frank, J. *Persuasion and healing (2d ed.).* Baltimore, Md.: Johns Hopkins University Press, 1973.

Ginsberg, L.H. (Ed.), *Social work in rural communities: A book of readings.* New York: Council on Social Work Education, 1976.

Ginsberg, L.H. Rural social work education. *Arete,* 1981, *6* (4), 13–17.

Ginsberg, L. H. Social work in rural communities with an emphasis on mental health practice. In P.A. Keller & J.D. Murray (Eds.), *Handbook of rural community mental health.* New York: Human Sciences Press, 1982, pp. 200–209.

Greene, V.L. *Premature institutionalization among rural elderly.* Paper presented at the Sixth Annual Institute of the American Rural Health Association, Jeffersonville, Vt., June 1982.

Hargrove, D.S. An overview of professional considerations in the rural community. In P.A. Keller & J.D. Murray (Eds.), *Handbook of rural community health.* New York: Human Sciences Press, 1982, pp. 169–182.

Hu, T. *Cost and utilization of social services for urban and rural elderly: An exemplary study.* Ithaca, N.Y.: Northeast Regional Center for Rural Development, June 1981.

Irey, K.V. The social work generalist in a rural context: An ecological perspective. *Journal of Education for Social Work,* 1980, *16* (3), 36–43.

Jackson, R.W. Delivering services to families in rural America: An analysis of the logistics and uniquenesses. In R.T. Coward & W.M. Smith, Jr. (Eds.), *Family services: Issues and opportunities in contemporary rural America.* Lincoln: The University of Nebraska Press, 1983, pp. 69–86.

Johnson, H.W. (Ed.). *Rural human services: A book of readings.* Itasca, Ill.: F.E. Peacock Publishers, 1980.

Johnson, L.C. The BSW delivers to small town America. In D. Bast (Ed.), *Human services in the rural environment reader.* Madison: The University of Wisconsin—Extension, 1977.

Keller, P.A., & Murray, J.D. (Eds). *Handbook of rural community mental health.* New York: Human Sciences Press, 1982.

Keller, P.A., Zimbleman, K.K., Murray, J.D., & Feil, R.N. Geographic distribution of psychologists in the Northeastern United States. *Journal of Rural Community Psychology,* 1980, *1* (1), 18–24.

Kim, P.K.H. Toward rural gerontological education: Rationale and model. *Educational Gerontology,* 1980, *5* (4), 387–397.

Kim, P.K.H., & Wilson, C.P. *Toward mental health of the rural elderly.* Washington, D.C.: University Press of America, 1981.

Kivett, V.R., & Learner, R.M. The rural elderly poor: Economic impacts and policy issues. In Community Services Administration, *Policy issues for the elderly poor.* Washington, D.C.: U.S. Government Printing Office, Community Services Administration Pamphlet 6172-8 (1981-341-509/2619), February 1981.

Kranzel, C.F. *The social cost of space in the yonland.* Bozeman, Mont.: Big Sky Books, 1980.

Martinez-Brawley, E.E. Historical perspectives on rural social work: Implications for curriculum development. *Journal of Education and Social Work,* 1980, *16* (3), 43–50.

Martinez-Brawley, E.E., & Munson, C. Systematic characteristics of the rural milieu: A review of social work related research. *Arete,* 1981, *6* (4), 23–24.

Morris, R. Government and voluntary agency relationships. *Social Service Review,* 1982, *56* (3), 333–345.

Munson, C.E. Urban–rural differences: Implications for education and training. *Journal of Education for Social Work,* 1980, *16* (1), 95.

National Institute of Mental Health. *Federally funded community mental health centers.* Washington, D.C.: Division of Mental Health Programs, National Institute of Mental Health, Department of Health, Education and Welfare, 1973.

Nelson, G. Social services to the urban and rural aged: The experience of Area Agencies on Aging. *The Gerontologist,* 1980, *20* (2), 200–207.

New York State Senate Research Service. *Old age and ruralism: A case of double jeopardy—A report on the rural elderly.* Albany, N.Y.: Senate Standing Committee on Aging, May 1980.

Nooe, R.M. *Clinical practice in rural settings: Curriculum implications.* Paper presented the Annual Program Meeting of the Council on Social Work Education. Los Angeles, Calif., March 1980.

Parkinson, L. Improving the delivery of health services to the rural elderly: A policy perspective. In P.K.H. Kim & C.P. Wilson (Eds.), *Toward mental health of the rural elderly.* Washington, D.C.: University Press of America, 1981, pp. 223–239.

Sauer, W.J. The elderly: Challenges for the rural community. In R.T. Coward & W.M. Smith, Jr. (Eds.), *Family services: Issues and opportunities in contemporary rural America.* Lincoln: University of Nebraska Press, 1983, pp. 186–203.

Schooler, K.K. A comparison of rural and non-rural elderly on selected variables. In R.C. Atchley & T.O. Byerts (Eds.), *Rural environments and aging.* Washington, D.C.: Gerontological Society of America, 1975, pp. 27–42.

Sleeper, D. Working for the rural public interest. *Country Journal,* 1981 (December), 60–67.

Southern Regional Education Board, Manpower Education and Training Project, Task Force. Educational assumptions for rural social work. In L.H. Ginsberg (Ed.), *Social work in rural communities: A book of readings.* New York: Council on Social Work Education, 1976, pp. 41–44.

Taietz, P. *The impact of area agencies on aging on the development of new services for the elderly.* Ithaca, N.Y.: Cornell University, Department of Rural Sociology, 1982.

Taietz, P., & Milton, S. Rural–urban differences in the structure of services for the elderly in upstate New York counties. *Journal of Gerontology,* 1979, *34* (3), 429–437.

Task Panel on Rural Mental Health, Final report. In President's Commission on Mental Health, *Report to the President—Volume 3*. Washington, D.C.: U.S. Government Printing Office, 1978, pp. 135–190.

Tremblay, K.R., Walker, F.S., & Dillman, D.A. The quality of life experienced by rural families. In R.T. Coward & W.M. Smith, Jr. (Eds.), *Family services: Issues and opportunities in contemporary rural America*. Lincoln: The University of Nebraska Press, 1983, pp. 26–40.

U.S. House of Representatives, Select Committee on Aging. *Rural elderly access to emergency medical services*. Washington, D.C.: Committee Publication Number 96-198, May 1979.

Wagenfeld, M.O. (Eds). *Perspectives on rural mental health*. San Francisco: Jossey-Bass, 1981.

Wagenfeld, M.O., & Wagenfeld, J.K. Values, culture, and delivery of mental health services. In M.O. Wagenfeld (Ed.), *Perspectives on rural mental health*. San Francisco: Jossey-Bass, 1981, pp. 1–12.

Walsh, M.E. Rural social work practice: Clinical quality. *Social Casework: The Journal of Contemporary Social Work*, 1981, *61* (10), 458–464.

Wodarski, J.S., Giordano, J., & Bagarozzi, D.A. Training for competent community mental health practice: Implications for rural social work. *Arete*, 1981, *6* (4), 45–62.

10

Policy Development
for the Elderly:
Rural Perspectives

Dennis A. Watkins and Julia M. Watkins

In 1974 Warner suggested the importance of examining "how the fundamental structures of national society differentially involve, represent, and affect rural people" (p. 307). More recently, the National Research Council (1981), in examining the need for a comprehensive data system reflecting the conditions and needs of rural America, noted that "the growing interdependence of rural and urban people causes the problems of each group to affect the other, and policies designed to meet the needs of either group will affect the other" (p. 193).

At a time characterized by severe economic downturn, volatile financial markets, high unemployment, rapidly changing demographic characteristics, and an economic base increasingly reliant on technological innovation, the interdependence of the fundamental social, political, and economic structures of American society is dramatically heightened (Bell, 1973; Bradshaw & Blakely, 1979). These interdependencies affect all people, be they rich or poor, young or old, urban or rural. Policy interventions designed to have impact on specific, circumscribed problems often activate these interdependencies with unanticipated and significant outcomes. Thurow (1980) observed that contemporary political economy is a zero-sum game in the differential allocation of societal resources and, therefore, adds to the complexity. In this chapter we will argue that rural areas, and particularly their elderly populations, more often than not have lost in competition with urban areas for scarce resources allocated by the political process (Ecosometrics, 1981).

The increasingly complex interdependencies of societal relationships must be acknowledged in the context of rural policy development (Watkins & Watkins, 1984). Failure to do so results in policy responses that risk being overly simplistic, ideologically based, and politically motivated for perceived short-term gains. The standard explanations of rural–urban differences (e.g., lower population density, small size and less complexity of organizational structures, extended distances among people, communities, and organizations, and a reliance on the care-giving capacity of extended family and informal resource systems) are primarily impressionistic rather than warrantable conclusions (Ecosometrics, 1981). Moreover, as a base for policy decision making, impressionistic judgments lead to superficial responses inadequate to the task of addressing the long-standing, fundamental structural problems of rural environments. In order to avoid this unproductive posture in examining policy development for the rural elderly and to unmask the complexities and interdependencies already suggested, we will analyze in this chapter three policy issues with significant implications for understanding the well-being of the rural elderly.

Policy Responses to the Needs of the Rural Elderly

Within the current political and economic climate several policy issues emerge as particularly relevant for our discussion. The current economic downturn, the cost-cutting initiatives by the federal government, and the increasing predominance of policies which augment the disparity between people with adequate incomes and those living on the margin of poverty (Clark, 1982) all increase the vulnerability of the rural elderly. Those who have historically suffered from the inequitable distribution of goods and services, including the rural elderly, will continue to be stigmatized and impoverished.

Policy strategies about which choices may be exercised and their impact on the rural elderly assessed include:

- *Income support versus service availability*. While federal and state policy is viewed as adhering fundamentally to either an income or a services strategy, the more important issue to examine is the appropriate mix of income support and service availability to foster maximum independence for rural elderly people. What level of income support and method of transfer will provide the most benefit for the rural elderly? How can services be structured to augment the care-giving capacity of informal resource systems in rural areas?

- *Generic/block grant versus age-specific/categorical programs.* General resource scarcity combined with the growing numbers of elderly necessitate a reexamination of policy choices between generic and age-specific programming. What is the potential for increased intergenerational conflict under age-specific programming? What will be the equity outcome for the rural elderly under generically based delivery systems?
- *Free market and competition versus systematic social planning.* The implications of social policy directed toward fostering a competitive service environment raises serious questions about social responsibility for disadvantaged groups like the rural elderly. Will a competitive service posture widen the already existing service disparity between rural and urban areas? What degree of congruity exists between the prerequisites of a free market and the characteristics of a rural setting? How do vulnerable populations fare in competitive market environments?

By applying the Warner (1974) suggestion of differential institutional participation to contemporary policy issues, the relative well-being of rural elderly people will be more clearly articulated. Moreover, this strategy will further the understanding of possible impacts of specific policy options as implemented in rural environments. From this strategy, future policy research issues may be inferred.

Income Support versus Service Availability

In general, the response of society to the needs of groups of people identified as vulnerable has been formulated around either an income- or a service-provision philosophy. That is, the way in which needs, as defined by a set of criteria, have been addressed is through a system of income or service provisions with program variation in the target population, the delivery of the benefit, the source of funding, and the flow of funding to the beneficiary population (Burns, 1956; Gilbert & Specht, 1974). The type of benefit, another dimension, is the focus of this section.

Social policy responses resulting in the provision of income benefits to a targeted population are designed with two primary issues in mind: (1) assuring a minimal level of income to those people who, for a variety of reasons, are not active participants in the labor force; and (2) addressing inequities in the income system through a transfer of income from one group to another to ensure that one group is not substantially below another group as defined by specified criteria. In American society, programs with a primary focus on the first issue are viewed essentially as public assistance benefits and for the elderly are represented by such programs as Supplemental Security Income (SSI), Food Stamps, and Medicaid. For the elderly, the second issue is addressed by programs of social insurance such as Old Age and Survivor's Insurance (OASI) and Medicare.

As a policy response, income strategies recognize the basic vulnerability of the elderly in a capitalist market system due to factors such as retirement disability, loss of a wage-earning spouse, and/or periods of acute medical intervention. Income strategies in which the benefit is made in cash are acknowledged as allowing the most choice for the individual at the point of consumption. However, this assumption is valid only when the income provided is sufficient to allow for choice and when the goods or services to be purchased are in adequate supply and accessible to the consumer. Furthermore, the income strategy as a way of addressing need suggests that the basic problem confronting the targeted population is an insufficient income and not the population itself.

A service response, in contrast, suggests that the elderly have needs which are poorly met by interactions with the economic marketplace. In this approach, factors other than income are acknowledged as substantial barriers to the access and use of a variety of services. The services strategy, the provision of a range of services by an instrumentality of society, assumes that the service consumer with access to usable and acceptable services will attain or maintain a more satisfactory quality of life. The services strategy, as noted by some authors (Estes, 1979; Estes & Harrington, 1981), tends to define the needs of the elderly as simply a lack of services while ignoring the more deeply troubling social and economic issues related to the discriminatory effects of sexism, racism, and ageism.

The implications of these two strategies for rural elderly Americans are many and diverse. Turning first to income strategies, issues related to employment, occupation, and income status are relevant to examine. Data reviewed in Chapter 2 demonstrated much higher incidences of poverty among the rural than urban elderly. This poverty is the complex result of lost or reduced income due to retirement, inadequate retirement benefits, below poverty level public assistance benefits, and considerable periods of underemployment. It has been noted, furthermore, that states with the highest percentage of rural poverty across all age groups tend to have the lowest public assistance benefits and substantial rural minority populations (National Rural Center, 1979).

What, then, is the impact of present income programs on the rural elderly? Social insurance entitlement benefits (OASI), which represent a substantial portion of the income for many rural elderly persons, are primarily a function of the amount of income earned during the working years. The fact that rural wages are at substantially lower levels than urban incomes (see Chapter 2 for details) suggests a reduced benefit level. Ozawa (1982) noted that the existence of a minimum benefit level subsidized OASI insurance for those who would have received low payments as a function of their work histories and, therefore, served to maintain some minimal income level, albeit inadequate. However, the recent abolishment of a minimum benefit level for OASI for those applicants eligible after January 1982 (Svahn, 1982) once again makes the insurance more closely related to work histories. Furthermore, the effect of a supplementary benefit from SSI serves potentially to reinforce the welfare stigma of the program—perhaps a particular problem for rural people who, although frequently underemployed, often have had strong, lifelong ties to work. In a sample studied by Ozawa (1981), elderly and disabled persons indicated feeling almost no stigma attached to receiving SSI, although the author noted that had the sample included more nonwhite, rural, and/or Southern respondents, the results might have been somewhat different.

Employment histories of a part-time, sporadic, or seasonal nature present a further dilemma for the rural elderly, namely, documenting a sufficient history of covered employment to qualify for OASI benefits. In addition, self-employed persons may not have reported sufficient earnings to qualify for coverage. Again, this latter predicament may be most damaging in rural areas, where LaFollette (1982) has reported a substantially higher percentage of self-employed persons (12.8% rural versus 6.9% urban).

Current proposals to raise the retirement age from 65 to 68 years for receipt of full OASI benefits have a projected discriminatory impact on the rural elderly. With higher levels of chronic disease and illness among rural elderly residents (McCoy & Brown, 1978), this proposal stands to further penalize the rural elderly, many of whom maintain attachment to low-paying jobs and self-employment beyond age 65. The most penalized group under such a proposal is the minority elderly in rural areas, who have both higher mortality rates and lower earnings during the working years than their urban counterparts or the nonminority rural elderly.

The rural elderly are eligible for public assistance payments, primarily SSI, providing they meet the means test of income need. The federal administration and funding of SSI with standardized benefit levels supports a more equitable distribution of resources between rural and urban populations. The determination of eligibility, however, which includes an assets test, is detrimental to the rural elderly who may have been self-employed. Carlin and Pryor (1980) have also noted that it can be detrimental for many rural people when long accounting periods are used to determine eligibility because income, while higher at one point in time, may be very low for a considerable period of time for many rural workers.

In spite of the fact that individual states may supplement the federal SSI benefit, only 16 states did so in 1980. States having the largest proportion of the rural elderly poor population characteristically have not provided an SSI supplement (National Rural Center, 1979). Because of increasingly severe fiscal constraints at the state level, there may be a further decrease in the number of states that provide an SSI supplement.

Turning briefly to the major health care programs, medicare and medicaid, which are considered by many policy analysts as in-kind income supplements, the differential impact on the rural elderly becomes strikingly clear. First, while medicare guarantees reimbursement to the provider for certain health and medical needs (aside from specified deductibles and co-payments), it does little to guarantee the availability of health care services (Roemer, 1980). Yet the rural elderly person pays the same "Part B premium" as does the urban elderly individual, and the same percent of social security payroll tax (2.6% in 1981) is earmarked for medicare whether one lives in a medically underserved area or one rich in health and medical resources. Somers and Somers (1977) have also suggested that the reimbursement mechanism for medicare and medicaid based on "usual and customary" fees and "reasonable" costs has tended to reinforce the maldistribution of health care personnel and facilities away from rural, underserved areas. A final point to be made relative to medicare and medicaid is the prevailing institutional bias in the reimbursement of services. This works against attempts to provide support and care for the elderly in a least restrictive environment. In particular it fails to support the care-giving capacities of friends and relatives who make up the informal resource system thought to be prevalent in rural areas (Johnson, 1980).

Any discussion of income strategies would be incomplete without an observation about work incentives devised to foster the acceptability of work over the receipt of public assistance. For rural populations in general this issue has different implications than for urban populations. It is documented that rural people have and maintain close ties to the work force, and yet are often underemployed (Carlin & Pryor, 1980). Thus, if equity in the distribution of resources is important, then benefit reductions based on earnings should be minimal for the rural elderly.

In contrast to an income strategy, the services strategy advocates for a wide range of services to be available for the elderly to support their maximum independent functioning. For the elderly population, this strategy is most strikingly apparent in the policy mandates of the Older Americans Act of 1965, as amended. Under Title III of that legislation, Area Agencies on Aging (AAAs) were established to develop comprehensive, coordinated systems of care for the elderly. Clearly, services were to become the cornerstone of federal policy for the elderly. To achieve this goal a variety of analytic and structural mechanisms have been suggested: continuum of care, case management, channeling, contracting, and advocacy.

The thrust toward a service strategy may, as suggested by Estes (1979), define the problems of the elderly as those of insufficient services or fragmented service delivery. Kammerman (1976), however, has asserted that service provision has developed to a more prevalent position in ways similar to income strategies because of a burgeoning group of older people who are living longer with more disability and whose families are no longer legally responsible for their care. Furthermore, Kammerman (1976) emphasized the similarity of needs for services among elderly people from varying economic strata. For Estes (1979) services may be viewed as instruments of social control and foster the bureaucratization of an "aging enterprise." Given sufficient income rather than services, the elderly could more effectively participate in the mainstream of economic activity by exercising choice in the purchase of services in the marketplace. This position poses additional issues which are discussed later in the chapter.

The services strategy for the elderly population is embodied in the concept of a continuum of care. While there is no clear agreement as to precisely what services constitute a continuum of care or how its delivery and administration are structured (Watkins & Watkins, 1981), it does serve conceptually to unify a system of community-based and institutional care (Benedict, 1978).

The policy importance of a continuum of services is reflected in the Older Americans Act, 1978 Amendments, in which resources of state and local agencies are to be directed toward "the development of comprehensive and coordinated service systems" (Sec. 301[a]) and to "provide a continuum of care for the vulnerable elderly" (Sec. 301[a][3]). Brody (1979) has suggested that a continuum of services has as its dual goals the assurance of a better level of health and well-being for elderly people living in the community and the prevention of the institutionalization of an undetermined number of elderly at some point in the future.

To this point, numerous service classification schemata have been proposed as constituting a continuum of care (Benedict, 1977; Brody, 1979; Glant & McCaslin, 1979; Philadelphia Geriatric Center, 1980; Tobin, 1975). The most salient difficulty with the continuum of care concept occurs as a result of constructing service typologies; once services are identified as constituting a continuum of care, there is a tendency to define need by the services which exist (Golant & McCaslin, 1979).

For the rural elderly population, services based on the concept of a continuum of care have several decided advantages as well as some clear disadvantages. First, a service system conceptualized as a continuum would provide service planners with valuable information about service gaps and deficiencies and suggest where resources could best be allocated in a community. Second, although services may be in short supply in the rural community, the mandates of the Older Americans Act may provide the leverage necessary to develop needed resources or to enter into contractual agreements with service providers in more distantly located communities. Third, Tobin (1975) has suggested that the development of local care systems based on the continuum concept may serve to reinforce local responsibility for the elderly, even if institutionalization becomes necessary, since the community-based and institutional components of the system are unified.

There are, at the same time, several disadvantages with a services strategy as represented by the continuum of care concept. If, as suggested by Golant and McCaslin (1979), services tend to define need, then the rural elderly are particularly disadvantaged as unneeded, yet available, services are overutilized and resources are not expended on the development of a more appropriate and comprehensive service system. Futhermore, when service dollars are dependent upon implementation of a particular mandate (e.g., a continuum of care), rural areas are at a decided disadvantage, initially, with fewer services to pull into a continuum and the need to expend more effort on service development. Finally, to carry out the mandated responsibilities of the Older Americans Act requires that local agencies (i.e., the AAA) have expertise in planning, contracting, and development, skills which are frequently in short supply given the propensity for professional human service workers to locate in urban rather than rural areas.

As a final observation, the services strategy neglects, for the most part, the structure and function of the informal resource system in rural areas. Shanas (1979) and Brody (1979) have documented the care-giving function of the family in support of an elderly family member. Krishef and Yoelin (1981) have shown the reliance of rural elderly blacks and whites on informal caregivers. These studies suggest the need to examine more closely the interface of formal services and informal caregivers in support of the rural elderly population (Froland, 1980).

Generic and Age-specific Programs

With the continually increasing costs of social programs in general, and those directed toward the elderly population in particular, an unmistakable requisite exists to reexamine the fundamental principles in support of either a generic or an age-specific policy for the elderly (Hudson, 1978). A generic approach to social program delivery identifies as its target population *all* persons with similar needs as they move through and confront the "crisis" points in the life cycle, such as illness, loss of job, or death of a spouse. Although movement through the life cycle is highly individualized and fluid (Hirschhorn, 1977), it is thought that vulnerable points may be identified and a rational system of services designed to meet needs (Martinez, 1980).

Age-specific programs, in contrast, represent a particularistic approach to service or income provision and rely less on demonstrated need than on attributed need (Kutza, 1981). When an entire group (e.g., all persons over age 65) is included as the target population, the program is easier to administer, derives more public support, and subsequently provides better quality service (Garfinkel, 1978).

The age-specific approach has strong ties to social advocacy as a way of strengthening the position of one group of people relative to other groups. The elderly, in this approach, are viewed as the primary population having certain identifiable needs. Furthermore, those needs are attributed primarily to age rather than assessed on the basis of a set of criteria. The sum result of age-specific programs, according to Myers, Weiler, and Fine (1982), is the creation of inequities "with some groups getting a richer service mix than others with nearly identical problems" (p. 178). These same authors have suggested that a particularistic posture encourages inefficiency since funds cannot be moved from one group to another to address pressing priorities.

The development of generic delivery systems as a response to the needs for service efficiency and coordinated delivery systems is currently represented by the block grant funding mechanism. Although programs funded under the Older Americans Act have remained age-specific, a major devolution of decision making from the federal to state and local governments has taken place—the Omnibus Budget Reconciliation Act of 1981 consolidated 25 health and human services programs into seven block grants. This hastening movement toward the New Federalism has also been characterized by a considerable decrease in funds allocated to the states (Beyle & Dusenbury, 1982). To enact block grants and at the same time decrease funding speaks ominously for rural, powerless people.

In a review of Title XX allocations in 1977, Schram (1979) reported that "in spite of the fact that Title XX gives states an opportunity to develop new patterns of social services, one problem with these block grants is that certain states simply have continued to distribute funds according to their states' historical patterns of providing social services" (p. 78). These findings are particularly significant since it was anticipated that the provision for citizen participation in Title XX would shift decision making to the local level and, thus, make outcomes more reflective of local needs. The analysis by Schram (1979), however, implies that this had not occurred since priorities remained as they had been previously.

In the context of long-term care, Hudson (1981) identified problems with the block grant mechanism and suggested that by combining the "management control" and the participatory approach to program implementation, the advantages of each are diminished. First, the state agency charged with implementing a block grant under decreased federal regulation and funding will at the same time lack federal organizational and bureaucratic support. Consequently, it will be vulnerable as the "scapegoat" for program failures and continually need to defend its actions—something which it previously could defer to the federal bureau-

cracy. Second, when providers and consumers participate in allocation decisions, factionalism among interest groups through competition for scarce resources may well develop. Third, as a function of
the decisions it makes, the state agency risks losing the support of
groups which it formerly relied upon in its interactions with the
federal bureaucracy.

On the more positive side, a generic delivery system based on
the block grant funding mechanism has several distinct advantages. The block grant does require the development of a state
level planning and assessment infrastructure. This, if at all re-
sponsive to local needs, can serve to promote efficiency and effectiveness at the state level. Second, the delivery system might more
readily address in a fluid, flexible manner the needs of individuals
as their statuses change, an important consideration as developed
by Hirschhorn (1980). For example, the elderly widow and the
young widow might participate in the same support program, or
the AFDC mother and the elderly couple needing transportation to
a distant medical facility might ride in the same van, which if only
serving one group might travel with empty seats or result in service inequities, as shown by Meyers et al. (1982). A third distinct
advantage, contrary to the factionalism mentioned earlier, is the
potential for increased program support as the constituency group
is broadened.

The advantages and disadvantages of a generic system resist,
at this point in time, absolute, clear-cut demarcation—a potential
disadvantage may well be an advantage under slightly different
circumstances. Nevertheless, some speculative observations regarding the rural elderly are offered as a means of gaining insight
into the complexities of policy decisions.

If it is correct to assume that many rural elderly are disadvantaged in their quest for a better quality of life, this position of
relative disadvantage can be expected to continue under a generic
delivery system (Nelson, 1980; Schram, 1979). There are other disadvantaged groups with greater public support (e.g., children and
families) and legal support (e.g., the physically handicapped and
the mentally retarded) and to them will go the greatest resources
(Myers et al., 1982; Schram, 1979). Advocacy for an age-specific
policy is diminished as advocacy for need across a more inclusive
target group is increased. Those with a specific need who lack
power and control over resources will continue to receive fewer
services than those with more influence.

The funding patterns that are currently in place will be difficult to change and priorities nearly impossible to modify with states already experiencing severely limited fiscal resources. Within the block grant mechanism itself, rural people who lack transportation or who must travel long distances to participate in public hearings are summarily excluded. If, however, block grants promote a greater responsiveness among decision makers to the local perspective, then the rural elderly, who often constitute a significant stable population group, may benefit immeasurably as the urban policy bias is confronted.

Second, if federal funding formulas continue to be based upon population rather than need, then the elderly residents of rural, geographically dispersed communities and low population states will continue to receive fewer benefits. Using the level of need and the cost of providing a given service as the base for funding decisions would serve the rural elderly more advantageously.

Finally, movement from an age-specific to a generic system would tend to expand the rural population base for a service. Funding formulas based on the amount of need for a service would increase under this approach. Furthermore, as the result of coalition formation there would be an increase in the political power of those people in need of a particular service. For the elderly population whose needs often include a range of long-term care services, Myers et al. (1982) have argued that a generic system would decrease the propensity toward institutional care by developing a more accessible and highly integrated system.

Increasing evidence shows that as a group the elderly have fared well under particularistic policies (Binstock, 1978; Hudson, 1978). Questions, however, have been raised about the continuation of such a "favored" status (Hudson, 1978). The further development of block grant funding with a more generic focus may, if the Title XX experience is generalizable, leave the rural elderly in a considerably disadvantaged position without strong advocacy on their behalf.

Competition in the Free Market versus Systematic Social Planning

Recent initiatives at the federal level have intensified a policy posture of fostering competition among service providers, developing partnerships between the public and private sectors, and relying on alternatives (e.g., voluntarism) to agency-based, professionally delivered services. These initiatives are based almost exclusively on the intent to reduce, or at least hold constant, the amount of federal tax dollars allocated to social welfare programs. Furthermore, the implementation of a variety of accountability mechanisms in the 1970s (e.g., cost effectiveness and cost benefit analysis, professional standards review, and health systems agencies) which failed to hold down service costs has further encouraged the search for alternative ways to allocate scarce resources.

Despite the current penchant for reliance on a free-market philosophy, competition as a mechanism for the allocation of scarce resources has serious limitations when applied to health and human services (Pruger & Miller, 1973). Moreover, these limitations intensify in rural settings as the assumptions of competition become even more inapplicable. Roemer and Roemer (1982), in a theoretical discussion of the relevance of a competitive mechanism in the health care sector, identified several preconditions for a competitive market structure. Those which seem to have the greatest relevance for rural, elderly populations are (1) an abundance of consumers and sellers in unconstrained exchange, (2) knowledgeable and informed consumers exercising choices in the purchase of a product, (3) low transaction costs for the item being purchased, and (4) insubstantial economies of scale.

In the rural setting, consumers (a term which connotes buyers in a competitive market) of most services are not in abundant supply. Providers of services are likewise more scarce than in urban areas. Aside from the paucity of consumers and sellers, the conditions leading to "buying" a service in and of themselves impose a good deal of constraint on the transaction. For example, the elderly woman living alone in a rural area and in need of transportation to a regional shopping center is constrained by lack of transportation services. Similarly, the elderly couple, one of whom needs immediate nursing home care, is constrained by financial considerations and the fact that the most accessible nursing home is many miles away. The relative lack of providers and the low demand for services, caused by a small population base, suggest a poor fit in the application of a competitive market to the rural setting.

In particular, within the health care sector the usual supply and demand functions of the marketplace are not realized. For example, the increase in the supply of physicians has not resulted in decreased prices. Indeed, Somers and Somers (1977) have suggested that physicians create a demand for their services and "generate expenditures throughout the entire health care system" (p. 141) through hospital admissions, referrals, and prescriptions. This occurs with little consumer choice.

In spite of an increasingly well-educated and informed elderly population, health and social service decisions require a level of technical information beyond that of even the most sophisticated consumer. Pruger and Miller (1973) have suggested that being a good client is easier than being a good consumer: the latter requires sufficient self-education for competent decision making. Moreover, the delivery system itself, with much lacking in terms of service evaluation data (Pruger & Miller, 1973) and professional sanctions against open advertisement of both services and their costs, increases the likelihood of a knowledge gap, and thus decreases the consumer's ability to make an informed service decision. The aforementioned barriers to informed consumer choice may be intensified by certain characteristics of rural elderly populations, e.g., lower educational levels, geographic isolation, high rates of poverty, and lesser institutional access.

Social and health services do not have low price tags. Services to rural elderly populations have a relatively higher cost because of transportation factors and greater assessed levels of need. When these high delivery costs are considered in light of relatively lower incomes and less access to resources, the service costs to the consumer become exorbitant.

While the competitive market mechanism depends upon multiple providers competing through efficiency of operation and innovative techniques to keep prices down, this in fact has not occurred in rural areas. Large monopolistic public agencies have in many instances been the single service provider. In addition, economies of scale through large organizations, frequently viewed as an urban phenomenon, are present in rural environments and significantly violate the competitive market mechanism. This is evidenced in the increasing trend toward urban-based hospital and nursing home chains acquiring and/or extending management services under contractual arrangements to rural health facilities and a concomitant loss of local autonomy and control. The subsequent responsiveness of these institutions to the needs and preferences of local older people is an issue requiring further examination. There is increasing evidence that small, voluntary agencies are not fulfilling a particularly innovative or advocacy-oriented role because much of their funding comes from the public sector through the purchase-of-service contract (Terrell, 1979).

Encouraging partnerships between the public and private sectors have been stimulated by rapidly expanding public expenditures for health and social services and issues of service effectiveness. The purchase-of-service contract, the cornerstone of public–private agreements in health and social services, has been used widely under Title XX of the Social Security Act and Title III of the Older Americans Act. These partnerships have involved primarily the private nonprofit sector. Increasingly, however, private, for-profit organizations have been included as contractees for public service dollars (Estes & Harrington, 1981; Somers 1978); proprietary nursing homes and hospitals are primary among this group. As this trend has accelerated, there have been questions raised about the quality of service being delivered (Fottler, Smith, & James, 1981).

In the area of income security, accelerated efforts to promote the establishment and growth of private pension funds by liberalizing tax incentives have generated a plethora of Individual Retirement Accounts (IRA) and private annuity plans. However, these initiatives benefit primarily upper-middle income people. Furthermore, the prevailing view that union-negotiated retirement packages, combined with OASI, will provide a substantial income at retirement is further evidence of the urban policy bias. Rural workers, less often unionized, will not benefit from this prevailing institutional structure in the same way as will urban populations.

The lack of a service infrastrucure, particularly a private or voluntary structure, in rural areas poses special difficulties for implementing public–private partnerships in service delivery. First, since the preponderance of formal services in rural areas has been under public sponsorship through branch offices, outpostings, and circuit-riding professionals, private providers aware of local needs and preferences are in scarce supply. In addition, with service reimbursement favoring institutional arrangements, the informal network receives little support even though it represents a substantial private, voluntary response to need (Brody, 1979).

Conclusions

Based upon Warner's (1974) insight that the fundamental structures of society differentially affect rural people, a number of observations critical to policy development for the rural elderly can be articulated. It must be pointed out, however, that the policy strategies discussed in this chapter will be affected by the larger forces in society, most notably the continued strength and composition of population inmigration to rural areas and the needed revitalization of the national economy.

The continued dependence of social insurance income transfers on earnings during the working years promotes a differential between urban and rural elderly populations. Income and work-related earnings, lower for the rural elderly with substantial underemployment, will continue at a lower level as reflected in retirement benefits. Basic human and social services designed from the perspective of an urban services infrastructure will be neither accessible nor effective in meeting the needs of rural people. Delivery patterns emphasizing a comprehensive array of services and reimbursement patterns favoring institutional providers will not only force the dislocation of elderly people to areas far from home yet rich in numbers of providers but also discourage the informal caring resources upon which so many rural elderly rely.

Program funding and delivery, either generic or age-specific, based upon population formulas rather than upon assessed needs of the rural elderly, will increase the financial pressures on agencies attempting to address a high level of need with high service costs. This disadvantage will be experienced by a highly dispersed rural population base. Futhermore, without substantial political advocacy, decisions made at the state and local levels will tend not to favor rural, powerless groups, including the elderly. The issues of what constitutes need and how service costs are determined emerge as priorities to address. Depending upon how these issues are resolved, policy decisions will have different impacts on the rural elderly population.

A competitive posture in the health and social services sector is clearly problematic in a rural setting. The existing planning and regulatory policies underpinning social programs, however, have not provided an adequate response to the unique configuration of strengths and weaknesses of rural settings. The potential benefits to the rural elderly of creative regulation and planning need to be examined. For example, policies and regulations supporting the availability of services and income transfers yet flexible in addressing the needs of diverse population groups are necessary.

Continued inmigration to rural areas is a trend warranting close scrutiny during this decade. The long-run implication of this trend and concomitant economic growth for rural–urban differences could greatly reduce the income disparity and subsequent retirement benefit differentials. Furthermore, the composition of the inmigrating population will have impact on expectations for quantity and quality of services. In contrast, should the rate of inmigration significantly decline and interact with other socio-demographic indicators, e.g., possible increase in the birth rate, rural–urban income disparities may in fact widen. Finally, the current policy preoccupation with broad economic issues obviates progressive social policy development directed toward the well-being of disadvantaged groups. Until an economic turnaround occurs, creative social policy responses to the rural elderly will remain in abeyance.

References

Bell, D. *The coming of post-industrial society.* New York: Basic Books, 1973.

Benedict, R. C. *Emerging trends in social policy for older people.* Paper presented at the 1977 National Roundtable Conference, American Public Welfare Association, Washington, D.C., December 1977.

Benedict, R. C. Trends in the development of services for the aging under the Older Americans Act. In B. R. Herzog (Ed.), *Aging and income.* New York: Human Sciences Press, 1978, pp. 280–306.

Beyle, T. L., & Dusenbury, P. J. Health and human services block grants: The state and local dimension. *State Government,* 1982, *55* (1), 2–13.

Binstock, R. H. Federal policy toward the aging—Its inadequacies and its politics. *National Journal,* 1978, *10* (45), 1838–1845.

Bradshaw, T. K., & Blakely, E. J. *Rural communities in advanced industrial society.* New York: Praeger, 1979.

Brody, E. M. Women's changing roles, the aging family and long-term care of older poeople. *National Journal,* 1979, *11* (43), 1828–1833.

Burns, E. M. *Social security and public policy.* New York: McGraw-Hill, 1956.

Carlin, T., & Pryor, S. A rural perspective of welfare reform: Part I— Issues. *Rural Development Perspectives,* 1980, *3,* 12–15.

Clark, T. Reagan's budget: Economic political gambles. *National Journal,* 1982, *14* (7), 168–285.

Ecosometrics, Inc. *Review of reported differences between the rural and urban elderly: Status, needs, services, and service costs.* Washington, D.C.: Administration on Aging (Contract No. 105-80-065), July 1981.

Estes, C. L. *The aging enterprise.* San Francisco: Jossey-Bass, 1979.

Estes, C. L., & Harrington, C. A. Fiscal crisis, deinstitutionalization, and the elderly. *American Behavioral Scientist,* 1981, *24* (6), 811–826.

Fottler, M. D., Smith, H. L., & James, W. L. Profits and patient care quality in nursing homes: Are they compatible? *The Gerontologist,* 1981, *21* (5), 532–538.

Froland, C. Formal and informal care: Discontinuities in a continuum. *Social Service Review,* 1980, *54* (4), 572–587.

Garfinkel, I. What's wrong with welfare? *Social Work,* 1978, *23* (3), 185–191.

Gilbert, N., & Specht, H. *Dimensions of social welfare policy.* Englewood Cliffs, N.J.: Prentice-Hall, 1974.

Golant, S. M., & McCaslin, R. A functional classification of services for older people. *Journal of Gerontological Social Work,* 1979, *1* (2), 1–31.

Hirschhorn, L. The implications of adult development for social policy. The National Conference on Social Welfare, *The Social Welfare Forum, 1979.* New York: Columbia University Press, 1980, pp. 94–102.

Hirschhorn, L. Social policy and the life cycle: A developmental perspective. *Social Service Review,* 1977, *51* (3), 434–450.

Hudson, R. B. Political and budgetary consequences of an aging population. *National Journal,* 1978, *10* (42), 1699–1705.

Hudson, R. B. A block grant to the states for long-term care. *Journal of Health Politics, Policy and Law,* 1981, *6* (1), 9–28.

Johnson, L. Human service delivery patterns in nonmetropolitan communities. In H.W. Johnson (Ed.), *Rural human services.* Itasca, Ill.: Peacock, 1980, pp. 65–74.

Kammerman, S. B. Community services for the aged: The view from eight countries. *The Gerontologist,* 1976, *16* (6), 529–537.

Krishef, C. H., & Yoelin, M. L. Differential use of informal and formal helping networks among rural elderly Black and White Floridians. *Journal of Gerontological Social Work,* 1981, *3* (3), 45–59.

Kutza, E. A. Toward an aging policy. *Social Policy,* 1981, *12* (1), 39–43.

LaFollette, C. More growth and less federal aid mean new problems for rural areas. *National Journal,* 1982, *14* (36), 1515–1517.

Martinez, A. Relating human services to a continuum of need. The National Conference on Social Welfare, *The Social Welfare Forum, 1979.* New York: Columbia University Press, 1980, pp. 39–44.

McCoy, J. L., & Brown, D. L. Health status among low income elderly persons: Rural–urban differences. *Social Security Bulletin,* 1978, *41* (6), 14–16.

Myers, B. A., Weiler, P. G., & Fine, R. R. Planning for long-term care: Population-specific or generic? The National Conference on Social Welfare, *The Social Welfare Forum, 1981.* New York: Columbia University Press, 1982, pp. 173–186.

National Research Council. *Rural America in passage: Statistics for policy.* Washington, D.C.: National Academy Press, 1981.

National Rural Center. *The rural stake in public assistance.* Washington, D.C.: National Rural Center, 1979.

Nelson, G. Contrasting services to the aged. *Social Services Review*, 1980, *54* (3), 376–389.

Ozawa, M. N. The fading issue of the stigma attached to income support programs for the elderly: A study. *Journal of Gerontological Social Work*, 1981, *3* (4), 51–63.

Ozawa, M. N. Who receives subsidies through social security, and how much? *Social Work*, 1982, *17* (2), 211–229.

Philadelphia Geriatric Center. Unpublished material presented at the Western Gerontological Society Meetings in Anaheim, Calif., March 1980.

Pruger, R., & Miller, L. Competition and the public social services. *Public Welfare*, 1973, *31* (4), 16–25.

Roemer, M. I. Health maintenance organizations—New developments of significance for the elderly in rural areas. Unpublished paper, 1980.

Roemer, M. I., & Roemer, J. E. The social consequences of free trade in health care: A public health response to orthodox economics. *International Journal of Health Services*, 1982, *12* (1), 111–129.

Schram, S. F. Elderly policy particularism and the new social services. *Social Services Review*, 1979, *53* (1), 75–91.

Shanas, E. The family as a social support system in old age. *The Gerontologist*, 1979, *19* (2), 169–174.

Somers, A. R. The high cost of health care for the elderly: Diagnosis, prognosis, and some suggestions for therapy. *Journal of Health Politics, Policy and Law*, 1978, *3* (2), 163–180.

Somers, A. R., & Somers, H. M. A proposed framework for health and health care policies. *Inquiry*, 1977, *14* 115–170.

Svahn, J. A. Restoration of certain minimum benefits and other OASDHI program changes: Legislative history and summary of provisions. *Social Security Bulletin*, 1982, *45* (3), 3–12.

Terrell, P. Private alternatives to public human services administration. *Social Services Review*, 1979, *53* (1), 56–74.

Thurow, L. C. *The zero-sum society*. New York: Basic Books, 1980.

Tobin, S. S. Social and health services for the future aged. *The Gerontologist*, 1975, *15* (1), 32–37.

Warner, W. K. Rural society in a post-industrial age. *Rural Sociology*, 1974, *39* (3), 306–317.

Watkins, J. M., & Watkins, D. A. *Toward a continuum of care policy framework for decision making by state units on aging and area agencies on Aging: Issues and opportunities in rural service provision.* Final Report, Administration of Aging Grant 90-AR-2073/01, Orono, Maine, 1981.

Watkins, J. M., & Watkins, D. A. *Social policy and the rural setting.* New York: Springer Publishing Co., 1984.

EPILOGUE

Philip Taietz

The epilogue is somewhat of a rarity in the social science research literature and therefore does not have accepted standards of style or content. There are, nevertheless, characteristics which distinguish it from other types of writing. For example, the readers can expect to find lamentations such as "we have just begun to scratch the surface," and "much well-trodden ground must be trodden again." Besides, what reader would be so ungracious as to decline the writer's invitation to take a brief look into the future of research? At the conclusion of the epilogue, the writer, overcome by the gap between what is and what ought to be, can only encourage the reader to be faithful to the high standards of scientific research and to hope for sustained financial support.

Thus, it was within this context that I accepted the invitation to prepare an epilogue for this volume. I am delighted to be a contributor to this endeavor because it represents a significant stride forward for rural gerontology. The time that has transpired between the release of the now-classic volume by Youmans (1967) and this contemporary collection represents a watershed period for rural gerontology—marking the end of an era of obscurity, negligence, and equivocation.

In reflecting on the past quarter century of research on aging and the rural environment, it is important to first note the changes which have taken place during this period in the broader "aging enterprise" (Estes, 1979). During this period we have witnessed the phenomenal growth of gerontology as a body of knowledge and as a set of occupations which have served to professionalize the field. The establishment of the Area Agencies on Aging through the 1973 amendments to the Older Americans Act provided new funds for local planning, needs assessment, coordination, and advocacy. Federal intervention has resulted in an overall increase in services to the elderly while at the same time significantly decreasing rural–urban differences, although substantial gaps remain. Associated with these changes have been the heightened expectations of the elderly and an increased awareness among decision makers about the special needs and life circumstances of the elderly. This seemingly optimistic picture of progress for the elderly of our nation has become somewhat clouded as we enter the 1980s. Recent cuts in the federal budget and a general retreat from the social programs begun in preceding decades have jeopardized the welfare and security of elders. Under these circumstances, it is difficult to predict what lies ahead for gerontological services or for the continued support of research on aging.

Much of the research reported in this book, as well as social gerontological research in general, has been concerned with psychological and social psychological variables. A smaller set of investigations has focused on environmental or structural variables. The recent growing interest in the rural elderly has produced some research which, while biased toward the individual level of analysis, nevertheless recognizes the necessity for both the micro and macro levels of analysis. Indeed, the greatest contribution of *rural* studies to the overall discipline of gerontology may well be their emphasis on dual-level analysis and policy-relevant research.

To continue to make contributions to the broad discipline of gerontology, however, rural-oriented research must overcome certain basic defects which continue to plague it and to detract from its effectiveness. A common defect is the absence of controls. Having uncovered rural–urban differences, many studies fail to ask whether the differences they observe could be explained away by age, income, health, education, or other control variables. An instructive example is provided by Sauer, Shehan, and Boymel (1976) in their reanalysis of a study of Hynson (1975). The latter examined rural–urban differences on four indicators of satisfaction: (1) satisfaction with family, (2) satisfaction with community, (3) general happiness, and (4) lack of fear. Hynson (1975) had reported statistically significant rural–urban differences in three of the four indicators of satisfaction. Sauer et al. (1976), however, found that when appropriate controls were instituted on the data used in the Hynson analysis, the rural–urban variable did not continue to have a significant effect on these indicators of life satisfaction.

But such findings do not necessarily indicate that residence is irrelevant. Rural–urban differences which are eliminated by controls on other variables may be spurious, or they may be interpreted as indirect effects of residence. A rural disadvantage attributed to the lower incomes of rural residents is a real disadvantage nonetheless, and its attribution to income provides a strategy for its amelioration. Research in this area would benefit greatly from increased use of causal modeling techniques to differentiate spurious relationships from indirect effects.

Another defect is the tendency to dichotomize rural–urban categories and, thus, to obscure or overlook the variation that exists within rural or urban environments. Coward (1979) emphasized the importance of rural heterogeneity for both practitioners and researchers, yet many analyses continue to rely on a bifurcated framework. In addition, many studies that purport to be comparative provide data for only a rural or an urban setting and infer the characteristics of the other.

As a consequence of the dearth of dual-level analysis and the persistence of the defects noted above, the actual number of published empirical studies of rural–urban differences with adequate controls and adequate samples is quite small. The results of a recent federally funded, exhaustive review of the literature in this area provide support for this conclusion (Ecosometrics, 1981). This project reviewed more than 600 research articles, reports, and monographs produced between 1970 and 1981 that dealt with either the status and needs of the rural elderly, the programs that serve them, or the costs of these programs. The report concluded that the literature on rural–urban differences did not thoroughly or systematically identify, discuss, or resolve crucial issues.

Two persistent themes in research on aging and the rural environment are (1) the differences that are presumed to exist between the cultural world of the small town and that of the city, and (2) the differences in values, attitudes and behavior of the rural elderly as compared with the urban elderly. The scenario that is often depicted is that of the "evil" city characterized by anonymity, impersonality, artificiality, and corruption which is then contrasted with the "good" small town identified with the simple virtues of hard work, honesty, frugality, and independence. There is little evidence to support the accuracy of these hackneyed images; indeed, most of them are mere assertions emanating from stereotypes rather than data.

Yet the results of past research have failed to correct, for most people, a number of myths with respect to rural–urban differences. For example, the belief that the elderly in rural areas are better off than their counterparts in urban areas in terms of the availability of informal support has not been consistently documented by research. Nor has the assertion that the rural elderly resist organized social services more often than the urban elderly been supported.

One of the conclusions that invariably follows from rural–urban comparisons is that there is a deficit in both the availability and the accessibility of facilities and services in rural communities. Such analyses often fail, however, to consider the crucial element of time. An exception is an investigation by Taietz and Milton (1979), who restudied 43 New York counties nine years after they had been studied in 1967 to assess changes in the level of services provided to older people. During the period between the first and second collections of data, the Area Agencies on Aging were established and a large increase in federal funds occurred for local services. Analyses demonstrated that federal intervention had produced an overall increase in services while at the same time decreasing, but not eliminating, the differences between rural and urban communities. Similar findings were uncovered in a study of 56 California counties (Taietz, 1982). We cannot necessarily expect this narrowing of the rural–urban differential in service provision to continue, however, since the unique events of the time period covered by this research (the establishment of the AAAs and the increase in federal funding) are not likely to be replicated in future years.

The current fascination with human ecology is in part an indication that in the arena of human affairs almost every policy, program, or service involves an environmental factor. An example of research in which the "environmental factor" is of considerable importance is the collaboration of social scientists, designers, architects, and medical personnel concerned with developing an optimum environment for the aged in such contexts as apartment houses or long-term care institutions.

Rural gerontological research has been advanced by Lawton's (1980) proposal that the behavioral and psychological state of an elderly person can best be understood through the dual analysis of both the macroenvironment and the microenvironment. During the past 15 years, a number of studies of the elderly have appeared which employed macrolevel variables such as the environment, the neighborhood, the residential unit, or the community in an effort to obtain a comprehensive understanding and explanation of the aging process (Lawton, 1980).

Although most studies of aging use a territorial area as a sampling context and examine some problematic aspect of old age within that context, not until recently have these studies utilized variables of community structure in their analyses. In a review of community research in social gerontology, Taietz (1970) identified two common defects in community studies: (1) studies rarely employed a sample of communities, but rather used the common practice of selecting a single community for investigation; and (2) studies seldom identified those variables of community structure which provided the rationale for regarding the community as a distinct area of investigation.

In recent years the community has been the subject of renewed attention along theoretical and research lines. Moving away from descriptive-analytic studies of single communities, community research is becoming comparative and now employs more sophisticated methodologies. This represents a considerable advance over earlier, single-community studies, since the effects of differing community structures cannot be ascertained unless multiple communities are studied simultaneously.

The structural differentiation of communities continues to be most commonly measured by population size. Structural differentiation can be measured more directly, however, by counting or scaling the specialized institutions of a community. For example, in a study of community structure and aging, Taietz (1970) developed seven Guttman scales of community specialization in a sample of 144 different-sized communities in New York. Separate scales of complexity were developed for social services, housing, retail trade, medical specialties, community planning, financial services, and political structure.

Employing the medical specialties scale as a measure of community complexity, Taietz (1975a) investigated the relationship of community complexity to knowledge of facilities (indexed by the presence of a senior center) in a subsample of 32 communities. Analyses of the data uncovered an interaction effect: the relationship between community complexity and knowledge was distinct within different categories of communities. There was a negative relationship between community complexity and knowledge of facilities for rural communities, but for large cities the relationship was positive. Taietz reasoned that it was possible to have knowledge of facilities in a small, undifferentiated community through informal, face-to-face communication. As the size and complexity of the community increased, however, immediate experience as the source of knowledge receded in importance and was replaced by secondary sources such as information centers, outreach programs, published directories, and the mass media.

Taietz (1975a) also identified communities, such as small cities, that were not large enough to rely predominantly on secondary sources but were too big for face-to-face communication. His data indicated that the less complex the rural community, the greater the chance that its members would have accurate knowledge about the existence of a center. The situation was just the opposite when large cities were involved.

Another example of the macrosociological approach is a study by Moore, Taietz, and Young (1973). These authors attempted to predict the presence or absence of 13 health and welfare institutions in selected New York communities. Each of these institutions, the findings showed, could be predicted by the structural differentiation of the communities as measured by a Guttman scale of medical specializations. Another structural dimension, centrality, was a predictor for eight of the institutions. The authors defined centrality as the degree to which the community and its incorporating system were linked by institutions that expressed mutual support and legitimacy. The decisive test of centrality was whether or not a community had some not widely available indicator of system level recognition, for example, county seat status.

Another measure of community structure which has been used is community solidarity (Young, 1970). There exist in communities certain structures which are created locally and have the implicit or explicit purpose of giving identity to the community, preserving its heritage, communicating its facilities and opportunities, and providing support for its programs. The concept of community solidarity illustrates the difference between the macro and micro levels of analysis. The macro level measure of community solidarity is but the other side of the coin of the micro level measure of the individual's satisfaction with, identification with, and commitment to the community. It would not be surprising to find a correlation between a community's level of solidarity and the levels of older persons' satisfaction with and commitment to the community. Research on the community satisfaction of the elderly has received some attention (Blake, Lawton, & Lau, 1978; Schooler, 1975); research on community solidarity is in a very formative state; and research relating the two variables is nonexistent.

It is evident from the contributions to this book that rural gerontology is replete with conflicting evidence. The first task of future research, therefore, is to design research projects aimed at resolving these contradictory findings. The task of reconstruction will affect a broad spectrum of gerontological research since the contradictory findings are not confined to a particular topic. The temptation to restudy, or indeed to study, everything at once should be resisted as it is likely to produce a large quantity of information that is of little cumulative value. Research centers and departments should set priorities which build on their strengths.

Rural sociology and rural gerontology share common substantive interests as well as a strong commitment to the application of research to planning and service delivery. Rural gerontologists and rural sociologists have made important contributions to our understanding of the role of elders in the resurgence of growth in rural areas during the 1970s. At the methodological level, rural sociologists have pioneered in the application of Guttman scaling to the measurement of community development and subsequently to the planning of services for the elderly (Eberts, 1978; Taietz, 1975a, 1975b; Taietz & Milton, 1979; Young & Young, 1973). Future research in rural gerontology should be characterized by a greater integration of the micro and macro levels of analysis using increasingly sophisticated techniques for employing controls and selecting samples.

References

Blake, B. F., Lawton, M. P., & Lau, S. *Community resources and need satisfaction: An age comparison.* Philadelphia: Philadelphia Geriatric Center, 1978.

Coward, R. T. Planning community services for the rural elderly: Implications from research. *The Gerontologist,* 1979, *19* (3), 275–282.

Eberts, P. R. *Conceptualizing community economic structures through Guttman scaling and input–output analysis.* Ithaca, N.Y.: Cornell University, Department of Rural Sociology, Bulletin No. 93, 1978.

Ecosometrics, Inc. *Review of reported differences between the rural and urban elderly: Status, needs, services, and service costs.* Washington, D.C.: Administration on Aging (Contract No. 105-80-C-065), July 1981.

Estes, C. L. *The aging enterprise.* San Francisco: Jossey-Bass, 1979.

Hynson, L. M., Jr. Rural–urban differences in satisfaction among the elderly. *Rural Sociology,* 1975, *40,* 64–66.

Lawton, M. P. *Environment and aging.* Monterey, Calif.: Brooks/Cole, 1980.

Moore, D. E., Taietz, P. & Young, F. W. Location of institutions in upstate New York. *Search,* 1973, *2,* 17.

Sauer, W. J., Shehan, C., & Boymel, C. Rural–urban differences in satisfaction among the elderly: A reconsideration. *Rural Sociology,* 1976, *41,* 269–275.

Schooler, K. A comparison of rural and non-rural elderly on selected variables. In R. C. Atchley & T. O. Byerts (Eds.), *Rural environments and aging.* Washington, D.C.: The Gerontological Society, 1975, pp. 27–42.

Taietz, P. *Community structure and aging.* Washington, D.C.: U.S. Department of Health, Education and Welfare, Administration on Aging, 1970.

Taietz, P. Community complexity and knowledge of facilities. *Journal of Gerontology,* 1975, *30,* 357–362. (a)

Taietz, P. Community facilities and social services. In R. C. Atchley & T. O. Byerts (Eds.), *Rural environments and aging.* Washington, D.C.: Gerontological Society, 1975, pp. 145–156. (b)

Taietz, P. *The impact of Area Agencies on Aging on the development of new services for the elderly.* Ithaca, N.Y.: Cornell University, Department of Rural Sociology, 1982.

Taietz, P., & Milton, S. Rural–urban differences in the structure of services for the elderly in upstate New York counties. *Journal of Gerontology,* 1979, *34,* 429–437.

Youmans, E. G. (Ed.). *Older rural Americans: A sociological perspective.* Lexington: University of Kentucky Press, 1967.

Young, F. W. Reactive subsystems. *American Sociological Review,* 1970, *35,* 297–307.

Young, F. W., & Young, R. C. *Comparative studies of community growth.* Morgantown: West Virginia University Press, Rural Sociological Society Monograph No. 2, 1973.

Index

Index